Pricing Guide

for Desktop Services

(formerly *Pricing Guide for Desktop Publishing Services*)

Fourth Edition

Street Smart Pricing for the Small Business Entrepreneur

by
Robert C. Brenner, MSEE, MSSM

Pricing Guide for Desktop Services
Fourth Edition

ISBN 0-929535-15-4

©1995, ©1996, ©1998 Robert C. Brenner. All rights reserved. Brief quotations of the material in this book may be used in other books, broadcast and print media, house organs, term papers, and presentations, provided full prominent credit is given as follows: "From *Pricing Guide for Desktop Services* by Robert C. Brenner. Published by Brenner Information Group, San Diego, California." For larger excerpts or reprint rights, contact the publisher.

Printed in the United States of America
FIFTH PRINTING

Published by

Brenner Information Group
P.O. Box 721000
San Diego, CA 92172-1000
(619) 538-0093

www.brennerbooks.com

Table of Contents

INTRODUCTION i

Chapter 1 - The Concept of Pricing
What's Included in a Price? 1
   What's Markup Got to do With It? 1
Factors Affecting Price 5
   Market Type 5
      One Seller, Many Buyers, No Price Competition 6
      Few Sellers, Many Buyers, Competition Drives 6
      Many Sellers, Many Buyers, Same Price 6
      Many Sellers, Many Buyers, Many Prices 7
   Market Size 7
   Demand 8
   Economy 9
   Competition 10
   Perceived Value 10
   Esthetics and Location 10
   Law and Government 12
   Profit Objectives 14
   Cost of Goods or Services Sold 14

CHAPTER 2 - Pricing Techniques
Reference Points 17
   Demand-Oriented Pricing 17
      Price Skimming 18
      Penetration Pricing 18
      Pricing the Prestige 19
      Differential Pricing (Price Lining) 19
      Odd/Even Pricing 20
      Demand-Backward Pricing 20
   Cost-Oriented Pricing 21
      Mark-Up Pricing 21
      Calculated Mark-Up 24
      Standard Mark-Up 24
      Accepted Reference Mark-up 24
      Cost-Plus Pricing 25
      Cost-Volume Pricing 25

Profit-Oriented Pricing 27
　Targeted Profit Pricing 27
　Targeted Return-on-Sales Pricing 28
　Targeted Return-on-Investment Pricing 29
　Competition-Oriented Pricing 29
　Accepted Customary Pricing 30
　Going-Rate Pricing 30
　Subjective Pricing 31
　Loss-Leader Pricing 31
　Composite Pricing 31
Estimating Demand 33
　Elasticity 34
　Factors Affecting Elasticity of Demand 36
　Determining Elasticity of Demand 37
　Actions in Each Demand Elasticity Situation 37

CHAPTER 3 - Developing a Pricing Strategy
Strategic Thinking 39
　Critical Factors in Your Price Strategy 42
　Eight Steps to Setting Price 46
　Establishing Pricing Objectives 46
　Studying the Market 47
　Determining Demand 47
　Studying the Competition 48
　Studying the Economy 49
　Estimating Your Costs 50
　Selecting Return on Investment 50
　Paying Back Loans 51
Perspectives on Pricing 51
　Notes on Pricing Service 52
　Is Price King? 53
　What Customers Really Want 53
　Looking Beyond Price 54
　Will Customers Pay for Added Value? 56
　Pricing Assumptions by Your Competition 56
　The High Price Myth 57
Creative Pricing Strategies 58
　Floor Price Plus Some 58
　Calculated Cost Plus 70% 59
　Percent Capacity Plus Margin 60
　Net Revenue, Inventory Sell Off 60
　Competing with the Competition 61
　Single Price, Any Customer Pricing 61

Tiered Pricing 62
Transaction Pricing 65
New Product - New Service Pricing 66
Leadership Pricing 66
Value-Based Pricing 68
"One-Half" Pricing 69
"2X" Pricing 69
"2.5X" Pricing 70
"3X" Pricing 70
Bottom Pricing 72
Only Pricing With Commas Accepted 72
Selling Service Contracts 73
On Donating Your Services 74
Adding Products and Services 75
Ethics and the Desktop Professional 77

CHAPTER 4 - Pricing Tactics
Tactical Pricing Actions 81
  Pricing Problems 82
  Taking Time to Price Better 82
Pricing Service in a Competitive Market 84
  Income Versus Profit 88
Productivity 89
  Calculating Shop Productivity 91
  Calculating Individual Productivity 93
  Factors Affecting Productivity 94
How Costs Vary During a Project 95
Finding the Break-Even Point 96
  Sales Volume Method 97
  Total Units Sold Method 100
  Short-Cut to Find Break-Even Point 102
  Break-Even, Overhead & Profit Margin 103
Margin Analysis 106
  Finding Optimum Order Size Using Margin Analysis 108
Selling at Reduced Prices 110
  Coupons 112
  Rebates 114
  Discounting 115
    Volume Discounts 118
    Discounting and the Law 119
  Adding Loss Leader Jobs 120
  When Price Cutting Works 120
  How to Handle the Price Cut 122

A Price Reduction Strategy that Worked 122
Raising Your Prices 122
   How Some Shops Handle Price Increases 124
   How Much Can You Raise Your Price? 126
   Subtle Ways to Raise Your Prices 126
   A Penny Here, A Penny There ...Adding Cents 127
   Handling Staff Objections to a Price Increase 130
   Easing Customer "Sticker Price" Shock 131
   Hold Your Price! 132
Pricing in a Changing World 134
   Analyze Your Customer Base by Profit 136
   Don't Give Away the Store 137
   Countering Cutthroat Competition 138
   How to Break Out Top Profits 144

CHAPTER 5 - Baselines, Standards & Budgeted Hourly Rates
Generating a Cost Baseline 149
   Fixed Costs 150
   Variable Costs 150
   Direct Costs 151
   Indirect and Overhead Costs 151
   General & Administrative (G&A) Expenses 153
   Overhead Factor 155
Project Cost Analysis 156
Standard Benchmarks 159
   Machine Standard 160
   Developing A Machine Standard Model 161
   Worker Performance Production Standards 164
      NAPL Standards 166
      NASS Standards 167
      BIG Survey Response "Standards" 168
   Generating Function-Time History 172
Baseline Production Standards 174
   Developing Baseline Production Standards 178
Budgeted Hourly Rates 183
   Budgeted Hourly Rate Example: Home Business 188
   Budgeted Hourly Rate Example: Store Front 197

CHAPTER 6 - Charging for Products & Services
Ready, Set, Charge! 207
   Charging by the Character and by the Line 209
   Charging by the Page 209
   Charging by the Hour 213

Charging by the Shop's Hourly Rate 214
Charging by the Job - Flat Rate Pricing 221
Additional Charges 224
  Preflight 225
  Dealing With Difficulty 225
  Use a Time in Tenths Chart 228
  Include the Cost of Meeting 229
Set-up Fees 236
Charging When Normal Time Limits are Exceeded 237
Charging a Minimum Rate 238
Charging for Rush Jobs 238
Charging for Alterations and Corrections 239

CHAPTER 7 - Estimating, Bidding & Negotiating
The Basis for Good Estimating 243
Applied Estimating 245
  Specifying a Job 245
  Create a Form for Estimating 246
  Estimating Example - Brochure 252
  An Estimate is Not a Bid 254
  Getting Bid Opportunities 255
  Responding to a Request for Bid 257
    Symptoms of a Poor Bid Response 258
    Bidding Against the Alligators 259
  The Case for Market-Based Bidding 260
  Submitting a Formal Quote 263
  Negotiating Techniques 265
    Using Body Language 270
    Getting Help on the Negotiation Process 278
  Put the Agreement in Writing 279
    Omissions in Many "Standard" Contracts 280
  Follow Up On Your Estimates 281
  When Estimating Your Next Job 282
  Tracking Bids and Buyer Decisions 283

CHAPTER 8 - Street Smart Operations
Do It By The Numbers 285
  Return on Investment 286
  Return on Assets 287
  Analyzing Financial Numbers 289
  Comparing Your Business With the Competition ... 292
    Measuring Profitability 293
    Making Your Own Profitability Model 302

What's the Maximum I Can Earn? 304
Making a Counter Price Book 306
Job Scheduling - Resource Allocation 309
Case Study: Break-Even Analysis - Color Laser Copier 311
Case Study: Estimating A Directory Project 317
Case Study: Trade Rate Rip-off 324
Case Study: What Billing Rate Should I Use? 326
Getting Paid 328
Guerilla Operations for Business Survival 335
One Final Word 342

Appendix
Profiles & Demographics 343
Publications 349
Associations 355
Other Books on Pricing 366

Introduction

"Price, not timing, can be everything."
- Normal Dolph, Success Magazine

Congratulations! You made a good decision. This is the fourth edition of a guide that has become the de facto pricing standard for desktop providers. Thousands of new and aspiring business owners are using this guide to develop sound pricing strategies and successful price quotes. It'll work for you, too.

Whether you're selling a product or offering a service, the price you set is critical to business success. Sometimes raising your prices will increase sales. At other times, cutting prices will increase sales. Pricing is a complex, yet exciting part of business. It's comprised of many factors, and the more you know about what affects price and a customer's willingness to let go of hard-earned cash, the more business you'll get and the more money you'll make.

Research consistently indicates that all too few business owners really understand operating costs and how to determine what prices to charge. Many owners fail to consider factors such as the time spent with customers as a cost. Many forget about preflighting a job to ensure that a customer's disk files are complete and suitable. Many are reactive and establish prices based on what everyone else seems to be charging—the "going rate." They're slow to raise prices when appropriate and don't test each price for its affect on sales. Many owners don't know how to analyze and establish optimum prices.

Pricing is a skill. It can be successfully applied only if you have the tools necessary to analyze and make good decisions.

This reference book was written to provide those tools. As a guide to product and service pricing, this book focuses on desktop publishing shops and prepress service bureaus, although once you've learned the "basics," you can apply the techniques in this guide to any business venture.

There are eight chapters in the *Pricing Guide for Desktop Services - Fourth Edition*. Chapter 1 covers the concept of price. In Chapter 1, you'll learn what's included in price, and the factors affecting a selling price.

Chapter 2 covers pricing techniques. In this chapter, you'll learn methods for setting price. This includes demand, costs, markup, your marketplace and moves by the competition.

Chapter 3 helps you develop a pricing strategy. Providing perspectives on pricing, this chapter explains what customers really want and are willing to pay for. And it includes examples of creative pricing strategies used by other business owners.

Chapter 4 helps you convert strategic planning into tactical operations. It's where the "rubber meets the road." This chapter shows you how to implement your pricing strategy in an operational environment. It describes ways to determine break-even and how to use margin analysis to determine the best product and service mix. You'll discover how productivity directly affects your bottom line, and how adding cents can significantly improve cash flow. It explains how to price in a competitive market and the affect of coupons, discounts and rebates on sales volume. Chapter 4 describes how to understand your customer and outfox the competition, when and how to raise or cut prices, and how to counter cutthroat competition.

Chapter 5 is about baselines and standards. It covers machine and production standards. Several industry production standards are discussed. Then you are guided through developing and implementing your own standards to establish budgeted hourly rates (BHRs) for every activity that your shop performs. Examples cover a home and a storefront business.

Chapter 6 describes how to charge for products and services. It covers pricing by the unit (character, line, page, etc.) and pricing by time expended (minutes, hours, etc.). Chapter 6 describes how to establish a shop hourly rate and how productivity affects this value. It also covers flat rate pricing and describes how you can use BHRs to price every service activity.

Part of your success is determined by how well you estimate and bid. Chapter 7 leads you through the estimating, bidding and negotiating processes. It describes the role of preflight in establishing project difficulty. An example shows you how to estimate a job producing a brochure. Then Chapter 7 takes you through the bidding process showing you how to respond to a request for bid (RFB). It explains how to make your bids responsive and more likely to win awards.

Chapter 8 describes operational tricks of the trade used by successful shop owners to break out top profits. The chapter also includes samples of forms and worksheets that you can adopt for making your business work better and more productive.

In the Appendix, you'll find useful information about the business of desktop publishing and prepress. This chapter presents survey profiles of desktop publishing and prepress shops in North America. It helps you understand what the competition looks like, what businesses structure is most popular and how much they make. The Appendix also includes the names and addresses of publications related to desktop services and associations mentioned by a majority our survey participants.

Our world is a kaleidoscope of text and colorful graphics. And we are being lifted up by an information wave that is changing our lives. Some people call this wave an "information highway" or "data highway." Whatever we choose to call this revolution, there are more opportunities in desktop services today than ever before in history. To succeed in this business, you need comprehensive information. This guide was written to help you win—to help you resolve your pricing concerns.

In producing this book, our goal was and still is to elevate the desktop service profession by helping struggling entrepreneurs set better prices. Shop owners work hard to succeed in business. And few professions have the intense learning requirement as the profession you have chosen. It is our desire to recognize your efforts and to do our part to bring the fee structure of desktop publishing and prepress more in line with the education and skills required—and with the work actually performed by today's desktop professionals.

This book was written for you. Get set for an informative and profitable reading experience.

1

The Concept of Pricing

"This is not a let's-just-wing-it operation."

An effective business strategy cannot be developed without a clear understanding of price. Yet pricing cannot occur in a vacuum. It requires the careful consideration of several important and interrelated factors. This chapter introduces the concept of price and explains why pricing is a dynamic business activity.

What's Included in a Price?

A fixed price is composed of a "standard" rate for that product or service, plus some time and materials pricing for the customized elements, and some value pricing based on the perceived value that a solution represents to a customer. Businesses charge the most for those things that have the most value to the buying public.

What's Markup Got to do With It?

A retail price can be roughly partitioned into two equal halves—the cost to produce, and the cost to sell. Related to the second half is the term *"markup."* Markup incorporates the selling cost plus projected profit. It could also include a return on your investment in the hardware and software required to make the product. Markup varies from product to product and from business to business. Some businesses mark products up 40%; others mark each product up a different amount depending on availability and customer desire.

Trying to find out a competitor's markup is like trying to find out what new toys are being developed by Hasbro. This information is kept proprietary. But you can calculate it based on knowing the wholesale cost, the selling costs, and an idea of a business' operating costs. Typically, a product's markup is directly related to how often that product sells (inventory turns over). A fast turnover suggests a lower markup—say 20%. A high price product with a low turnover typically has a high markup—say 55%.

Retail department stores typically set prices at two times the wholesale price (100% markup). This is called a *"keystone markup."* Sometimes they tack on an additional 10% to the selling price if the product is imported or is a private-label. This lets them sell the product at "half off" and still make money.

A discount store generally has a lower selling cost so they typically use a 40% markup. An "off-price" retailer typically marks up its products by about 35%. Although these are typical, markup can vary within the same store.

When a store offers a "Percent-Off" sale, the fun really begins. The initial markup is never as important as the final selling price.

The difference between the actual selling price and the wholesale price is called *"gross margin"* or *"gross profit"* as shown in Figure 1-1. The wholesale price includes the cost to produce that product. Gross margin is expressed as a percent of revenue. Out of this, you pay expenses such as sales, marketing, and general and administrative costs.

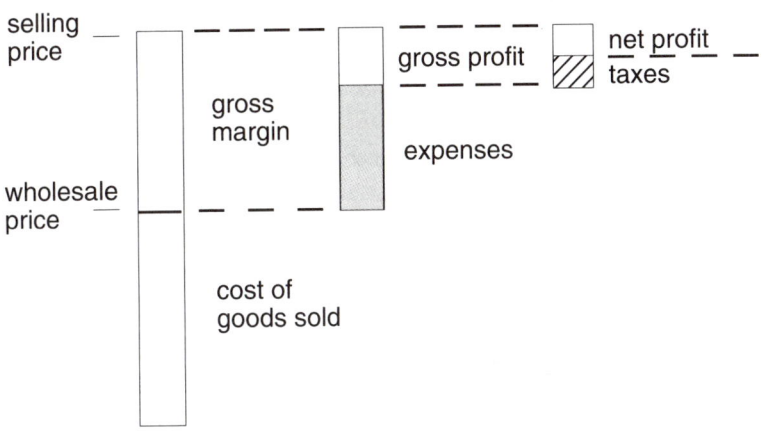

Figure 1-1. Relationship between gross margin and gross profit in a retail business.

Gross margin is closely held information by most retail outfits, but we have clues to what it should be by studying the trade publications. Computer manufacturers operate at approximately 50% gross margin. Software companies typically achieve gross margins in the 80% area. Desktop publishers and prepress service bureaus typically operate in the 30% - 40% range of gross margin.

In a service business, gross margin is determined in a similar, but different, way. As a service provider, your major expense is direct labor. Therefore, as shown in Figure 1-2, gross profit is equal to gross revenue less direct labor. Dividing gross profit by gross revenue yields your gross margin. Thus, gross margin for a retail store is typically larger than the gross margin for a service bureau. This is because the gross margin for a retail store is determined *before* direct labor and other expenses are deducted.

In addition, Figures 1-1 and 1-2 show that gross profits for retail and service businesses are somewhat different. Notice that gross profit in a retail business is established before taxes are deducted. Fixed and vari-

4 - Pricing Guide for Desktop Services

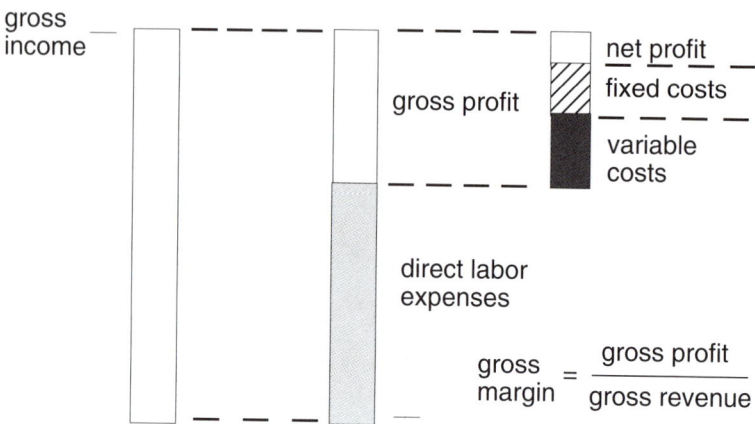

Figure 1-2. Relationship between gross margin and gross profit in a service business.

able expenses have been deducted. In the service industry, gross profit is established before fixed and variable expenses (such as taxes) are deducted. Only the direct labor variable expenses are deducted out of gross revenue.

Gross margin is a way to isolate profitability regardless of other costs that may cloud the profit picture. Gross margin is also an indicator of the value of a product or service. A gross margin can tell you when you're selling a service that has become a commodity in the market. As black and white laser printer output prices have dropped from $1 a page to around 25¢ a page, this service becomes a commodity item such as copier output.

In addition, as more shops offer the same service, prices settle at some nearly uniform level with a lower gross margin. When gross margin drops below 30%, the service or product is becoming a commodity. Many shops focus on higher margin products and services.

Factors Affecting Price

As shown in Figure 1-3, price is affected by many related factors—the type and size of the market, customer demand, competition, government regulations, and so on.

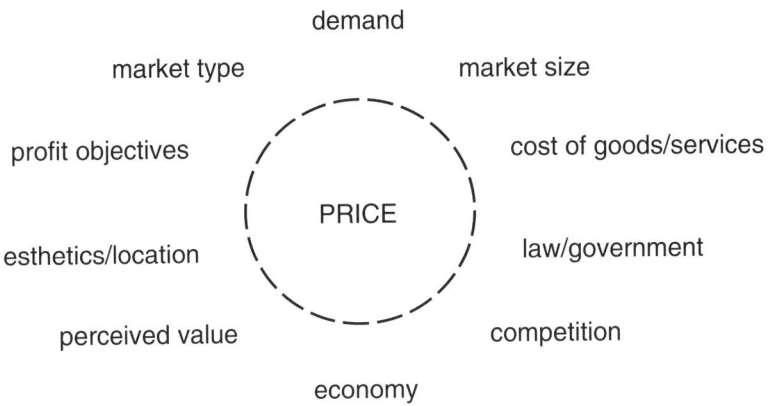

Figure 1-3. Many factors affect the price of your service or product.

Market Type

How you decide to price your product or service often depends on the type of market in which you will compete. If there are many DTP shops and service bureaus in your area, you adopt a different pricing strategy than if you operate in a community in which you are the only business of your type. Basically, there are four types of markets in which you may operate—monopolistic, oligopolistic, purely competitive, and monopolistic competitive. It's important to know where you stand before you decide where you want to stand.

One Seller, Many Buyers,
No Price Competition In the jargon of economists, this is a *"monopolistic"* market. You operate the only shop in your area and you have many customers. The nearest competitor is in the next town so you don't really have a price competitor to deal with.

When you're the "only game in town," you should price carefully so you don't cause buyers to select other alternatives to get the service they need (e.g., hire students, hire support from out of town, etc.). You also don't want another entrepreneur to start a competitive business in your neighborhood. Therefore, you price your products and services to cover costs and return good profit without encouraging competition.

But if your shop is the only source of a unique service, you are able to charge more. It's like operating a gas station along the highway in the Mojave Desert. Gas is priced 30¢ higher, but this station is the only source of gas for 150 miles.

Few Sellers, Many Buyers, Competition Drives This is called an *"oligopolistic"* market. In this market, high start-up costs keeps the participants low. So, few people operate this type of business. For those that do, all the competitors offer a very similar product, so the pricing strategy depends on not only what the customers prefer, but also on what the other competitors do.

If this is your market type, reducing your prices will cause your competition to reduce theirs. Raise your prices, and they may or may not raise theirs. If they don't, you may have to retract your price increase just to keep customers.

Many Sellers, Many Buyers, Same Price In this *"purely competitive"* market, the product is the same. You can't charge more than your competitor because a customer knows that the same product is available for a lower price elsewhere in town. This makes both buyer and seller price-takers rather than price-makers.

The inability to offer a different product, means that all of the sellers must price the same. Your only advantage is to be where most of the customers go to shop. The only way to get away from a purely competitive market is to offer additional products or services to make you different—faster service, longer hours, credit, better quality, etc.

The homogeneous product becomes essentially a lost leader. You make your money on differentiation.

Many Sellers, Many Buyers, Many Prices In economic terms, a *"monopolistic-competitive"* market is one in which you can succeed and have the most fun. This market has product and service differentiation. You try for maximum differentiation so you can achieve maximum profit. The customer determines price so pricing analysis and strategy become important. This is where goodwill, advertising, capability, and all the other aspects of business can have the most affect. For most of us, this is the market in which we operate.

Market Size

If you plan to operate in a small town, your local market may be too small to make your business successful. Four sales a week at $20 a pop won't pay the rent and feed the family too. You'll have to draw business to you from outlying areas by advertising outside the county or state. Every entrepreneur seeks the largest market with the least competition.

With our world rapidly becoming a global sales floor, don't be afraid to seek business from across the state (or country) or even on-line.

One colleague that I met operates a graphics design and desktop publishing business in Hawaii. She advertises in a national publication and draws business from all over the U.S., yet she operates from a island thousands of miles from the mainland. The world is literally an open door market for desktop publishing businesses today.

Electronic commerce is in its infancy. Entrepreneurs are exploring selling using on-line services. As this form of electronic stores develops, the whole world opens up for you to sell products and services anywhere on our planet. Many cautions and risks exist, but as business relationships evolve, the smart entrepreneurs will find a way to make it work.

Monitor the number of magazines and newspapers establishing a World Wide Web on the Internet and the number of editors who accept articles over electronic mail, and you get a feel for the potential for this greatly expanded market.

An entrepreneur no longer needs to feel isolated on the rolling range land in Montana. This person can operate from a home office and market to customers in every country. The potential is staggering.

Demand

While the market place continues to grow, it is the demand for your products or services that makes you a successful enterprise. The capability to generate a really nice product is useless if no-one cares. Without demand for your products and services, your business cannot survive. Nor can you make it if your products are obsolete.

A typing service using manual typewriters will fall on its face trying to compete with a word processing shop providing the same service but using computers and laser printers.

Selling newsletter design services using dot-matrix print output will never successfully compete with a shop providing the same service but based on laser print output. You need to develop quality products and services that are unique and are in the form that customers want. The adage for success is simple: Find a need and fill it. Doing this may be more difficult. Only by knowing the marketplace and your business can you be sensitive and recognize opportunity. If you can provide a product or service that meets a high demand, your business can grow significantly. When Christian Riese Lassen adopted his creative surfing skills to painting multidimensional ocean scenes, he created products that touched the emotion of people. His unique products sell for $1,500 to $500,000 each. Demand for his paintings is based on the uniqueness of his work. Find a niche and fill it.

Economy

Fifty years ago, Abraham Maslow developed a hierarchy of needs to describe people and what they perceive as important. A similar hierarchy of needs can be developed based on the economy. Buyers look at a product based on perceived value. This value can rise or fall depending on personal need, future plans, current finances, and the economic outlook.

As the economy sours, most people conserve more and reduce spending. They increase bargain shopping, select less expensive solutions, and put off major purchases. Many businesses cut prices, extend credit, and offer more for less as they try to stimulate sales. In other words, they alter their products or services to provide lower-cost alternatives. They cut the frills, unbundle certain services, and may also offer self-directed document generation opportunities.

As the rate of inflation increases, buying power declines and shoppers become even more price sensitive. So businesses stress lower prices and better values. The rate of inflation strongly influences how customers perceive price.

Competition

If your service isn't selling, you can always consider lowering your prices to create volume. But cutting your price by 50% won't increase your sales volume by 400% (which is usually what you'll need to net the same profit).

Let's say you have customers who want laser-printed sheets. Some shops use several pricing grids. One is based on the total number of sheets handled. Another is based on the total number of pages per original. And a third is based on the amount of toner coverage on each sheet. These pricing grids are based on the time to print and the toner expended. The total number of pages printed per original provides volume discounts and is more favorable to the large-volume customer.

Customers who want special features such as color printing have expectations that this will cost more and price doesn't seem to be a major factor to them. Therefore, the average cost for a color output page is $4—far more than the 25¢ per page average for black and white 300 dpi laser printouts.

Combining competitive pricing with quality products is hard to beat.

Perceived Value

A service product can command a higher price if it's marketed as different and of premium quality. Purchasing decisions are often driven by the emotional and psychological character of the buyer. After committing to a sale, many buyers use logic to rationalize the wisdom of their decision. They were drawn to your shop by the value that they perceived in your products and services.

By being considered preeminent in your field, you can successfully charge a "premium price" for your service. In this case, your "premium price" is an aggressive advertisement for quality. However, you must deliver on the perception. If you get tainted with a bad job, your image and prestige will suffer. So will your sales.

When a customer falls in love with a product, you can increase its price and they'll still buy. This added price is the *"WOW"* content. Price is really what a customer is willing to pay. If they'll pay more, then most retailers charge more. The McDonald's fast food restaurant chain calls this *"value pricing."* They generate a "value menu" as a long term phenomenon rather than simply use it as a tactic to meet competition. McDonald's knows what products customers really prefer. They set higher margins on french fries and soft drinks because these are the most common sales that accompany combination meals and sandwich orders. They compete on hamburgers. They profit on french fries and drinks.

Esthetics and Location

There is a distinct difference in how some customers perceive a business that operates out of a garage, out of a "hole-in-the-wall" strip center, or out of a professional business park.

When a customer comes to you, esthetics and location become important in how you price your products and services. Each of these three locations can be a successful business. But each will cater to a different customer mix. That "mix" may include customer location.

Therefore, decide what customer base you want to target. Then learn all you can about your customer. Based on this knowledge, organize and operate your business accordingly.

Law and Government

Pricing directly affects both consumers and businesspeople, so local, state, and federal regulations have been implemented to keep customers and competitors from being treated unfairly. Before you start a business, and certainly while you operate your business, you must be aware of the laws and ordnances that affect how you can function.

Your local Chamber of Commerce and government offices can help you determine the local, state, and federal regulations that you must follow. Each state has its own version of an Unfair Sales Practices Act that limits the mark-up you can place on certain items.

The minimum mark-up is regulated. You can charge more, but not less than specified mark-ups allow. These "minimum mark-up" laws allow sales of old or outdated products, but they are designed to protect small businesses by forcing discounters to apply at least a minimum mark-up to their products. This lets a small operator remain competitive with a larger operation.

In 1936, the federal government passed the Robinson-Patman Act to prevent price discrimination. This act makes it illegal to charge a lower price to one customer than you charge to another similar customer. You should not induce, give, or receive discriminatory prices. What you charge (or pay) must be consistent for all. For example, you can't give a discount to one party without offering the same discount to everyone else. This helps you when large retailers demand a wholesale discount even though they may purchase in small quantity.

The Robinson-Patman Act does enable cooperative advertising and promotions as long as the same opportunities are offered to all customers on proportionally the same terms.

There are two provisions in the Act that may appear discriminatory, but are accepted. The first allows you to charge one customer a lower price if your purpose is to meet the same low price offered by a competitor. Thus, a customer who brings you an ad for the same services offered by a competitor at a lower price can realize a savings if you are willing to lower your price to match the competitor's price. You can meet a competitor's lower price without violating the intent of the Act.

The second provision lets you price a product differently between buyers if you can prove that the difference represents a pass-through of costs saved by selling to one buyer over another (e.g., one buyer is local and doesn't require products to be packaged and shipped).

The Federal Trade Commission Act established a watchdog agency to monitor how businesses operate in the United States. Both the Robinson-Patman Act and the Federal Trade Commission Act were designed to protect consumers and small businesses. Congress also passed the Sherman Antitrust Act to deal with price. Only by keeping current on local, state, and federal business legislation can you operate with some assurance that you will avoid legal troubles.

Price fixing charges are in the news periodically. The airline and automobile industries have both dealt with this issue. The point is that groups of similar businesses must not organize to set "standard" prices on products and services. The Sherman Antitrust Act, the Clayton Antitrust Act, and the Federal Trade Commission Act all make it illegal for a group of competing businesses to collectively set prices. Each business must price independently. This doesn't mean that each business should not try to find out what the other is charging.

Many owner-operators have not learned how laws, ordnances, and regulations can affect their business. Many are operating in gray areas of legality. And some are actually conducting business in violation of law.

If you notice a competitor "operating outside the law," rather than sending "the feds" to catch this person, give the competitor a call and let them know that they may be breaking the law. Most small business owners do not intentionally violate the law. They simply have so much to learn and handle, that unintentional oversights or improper activities occur. However, ignorance is no excuse. It's better for all of us to look out for each other, than for us to look out for the law. We should not be in this to drive each other out. We should be in this so all of us can win and enjoy our business adventures.

Profit Objectives

There are two ways to increase your profit margin—lower your percentage of costs or dramatically increase demand. A business with the largest market share should also have the lowest cost. Both material and labor costs are directly proportional to market share.

Trading short-term profit (through lower prices) to gain market share may be a good long-term strategy if your material costs decrease as sales volume increases. If not, be careful of quick profits with long term losses.

Higher demand with relatively fixed cost of goods can enable you to charge more and effectively net a higher profit margin.

Cost of Goods or Services Sold

No consideration of pricing should occur without a clear understanding of the cost basis that is unique to your own shop. Each time you purchase new equipment or a new application program, there are two costs involved—the purchase cost and the ownership cost. We can negotiate various purchase prices depending on where and how we buy. Once the purchase is concluded, the cost becomes the basis for any tax-related depreciation we are able to assume.

The cost of ownership is different. It includes those expenses related to operating and maintaining the system. It takes time and energy to learn and exploit the power in the hardware and software used in your business. With software becoming more complex and hardware becoming more powerful, you cannot assign operating tasks to just anyone. You must first become proficient yourself. Then you must teach those who support you.

With processing power dispersed throughout your shop, the functions and capabilities can become more than one person can handle well. This means that you may have to hire expertise to help cover unfamiliar tasks. You'll have to rely on others to perform. This will require management, leadership, and education. Each of these factors has an associated after-purchase cost.

Maintenance cost is another direct expense that you must understand and control. Hardware and software each have an associated maintenance cost.

For hardware, it includes cleaning, diagnostic checkups, and repair actions when necessary. It could include a service agreement for third party support.

Software maintenance can include paying for on-line technical support or the cost to customize a program for your business. Configuring a program to work with other programs may require hiring someone to perform the integration. An accounting package needs modifications to incorporate changes to the staff, to add new benefits, to change the tax and social security structure. A database used for market analysis and customer contacts needs update and clean-up. A spreadsheet needs modification to incorporate new information or to produce a different output. Each action has an associated cost.

Then there are the less-obvious costs—the indirect costs. These include upgrades, trade-ins and system availability. We upgrade our hardware and software to keep at the forefront of technology, or to increase our capability as business grows. Sometimes we trade in older equipment for new hardware. And sometimes we wait for advertised hardware or software that never becomes a reality—*"vaporware."*

In the past several years, a growing number of products have been touted, hyped, and promised. But delivery was woefully late, or nonexistent. Basing your business plan on hardware or software that becomes vaporware has a cost. Don't believe the optimistic schedules of marketeers. Plan implementations far enough ahead that you can work out the bugs and operational idiosyncrasies (or implement alternatives) long before you put your new system on line.

Summary

Pricing is part art, part science. As this chapter explained, pricing has many facets and is affected by many factors. Understanding price and the marketplace gets us ready to explore the techniques for pricing—covered next in Chapter 2.

2

Pricing Techniques

"Intuitive pricing is a fool's folly in today's highly competitive world."

Pricing has been described as one of the most challenging parts of business operation. Pricing is a multi-faceted animal with many inter-related factors. To become successful in business, you need to learn the ropes—the techniques that others use to price products and services. This chapter deals with method, with technique. It is a critical part of your success formula.

Reference Points

There are basically four reference points from which you can price your products and services—demand, cost, profit, and competition. Some businesses develop a composite of two or more of these approaches to pricing.

Demand-Oriented Pricing

This approach places more emphasis on customer tastes and preferences than it does on cost, competition and profit. There are six types of demand pricing—skimming, penetration, prestige, lining, odd-even, and demand-backward.

> **DEMAND ORIENTED PRICING**
>
> Price Skimming
> Penetration Pricing
> Prestige Pricing
> Differential Pricing
> Odd / Even Pricing
> Demand-Backward Pricing

Figure 2-1. The six elements of demand-oriented pricing.

Price Skimming In *price skimming*, a high initial price is charged for a new product. Customers who want the product are less sensitive to price because they perceive high value in the product. As demand by this group is satisfied, the price is reduced to attract the next (more price-sensitive) consumer group.

Skimming is effective when customers line up to buy the moment a product is released. The product is perceived to have high value and high quality. However, the high initial price must not be so high that it attracts competitors. The early appearance of competition can prevent you from using a higher initial price to offset high start-up production and marketing costs and from achieving lower follow-on production costs with lower selling prices later in the product life cycle.

Penetration Pricing In *penetration pricing*, a low introductory price is used to generate large mass appeal. The intent is to gain as much market share as possible before competitors move in. This strategy works when the marketplace is price sensitive.

Production costs can be dramatically lower as sales volume increases. The low initial price acts to discourage competition.

Some businesses implement price skimming when a product is first released to recoup initial development and promotion costs. Then, some months later, they implement penetration pricing to attract a larger segment of the market. The electronics industry follows this strategy.

Pricing the Prestige Perceived value can demand a higher sales price. When a product or service is perceived as high quality or a "status " purchase, a high price works well. In fact, lowering the price can reduce demand because the customer may perceive the change as a lowering in quality. If your customers expect to pay more for your services, why deny them the satisfaction?

This form of psychological pricing matches perceived value to selling price. When service is seen as having added value, demand rises and the price is adjusted upward. Customers who don't place a high value on service are offered a lower-priced service product. This is a form of *"price discrimination"* that can be used effectively as long as you have a solid understanding of the marketplace.

Differential Pricing (Price Lining) A business with a line of products can partition the products into categories with specific prices for each category. Each line of products is targeted to a specific type of customer. Even when products are purchased at the same cost, they may be marked up differently based on color, style and expected demand.

For example, when I was a teenager, I worked at a salt company where standard salt and Kosher salt both came from the same raw material bin. Both products received the same processing, yet the Kosher salt was poured into a container with a different packaging label. This enabled the company to sell Kosher salt to distributors for almost twice the price of the regular salt. Yet both came from exactly the same raw material source.

Price lining can also be applied when demand varies in different markets. Here you typically sell at a higher price to those markets in which a lower price won't increase bottom line revenue. You then sell at a lower price in those markets that are sensitive to price.

U.S. manufacturers often sell products overseas for much more than the added cost of doing business internationally simply because U.S. products are perceived as having higher quality.

A business applies *differential pricing* by considering each product or service relative to time, season, location, and customer. For example, a custom Christmas newsletter service could be introduced in the fall and priced at maximum in November and December. Then you can offer special prices for jobs placed during off-times and off-days. You can change the packaging of a product (e.g., fancy covers on reports designed for large corporate customers), and you can offer different prices to outlying areas or locales.

Odd/Even Pricing The *odd/even* approach uses the cents (or points) to promote a lower price than reality. Selling a product for $2.99 instead of $3 gives the impression that the customer is paying "just over two dollars." You'll learn more about this in the strategy section (Chapter 3).

Demand-Backward Pricing Here, a company estimates a price that customers will be willing to pay. Then it works backwards through the calculations to arrive at an acceptable manufacturing quality and production cost that enables the business to make money at the pre-determined selling price.

This is what happened in the modem industry. Modem manufacturers knew that they needed to get the selling price of the 9600 bps modem below $1,000 to increase sales. So they backed into the price and designed a product that could be built at a cost that would allow sales at $995 or less and still produce acceptable profit.

If you know that short-run publishers are growing at a rapid rate yet they consistently face "large run" prices, why not develop a product and service that you can offer at a production cost low enough to meet the price they are willing to pay?

Cost-Oriented Pricing

Establishing price based on cost is the most frequent pricing method used in business. Usually, minimal consideration is given to the effect price will have on demand. The focus is on cost, not demand. There are three forms of cost-oriented pricing—mark-up, cost-plus, and cost-volume.

```
COST-ORIENTED PRICING
— — — — — — — — —
Mark-Up Pricing
Cos-Plus Pricing
Cost-Volume Pricing
```

Figure 2-2. The three elements of cost-oriented pricing.

Mark-Up Pricing In the *mark-up pricing* form of cost-oriented price setting the sales figure is established by adding a predetermined percentage to the cost of a product. This amount can be a percentage of the wholesale price, or a percentage of the cost. The total markup represents operating expenses, overhead and profit.

Mark-ups differ based on the product, competition, turnover, and sales risk. However, many businesses use a "standard" mark-up for each product category. Clothing is typically marked up by 40-60%. Staple food items such as bread and milk are marked up by 10-23%. Snack foods receive a 27-47% mark-up, and so on. In reality, there's a mark-up at each stage in the development of a product—manufacturing, distribution, and final sales. The net result is a product or service that has been marked up several hundred percent over its initial raw material cost as it passes through each stage in the manufacturing-to-customer process.

If a product cost $10 from a wholesale supplier, a business owner will add a portion of overhead costs (rent, utilities, insurance, salaries, etc.) and profit to this base cost to arrive at a selling price. To get this selling price, divide the wholesale cost by one minus the percent overhead plus percent profit (both expressed in decimal) as shown in the formula below. If overhead represents 25% of your costs and you want a 10% profit, you would mark up a $10 product by 53.8% to achieve a selling price of $15.38.

$$\text{Selling Price} = \frac{\text{Wholesale Cost}}{1 - (\text{overhead} + \text{profit})}$$

Thus

$$\text{Selling Price} = \frac{10}{1 - (.25 + .10)}$$

$$= \frac{10}{1 - 0.35}$$

$$= \frac{10}{0.65}$$

Selling Price = $15.38

To get the markup percentage, apply the formula

$$\% \text{ Markup} = \frac{\text{Selling Price - Wholesale Cost}}{\text{Wholesale Cost}} \times 100$$

$$= \frac{15.38 - 10.00}{10.00} \times 100$$

$$= \frac{5.38}{10} \times 100$$

Percent Markup = 0.538 × 100

= 53.8%

    Several variations of mark-up pricing exist—a calculated mark up for each product or service, a standard mark up on all products, and a markup based on some accepted reference. Basing your price on covering total costs, including overhead, with a pre-determined mark up for profit is called *full cost pricing*. If your price covers the variable costs of doing business with a predetermined mark-up for profit but not all of your overhead, you are applying *incremental cost pricing*. This method assumes that your mark-up will cover overhead and provide a fair profit. It is only effective for those skilled in pricing.

    The formula on the next page can be used to calculate price using cost plus mark-up:

Price = (Direct Matls x Mark-up) + (Est. Time x Hourly Rate)
= (Total Production Costs) x (Mark-up)

Calculated Mark-Up In the calculated mark-up approach, each product and service is analyzed to determine its associated costs. Then a mark-up is applied to each product or service based on demand, perceived value, and similar factors. *Mark-up* or *cost-based* pricing is often used on time and materials contracts.

Standard Mark-Up In this method a business owner partitions the products and services into specific categories. Each category is assigned a *"standard"* mark up. The appropriate mark-up is then applied to each element in a category.

In a retail store, various products have different mark-ups that are possible (driven by competitor prices or industry-standard markups).

In the service industry, one form of standard mark-up is to allocate a basic rate to each cost center and then to use these rates and the productive hours available to estimate and price a job. This approach is called *budgeted hourly rate* pricing.

Accepted Reference Mark-up There are two versions of the *accepted reference mark-up* approach to mark-up pricing. One is to establish base prices for all products and services by analyzing the actual operating costs and then adding an appropriate mark-up to each service. The final "standard" prices are then published in an "in-house" price list. The retail price list page is shown to customers. Some shops call this the *"counter price sheet."*

The second approach is to purchase a book of industry standard rates for the products and services that you offer. This book is then consulted each time a job estimate is required. The Industry Standard Rate book is most useful when it accommodates location and market conditions.

Except for competitive bid situations, mark-up pricing is probably not appropriate because it doesn't maximize profit when the possibility exists to charge as much as the market will bear. In addition, the cost basis for service is often difficult to determine. Nevertheless, mark-up pricing is often considered the fairest pricing method for both buyer and seller.

Mark-up pricing is the norm in the retail world.

Cost-Plus Pricing In *cost-plus pricing*, the customer pays for the cost of developing a product plus some percentage or fixed amount above cost. For example, a customer brings a complex and inter-dependent project to you. There are elements in the project whose costs are uncertain. Instead of trying to "guesstimate" your costs, you offer to do the job for your costs plus a percentage.

I've successfully implemented this strategy when a customer wants services that I don't provide. I subcontract the job and provide my client with a copy of the actual invoice from the subcontractor. On my invoice, I add a percentage to the subcontractor charge for my administration of the job.

Cost plus percentage pricing varies from 10% to over 40% depending on the tasks, the location, and the business.

Cost-Volume Pricing In this form of cost-oriented pricing, a cost-volume curve such as that shown in Figure 2-3 is generated to equate the volume of sales income to manufacturing and overhead costs. It shows graphically that as you increase sales, the net unit manufacturing costs decrease. A percentage of the cost of sales will expense out as overhead, so as volume increases, the cost of goods or services sold (per unit of product or service) actually decreases. This suggests that if you lower your sales price, more people should buy, and the added volume should further increase your profit.

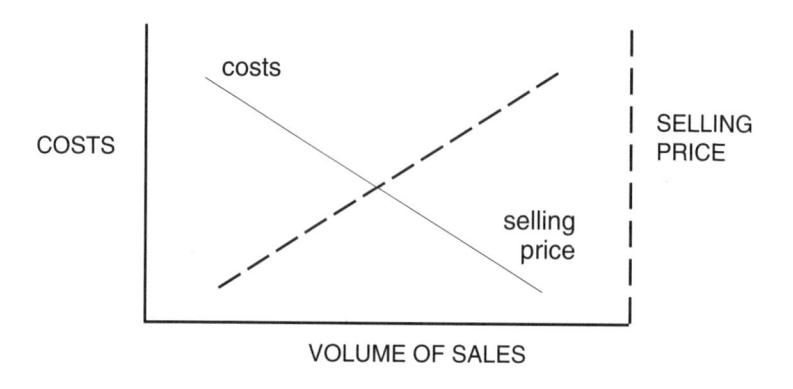

```
                        |
         costs          |
COSTS    \         /    | SELLING
          \       /     | PRICE
           \     /      |
            \   /       |
             \ /        |
              X         |
             / \ selling|
            /   \ price |
           /     \      |
          /       \     |
        VOLUME OF SALES
```

Fig 2-3. A typical cost-volume curve.

Some people call this approach *"doing yourself in."* It's risky because it presumes that your competition will sit still while you manipulate prices in the marketplace. This approach is based on your having an accurate assessment of the customer base and of your competition. And it assumes that you clearly understand your costs on a product-by-product and service-by-service basis.

The Cost-Volume approach is often a trap, because as you lower your price, your competition usually lowers theirs in response. You effectively become a price leader on the way down toward insolvency. The inherent risks are simply too great for most shop owners to attempt. Trying to optimize sales using a cost/volume curve is risky.

Profit-Oriented Pricing

In this pricing technique, the sales price is based on the profit desired. There are three forms of profit-based pricing—targeted profit, targeted return-on-sales, and targeted return-on-investment. In all three methods, you balance revenues and costs to establish a selling price.

PROFIT-ORIENTED PRICING

Targeted Profit
Targeted Return-On-Sales
Targeted Return-On-Investment

Figure 2-4. The three elements of profit-oriented pricing.

Targeted Profit Pricing In this method, you set an annual profit target of a specific dollar amount. You determine your fixed and variable costs. Then you estimate how many units of a product or service you can sell and how sensitive demand is to price. Next, you set a target profit value and decide what price you can charge.

Since profit equals revenue less costs, we can use the following formula to derive a price.

Targeted Profit = Total Revenue - Total Cost

where

Total Revenue = (Price) x (Quantity)

Total Cost = Fixed Cost - (Variable Costs x Quantity)

Therefore,

Profit = (Price)(Qty) - [Fixed Cost - (Variable Costs x Qty)]

Solving for price, we get:

$$\text{Price} = \frac{\text{Profit + Fixed Cost + (Variable Costs x Quantity)}}{\text{Quantity}}$$

This simplistic formula assumes that the price you select will not change the quantity of sales realized from those estimated. It also doesn't account for the investment needed to achieve the sales volume (cost of goods sold).

By knowing your cost of goods, the revenue you want and the profit you want to earn, you can back into this formula and determine the best quantity and the best selling price to use by changing the variables in your "what if" cost/price breakdown spreadsheet.

Targeted Return-on-Sales Pricing This method focuses on achieving a minimum percent return on each sale. In this case, you use the same fixed and variable costs established for the Targeted Profit pricing method, with the same quantity of sales. Then apply this data to the following formula:

$$\text{Targeted Return} = \frac{\text{Targeted Profit}}{\text{Total Revenue}}$$

$$= \frac{\text{Price x Qty - [Fixed Cost + (Vble Costs x Qty)]}}{\text{Price x Quantity}}$$

Solving for price we get:

$$\text{Price} = \frac{-\text{Fixed Cost} - (\text{Variable Costs} \times \text{Quantity})}{\text{Quantity} (\text{Targeted Return} - 1)}$$

The negative values in the top and bottom of the formula cancel out, resulting in a positive price value.

Targeted Return-on-Investment Pricing The *targeted return-on-investment* pricing method assumes that you can obtain at least as good a return on the money that you invested in a business as you can by investing in financial securities. If you feel that you can get a 15% return by investing in stocks, bonds, mutual funds, etc., then you can develop a business model that relates price, quantity, unit variable costs, fixed costs, overhead, taxes, etc. to yield the same 15% return on investment for a number of variable business options.

In this method, you select a profit and then work backward to determine what pricing will cover your expenses and still yield your desired return.

This is a sophisticated version of cost-plus pricing. The profit-oriented pricing methods are ideally suited for computer spreadsheet analysis.

Competition-Oriented Pricing

In *competition-oriented pricing*, you establish prices based on what your competition is doing. Referencing your prices to what the competition charges is a common business practice.

This approach includes price matching and percent-above or percent- below pricing strategies. The options that you can use include accepted customary pricing, subjective (at, above, or below market) pricing, and loss-leader break-even pricing.

> **COMPETITION-ORIENTED PRICING**
> ─ ─ ─ ─ ─ ─ ─ ─ ─
> Accepted Customary
> Going-Rate
> Subjective
> Loss-Leader

Figure 2-5. The four elements of competition-oriented pricing.

Accepted Customary Pricing Here, the customer expects to pay a "standard" fee for certain products or services. For years, black and white copies cost 10¢ each. To raise your price to 15¢ would exceed the accepted price threshold of your customers and they would shop elsewhere. When paperback books were priced at $3.95 each, and printing costs increased, a publisher would change the quality of the paper, or the quality of the binding to keep manufacturing costs low so they could hold the $3.95 price constant for the buying public.

Bucking the accepted standard price can also be risky. Lower price too much and customers think they're getting poor quality. Raise prices too much and customers think you're too expensive. Competitor pricing and market expectations drive your pricing decisions.

Going-Rate Pricing This method is common. It's based on charging what the competition is charging. It doesn't require analysis to determine the best prices for a profit objective. And it assumes that your competition is being successful by charging the prices that they charge.

There's a risk involved when you assume that your competition knows what they're doing. They could be selling at a loss or below acceptable profit levels without your knowing it. If all the competitors begin matching each other, everyone can lose money together. Some say "misery loves company," but this is taking the adage too far.

Subjective Pricing After years in the business, an owner gets a "feel" for what a price should be. Using this subjective feeling, the owner can price products and services at, below, or above this benchmark.

Businesses that target their products and services for a specific market, will price accordingly. If you want to sell to the high-end corporate customer, you will price your products and services to meet the expectations of this market. You will base your prices on market research and your opinion of what is acceptable.

Loss-Leader Pricing In *loss-leader* pricing, a product or service is sold at break-even or just below cost to attract customers to your business and to sell them on your other products and services.

Your goal is not to increase sales of the "no-profit" product, but to attract sales of higher-margin products and services.

In a retail store, magazines are not very profitable (20% gross margin), but magazine purchases often accompany purchases of candy and drinks. These other products have higher margins. Thus, the magazines are almost loss-leaders just to sell more snacks and soft drinks.

Composite Pricing

You can combine pricing methods to produce your own composite pricing technique. For example, you can establish one set of prices for established products and another for new products. You can price for flexibility to sell to a particular market niche, bundle your products, price for leadership, and price for market share.

```
Demand  ──┐                    ┌── custom
Cost   ──┤   PRICING          ├── prices
Profit ──┤    MODEL           ├── for each
Competition ──┘                └── product or
                                   service
```

Figure 2-6. The optimum price model considers all forms of pricing.

Each method assumes different goals, objectives, assumptions, and requirements. Each method also has its own deficiencies. The optimum way to price is to develop a composite that includes the best things from each approach.

Use the industry standard rates. Consider the competition's pricing. Do a cost analysis on your own business. Determine the time it takes you to perform certain tasks. Place a value on your skills and your experience. Then, wrap all this into a custom price list that works for you.

Once your draft price list is complete, adjust and fine tune the basis for each price to create your own final rates. By developing a custom rate pricing structure, you can quickly and accurately provide an estimate without having to spend a lot of time re-constructing your business cost basis. With your composite pricing guide, you can bid on jobs with full confidence that a desired profit margin is already integrated into each price quote. A computer spreadsheet program can be used to develop pricing models that you can adjust to find the optimum strategies for each product and service.

Chapter 5 describes how to establish production standards and budgeted hourly rates so you can bid firm fixed price on job opportunities.

Estimating Demand

Demand for your products and services is directly influenced by the customers that you target — their tastes and preferences, their income, the size of this market, and the price and availability that you establish.

These demand factors can be represented in a curve that graphically shows the maximum number of products and services that you believe customers will buy at a given price. In the demand curve shown in Figure 2-2, the vertical axis is price. The horizontal axis represents quantity of sales. The curve shows how changes in price affect changes in the quantity of a product or service demanded by the customer base.

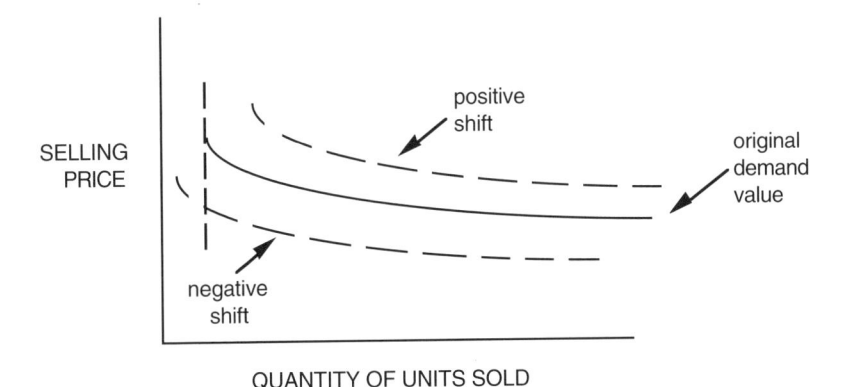

Fig. 2-7. A typical demand curve.

The trick here is to determine where the curve should be on the graph — selling price versus quantity sold. An increase in the size of the market causes the curve to shift to the right (positive). An increase in competition causes it to shift to the left (negative). An increase in the average income level of your customer base causes a positive shift to the right—more products are demanded. An introduction of new technology can cause a negative shift of the curve (to the left). An increase in the need for desktop publishing and prepress services will cause a positive shift of the curve (to the right).

Therefore, as you encourage the corporate and private users to buy more DTP and prepress services, the profession as a whole will benefit. This is why associations and other organizations are so important in making business better for the good of an industry or profession.

Elasticity

The slope of the demand curve is called its *"elasticity factor."* If the market for a product or service is price sensitive, demand is said to be *"elastic."* Sales will respond to price.

A decrease in price can generate enough additional sales to increase the total revenue because the product demand is elastic. If a change in price has no effect on total revenue, the demand curve is said to have *"unitary elasticity."*

And if a reduction in price actually results in a decrease in revenue, the demand is said to be *"inelastic."* In this case, raising the price will generate more revenue because of the higher price received for each unit sold.

Figures 2-8, 2-9, and 2-10 describe the elastic, unitary elastic, and inelastic demand conditions.

Figure 2-8. Elasticity of demand (Elastic).

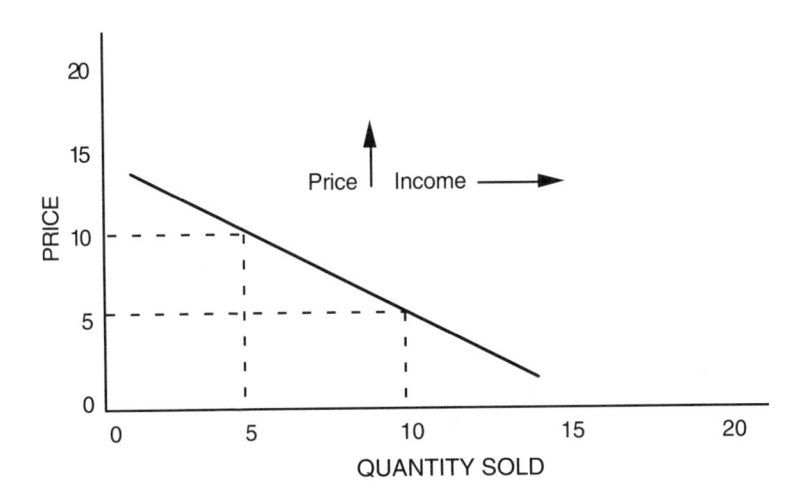

Figure 2-9. Elasticity of demand (Unitary Elastic).

36 - Pricing Guide for Desktop Services

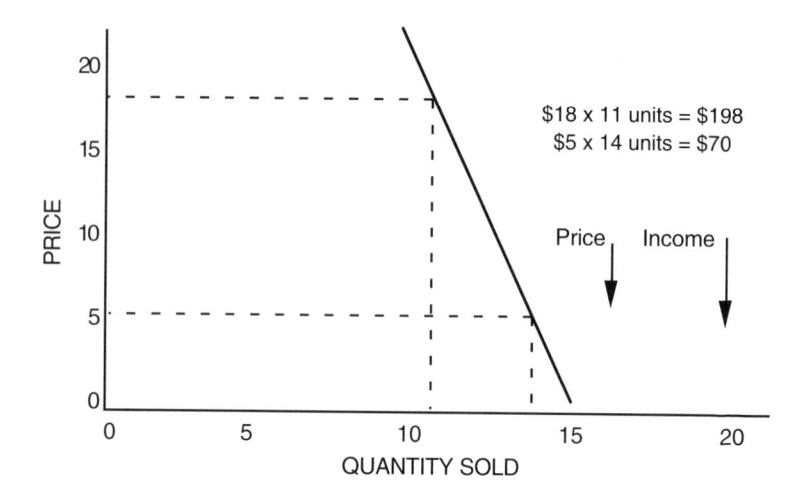

```
        $18 x 11 units = $198
        $5 x 14 units = $70
```

Figure 2-10. Elasticity of demand (Inelastic).

The shape of the elasticity curve varies by product or service and by time. A product with a wide customer-base appeal is more price elastic than one with a limited appeal.

Factors Affecting Elasticity of Demand Two factors have the most influence on elasticity—the relative importance of the product to the customer's budget, and the availability of alternative products. A high-cost job can make a customer price sensitive (demand becomes elastic), but an inexpensive job such as getting a 3-page letter printed out on a laser printer has little impact on a budget, so price sensitivity does not play an important role in their buying decision.

This is why there are more promotions for support on larger projects than there are for relatively minor sales such as disk copying, data conversion, and simple hard copy printouts.

However, the availability of alternative products and services does have a significant influence on demand. When there are dozens of DTP and prepress shops offering the same products and services, the customer will shop for the lowest price. This elasticity makes them price sensitive, and they will have little or no shop loyalty. To hold these customers, you must be price vigilant and offer to renegotiate if a customer discovers a competitor offering lower prices.

However, be cautious that you aren't being duped by the customer. And, also be careful that you don't accept a job at a loss. You're in business to make a profit.

Determining Elasticity of Demand Elasticity is difficult to measure. The key here is to tap every available resource to determine all you can about the shape of the demand curve for those products and services that you offer.

Typical resources include market analysis, special reports, statistical analysis, market surveys, experimentation, and experience. Use your modem to access relevant on-line services. Contact your local libraries to get research support. Work through your local and national business organizations to gather information. Ask your colleagues. Ask your customers. Ask your competitors. Attend business lunches and networking groups. Gather intelligence wherever you are and whenever you can.

A recent study found that a price increase between 10% and 20% had little affect on reduced purchases, but an increase of 40% or more prompted customers to seek alternatives, including going out of town for support.

Actions in Each Demand Elasticity Situation If demand is elastic, make every effort to price competitively. If demand changes little as price is varied, change your product or service to make it more elastic.

If revenue decreases as price is increased (inelastic), consider raising your prices to generate more revenue (even with fewer sales). You could also compete based on non-price factors such as the expertise of your staff or the speed of your response.

Summary

Price and pricing comprise a fascinating and dynamic aspect of business. Now that you understand price and how it affects the success of your business, you can see that many factors are involved in the prices that you set. In the next chapter, you'll explore pricing strategies and discover how to develop a success strategy for your own business. You'll also learn how to break out top profits in a competitive market.

3

Developing A Pricing Strategy

"Think of pricing as a marketing strategy."

Pricing has been described as one of the most challenging aspects of operating a business. To succeed in business, just as to succeed in sports, you need goals, objectives and a strategy. In your business plan, you established your goals and objectives. This chapter will help you establish a strategy. Besides learning how to develop a strategic plan for successful pricing, you'll be exposed to creative pricing techniques currently being used by shop owners around the country. You'll also learn when and how to raise prices, and when and how to reduce prices while continuing to grow a profitable business.

Strategic Thinking

Pricing decisions are often the result of hunch, gut feel, intuition, or "let's charge that price, too" reactions. Yet there are practical ways to make good pricing decisions. These methods become tools that a business owner uses to conduct market analysis and to develop business strategies.

Each prospective customer has a need that requires intelligent response to price, quality, and schedule. You add value by the way that you handle these factors. If you can offer the greatest value in at least one of these three areas, you should get more than your share of the available business.

There are two distinctly different types of customers that you must deal with in pricing your products and services—the *commodity customer* and the *solutions customer*. The commodity customer wants to buy a product at the lowest cost and neither wants nor desires hand-holding. The solutions customer wants the best price but also wants a source for answers when operations become too complex and confusing.

Many businesses offer basic products without technical support. Other businesses thrive on the premise that the customer needs information and place customer service and support paramount in their strategic decisions.

In today's economic climate, most customers seem motivated only by price. They'll quickly take their business elsewhere when problems arise or your quoted price exceeds their threshold. Although little customer loyalty exists (or business-to-customer loyalty, for that matter), the customer's expectations and attitudes still lag whatever business loyalty that may exist.

However, contrary to what you may currently feel, the solutions-oriented business will likely supersede the commodity-oriented business within the next four or five years. Technology and information transfer are becoming too complex for simple solutions. The company that can guide a customer through a project will likely earn respect and more business. For customers interested only in price and output, you can establish a special rate structure for them (differential pricing). Or, let them seek out and purchase from the "canned-product" low price shops.

To develop your strategy, you must think like a customer. This means that you've truly got to know your customer. What first attracts them to a business? Price? Quality? Response time? If it's price, then you must be competitive. I didn't say charge the lowest price in the area. Nor did I say be the most expensive (although there's much to be said for being among the higher priced companies). The key is to provide sufficient perceived—as well as real—value to warrant the prices that you charge.

A pricing strategy that encourages higher sales volume in an elastic market can produce stronger profits. If you adopt a pricing strategy based on maintaining a high profit margin, you may find your customers moving to another competitor. This causes some shops to focus on unique and special services. With something distinct to offer, your margins are higher and the competition is reduced. The personal computer industry once enjoyed this position, but high margins brought in more competitors until price cutting erupted. Today, the PC is simply a hardware commodity. Profit margins on these products have gone into the tank.

A similar thing is happening in laser printing and imagesetting services. Some businesses have reduced their prices to a point that, although their volume is high, their margin is so low that profit is minimum. These businesses use the laser and imagesetter services as "loss leaders" while pushing other (added) services such as image cleanup/retouching to recoup a healthy net margin.

One school of thought suggests that shops bundle services to minimize the complexity that the customer can perceive, offering a "total" solution to any job. Some customers prefer not to get involved in the difficult stages of document design and printing. Anything that you can do to help in this process lends value to your business.

Typically, larger companies prefer a "bundled solution" approach. Small businesses will likely opt for the unbundled approach and purchase only those services that they can't provide themselves. They are reluctant to pay for services that they don't need or can do themselves.

Talk to any customer, and they'll say that quality is very important. Yet, when push comes to shove, many customers are willing to accept lower quality to get a better price or response time. It's up to you to find what quality level they will accept and then produce to this standard.

To many business people, fast response is key. They are typically rushed on most projects and appreciate a support organization that can work evenings and weekends (if necessary) to get out a job that is well done and meets their harried schedule. Some shops find that over 60% of their business involves rush jobs. Chapter 6 covers pricing surcharges for rush work.

Critical Factors in Your Price Strategy

As shown in Figure 3-1, five factors define the range of options that you have in setting price —real costs and profits, the customer's perceived value of your products and services relative to alternative choices, the differences in the various segments of your market, likely reactions from competitors, and your company's marketing objectives. Each of these issues should be considered when you develop your strategy for pricing.

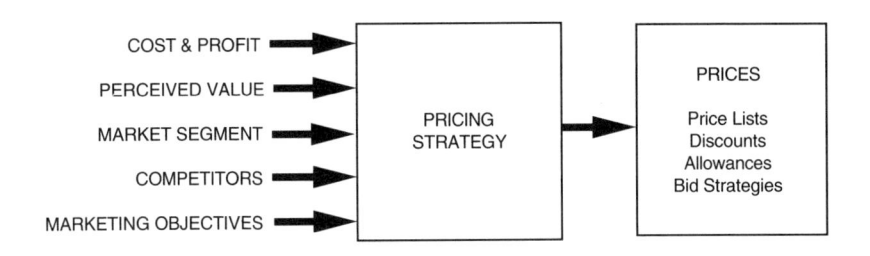

```
COST & PROFIT        ──▶
PERCEIVED VALUE      ──▶                              PRICES
MARKET SEGMENT       ──▶    PRICING       ──▶         Price Lists
                            STRATEGY                  Discounts
COMPETITORS          ──▶                              Allowances
                                                      Bid Strategies
MARKETING OBJECTIVES ──▶
```

Figure 3-1. Five factors affect the prices you charge.

Notice that I said strategy. Many businesses are followers. They price goods and services based on what competitors charge. But what happens when all shops are doing the same thing? There is no leader, just price confusion. You need a logical way to determine what your prices ought to be. Then you can decide what you want them to be. At least you'll know the difference. And you'll feel comfortable that you're pricing for profit, not for paucity (scarceness, or meager income).

You need to clearly understand why you're in business. Is your goal to build a retirement nest egg? Is it to build a large, thriving business to turn over to your kids? Is it to just have fun in life? Is it to earn all the money that you can by a certain age? Is it to return good service to a country that has served you so well? Whatever the reason, you need to recognize and accept why you are operating your business.

Next, you must decide the real nature of your business. Is your business to provide solutions? It is to provide time for others to do different things? Are you offering a profit opportunity for your customers? Are you selling layout and design, or are you selling worry-free publishing?

Consider the "Gillette safety razor" strategy. Gillette made his profit by selling blades, not by selling razors.

He sold his razor at a loss so he could really sell the patented blades at a comfortable mark-up. What the customer wanted was a cheaper shave. Gillette sold a way to get a one penny shave—substantially less than going to a barber at the time.

Xerox adopted the Gillette razor pricing strategy and developed a huge market by selling a copy of a document, not by selling a copying machine. There could be a Gillette razor in your business too.

From your analysis you can develop a mission statement that explains why you're operating your business. Take time to write a brief mission statement describing what kind of company you are and where you intend to go. Chart your course.

With this statement clearly in mind, gather your staff and begin an analysis process leading to goals and objectives. Look at your products and services. Are you providing the right products and services to the right markets in the right time frame? What about your competitors? What products and services are they offering? What is their market position? What can you determine about the area they cover, the prices they charge, and the extent of their business? Can you spot any weaknesses in their strategy?

Based on this assessment, establish short term and long term goals for your business. Decide where you plan to go, what you plan to do, and where you plan to be three years from now. Do you want to improve efficiency? Quality? Market share? This self-introspection process is best accomplished as a team—all of your full time staff should be involved.

The goals that you establish form the basis for your marketing plan—your road map for operations. A key to surviving a competitive market is good planning followed by good plan execution.

After a look at the long range, take a shorter view and answer the same questions for the near term. What do you want to accomplish each year between now and three years from now? This is the basis for your tactical plan.

Based on the strategic (long term) plan and your tactical (short term) plan, carefully establish business objectives. These objectives should be specifically expressed and be both achievable, and measurable. Each objective should have an associated responsible person and a deadline for accomplishment.

Part of these objectives address pricing. Based on these objectives, develop a pricing strategy that represents a framework in which your pricing objectives can be translated into pricing tactics. These tactics become the specific decisions or actions that you'll follow to carry out your formula for success.

Once you've clearly defined the goals and objectives for your business, communicate these to your staff. It is from these goals and objectives that you establish specific tasks for each of your employees.

As you implement your plan, monitor the daily operations and periodically measure quantitatively how you and your team are doing in meeting your objectives. When an objective has been met, tell your staff. Then reward everyone for their part in making success happen. Many companies are giving bonus awards for performance. Returning 10% of net profit for realizing a goal is not out of line. Just remember to reward everyone who was responsible for making that goal a reality.

If your goals become unrealistic, change the formula, change the ground rules, or change the players (if necessary). It's important to accept change in your formula for success. Change will occur. And only by revising your goals and objectives can you keep everything on a known path.

Eight Steps to Setting Price

There are eight steps that you must perform to arrive at the price for a product or service.

1. Identify the constraints and objectives in your pricing strategy.
2. Estimate the demand for your services.
3. Estimate the demand elasticity associated with your product or service. You need to know the pros and cons of each of your products and services. You need to determine how customers and your competitors may react to any price change you make. To help, get input from people outside your company—customers, vendors, colleagues, and your competitors.
4. Estimate the possible sales revenue.
5. Determine the cost, and analyze its relationship to sales volume and profit.
6. Select an initial set of prices based on demand, cost, profit, and competition.
7. Establish the pricing policy on which you base your list or quotable prices. This can be a single price policy, a flexible price policy, or an incremental cost-revenue balancing policy.
8. Make adjustments to your list of quotable prices based on discounts, or special allowances.

Establishing Pricing Objectives

Pricing objectives are the overall goals or targets that you want to reach.

Typically, short term objectives focus on achieving some level of profit, surviving a down economy, protecting your market share, discouraging or weakening competition, preventing a rival with a cash flow problem from disrupting the market, getting a specified return on investment, or achieving some level of personal satisfaction and reward.

Long term objectives can include becoming a recognized leader in the marketplace, achieving top quality in a particular niche, reaching some specified sales volume, or positioning your business for a financially rewarding sellout.

Whatever you decide, be sure to make your objectives consistent with the mission statement that describes your business. Some businesses use return-on-investment (ROI) as a measurement. Others use inventory turnover and number of sales to help decide if an objective has been met.

If you decide to target the upscale and more sophisticated customer, then design your shop and your business forms to reflect this ambience. But don't then set your rates to appeal to the price-sensitive customers. If you want to be unique, then your prices should reflect this. They also should be in line with your expenses.

Studying the Market

Make a thorough study of the potential in the market that you've selected.

How many people are buying your products and services? How many are located in your immediate area? What's the demographic trend for the future? What is the purchasing power of your market? What prices are customers willing to pay right now? Who are your customers? What businesses are they in? What businesses will they be operating in five years?

Determining Demand

To settle on a strategy for pricing products and services, you need a feel for the demand for what you offer. As you discovered in Chapter 2 market demand can be elastic, inelastic or somewhere in between. Only you can estimate the demand elasticity of your products and services.

Do your research to determine if there really IS enough demand for your services to really warrant offering these. As you notice that fax machines are rapidly being brought into the home office, should you still offer fax services?

Demand is an interesting human phenomenon. And it can change almost overnight. Look at what happens when a successful motion picture comes out. People flock to buy T-shirts, posters and toys depicting scenes or characters from the movie. When color copying was introduced, demand grew as business people began flocked to those businesses that could offer this service.

You must keep aware of new technology and new concepts. Demand can grow rapidly. Those shops, who are quick on their feet, can reap a terrific harvest by being there with the right service at the right time.

Studying the Competition

Take a long, hard look at your competitors. What are they doing right? What are they doing wrong? How are they pricing their products and services? What "extras" are they offering? Who are they? Where are they? How successful do they seem? Where do they advertise? How often? How large an ad do they place? What professional groups or organizations do they join? What does their financial statement (10-K financial report) tell you about how successful they are? What markets do they seem to be serving?

Then make some strategic decisions based on your findings. Should you price to match your competition? This serves to stabilize prices and avoid costly price wars. But it can stagnate your business. Is a niche market developing that is not being served? Should you focus on this niche market and then price to avoid competition? This action lets you make a reasonable profit without attracting new competitors.

If your products and services are in strong demand and there's a shortage of businesses like yours, you could maximize your profits by raising prices to "the most the market can bear." Be aware that this high pricing could be perceived as "gouging" and "unethical" by customers and business colleagues.

The customer eventually dictates price. And if a competitor is attracted to your niche, those over-charged customers have memories like an elephant. The trick is to set your prices high enough to keep customers, but not so high that you attract new competitors, or so high that the legality of your pricing becomes an issue with government or other local businesses. Remember, if you charge very high prices over a short term, you risk losing market share to competitors who are willing to offer the same or similar services at lower prices.

Studying the Economy

Make an assessment of current economic conditions. What is the business climate? What is it expected to be next year? Who are the winners in this economy? Which businesses are growing? Which are stagnating? Which are declining? Who's reducing staff—laying off and offering early retirements? Are there opportunities for short term business with those companies that have reduced staff yet retained document-generation requirements? What are the current governmental fiscal policies expected to do to businesses in your state? Which companies are headed toward Chapter 11 bankruptcy? Which are already there?

During uncertain times, there are several actions that you can take to ease the economic affects on your business. You can eliminate credit. You can modify your discount policies so your customers get a larger discount for paying early. You can even reduce the discount that you offer. You can reduce the net payment due time. You can unbundle products and services to offer more selection to price-sensitive customers. You can also price for delivery from your shop and not include shipping or free pick-up and delivery as part of your own cost of doing business.

Estimating Your Costs

Few shop owners know their actual costs. In fact, when owner-operators calculate their true costs, some have discovered to their dismay that their operating costs exceed revenue. They are actually paying more to earn less.

But what is cost? And how does cost relate to productivity and profit?

There are several types of costs that you must incorporate in your pricing strategy. These include wages, overhead expenses, return on investment, and profit. Your costs are also influenced by the productivity of your shop. Each of these will be discussed in some detail in Chapters 4 and 5.

Cost can also include what you pay to make your market aware of and understand your product or service. Your price structure should take into account the cost for advertising. According to an article in *Entrepreneur*, advertising costs can be as much as 60 percent of sales revenue. The article described how Orville Redenbacher popcorn has a higher price than competing products because they spend more money on advertising to convince customers that their popcorn is better than other brands. This advertising costs is reflected in their price.

Selecting Return on Investment

Not many shop owners take time to think about or calculate the amount of money that they've invested (poured) into their business. But if you borrowed money to buy computer equipment or software, you would surely pay interest on the loan. The same holds true if you were to "loan" money to a business—your business. You deserve at least the same interest earnings on your loan. This is called *"return on investment"* or simply *ROI*. If you put money into your business, but don't consider it a loan that earns interest, you're cheating yourself.

Even a modest return of 4% on your investment will just keep up with inflation. You should calculate the ROI "cost of seed money" to capitalize your business, and include ROI as a repayment cost factor when you establish your prices and service rates.

Paying Back Loans

Paying your company back for loans to buy hardware and software is called *"debt servicing."* As you periodically update your equipment and upgrade your software, you'll deal with depreciation. You'll also deal with servicing the debt.

Your prices should incorporate and accommodate paying back loans. If you can operate debt-free, great. But if you're like most shop owners, you'll find a need to get loans to purchase or lease larger, more capable equipment. To pay back these loans integrate debt servicing into your pricing formula.

Perspectives on Pricing

The way service is priced is changing. The mood is away from selecting a winning proposal based on the lowest bid. Although price will always be important, the buyer's perception of your ability to perform at an agreed price is becoming paramount.

In the past, many businesses earned a reputation for taking a loss on the first contract to "get their foot in the door." After the contract was awarded, they then tried to "get well" by promoting changes for which they could charge higher fees. In the desktop publishing and prepress professions, as competition increases, customers look critically at differentiating factors such as quality, professional attitude, and value-added service. These factors should be considered part of your total pricing package.

Customers want to know how your service will be implemented. Will you use quality paper? What is your best print resolution? Will the layout be easy to modify? Can you expand your support as a need develops for other services? Are you able to consistently provide outstanding service?

The concept of quality is beginning to sink into the minds of buyers. The trend is for customers to make price a secondary issue. Many will be willing to spend more to get quality products and service. This phenomenon will be affected by economic downturns, but the trend strongly suggests that customers will gravitate to businesses that consistently offer quality service.

Notes on Pricing Service

In-house hourly service rates vary from $20 to $95 (some prepress system work is billed out at over $150 an hour). Few owners (18%) charge for travel time if they have to go out to a customer's site. Most shop owners place no value on the difference between a client bringing a job to them or to their sending someone out to pick up the job. They are accepting added costs without adding income at the other end.

A sad commentary is that few shop owners understand why they should charge a different rate for different types of service. Many owner-operators leave a lot of money on the table when they price a job.

Take a hard look at all the services that you provide. Assess the worth associated with the value of each function or output. Then review, implement, and adjust your rates accordingly. Recognize and then consciously decide if you still want to provide a service free.

Is Price King?

How much value do your customers place on your level of service? Depending on the type of customers to which you focus your marketing and advertising, the value can be significant.

Some business owners openly list prices 15 to 20% higher than competitors. But, usually these shops have earned a reputation for providing the best customer service in the area. Corporate customers will pay more when you make them feel that they're important to you and that your service is high quality and fast.

What Customers Really Want

A recent letter to the editor of *Entrepreneur Magazine* succinctly explained why customers buy. There are four basic reasons for exchanging money for products or services: to make more money, to save money, to save time, or to increase productivity.

A prospect coming into your shop is seeking answers and solutions. And they seek value. The service and support provided by your business is rated by your customers based on responsiveness and the quality of your work. It's also rated on the knowledge that your team has of the customer's business.

Many customers want to know how your particular service and support can give them an edge over their competitors. If you can show them solutions—good output that you've produced—if you can show them designs that won awards, or that have been touted as among the top response-pulling ads in a publication, you'll win their business. Consistently strive to be the best.

Then, find out what your customers really want. Develop an ability to listen well and be consistently sensitive for market intelligence. Go to great extremes to learn the business of each client. Many of them operate on a minute-to-minute schedule and can't afford delays. Discover their concerns, problems, and frustrations. See if you can provide solutions to part of their needs. Understand their document generation problems and then make a sincere effort to help them solve each one.

Customer surveys suggest that the most important factors driving purchase decisions are price, quality, and commitment to customer service—in that order. There is no common reference for the meaning of price. Each customer has their own measurement. The key is that customers buy because they are willing to trade dollars for perceived benefit—price for value.

Looking Beyond Price

Once a prospect gets attracted by your price, other factors come into play.

Shop image. This is produced by the way your people answer the telephone, how they react when customers enter your shop, and how you and your people treat each customer during and after a sale.

Ability to meet specification. Don't advertise or suggest capabilities that you don't have. Focus on what you can do best given the people, the equipment, and the time that you actually have.

Work samples. Have a portfolio of samples to show your prospect. If possible show them how they were produced. (e.g., Let them watch you prepare a sample application in the computer and then print it on your laser printer or imagesetter. Let them see you cut, trim and bind some workbooks for a local company.) Not only does this give them an idea of your operation, it may spark ideas of other projects they may want to have you do for them.

Pick-up and delivery. Time is money. If a client can hand off a job to you and then focus on what they do best, everyone wins. Explain to them that their time may not be well spent driving across town to bring a job to you or to drive over to pick up completed work. Suggest that you pick up and deliver the work (for a modest fee).

Distance from customer. Increasingly, businesses are seeking local support. Therefore, concentrate the majority of your marketing and advertising in your own neighborhood.

References. You may convert a reluctant prospect to a solid customer by offering to let them talk to other companies to whom you've provided products or services. Be sure to get permission from each reference before you suggest that a prospect call them.

Quoted versus actual delivery date. Delivering a product 10 days early may be as bad as delivering it 10 days late. An early response could introduce possible storage and loss or damage problems for the customer. It's best to negotiate a delivery date and then to deliver on that date or a day earlier. Avoid late deliveries. These can cause the loss of repeat business.

Payment terms. We all want cash up front, but America is a country based on credit. So, develop a "terms and conditions" strategy that is comfortable for everyone. On small jobs, let customers pay in full upon delivery. On larger jobs, get a percentage up front, a percentage upon completion of some agreed milestone event, and a final percentage upon completion and sign-off of the job. For loyal repeat customers, work out a net payment time for your work, but be open and up front with them regarding the need for working capital to do the best job you can for them. Since most of your customers will likely be small business entrepreneurs, they will understand cash flow and are usually easy to work with on payments. Frank and honest communication is the key.

Will Customers Pay for Added Value?

Everyone wants more value added to a product or service. But few seem willing to pay for it.

Those companies that boast many forms of added value—free pickup and delivery, overnight response, special document design classes, etc. will find a ready market for the "free" part of their service. But, with desktop publishing becoming so common, some customers perceive that the availability of desktop design makes document layout a commodity form of service. They have difficulty accepting that good layout doesn't just magically occur.

As more and more of them actually attempt DTP on their own, they begin to realize that a lousy design on a powerful computer with very capable software is still a lousy design. Education and experience make believers (and ready customers) out of these people.

However, many of them become quite adept at spotting the new business offering "added value" at little or no cost. They swoop in on inexperienced business owners and literally suck the energy and capability out of these unsuspecting operators, leaving a broke and broken relic, milked into giving quality work at pauper-producing prices.

Pricing Assumptions by Competitors

If your pricing strategy is based on inadequate sample sizes, or bad information, you could put your faith in, and make pricing decisions on data that may be grossly in error.

If your competitors are reacting to each other's pricing moves, they may follow themselves and consistently be losing money. Don't mirror the competition. Never assume that they know best. They usually don't.

Do your own analysis. Develop your own desired prices. Then compare these with the competition to see how prices vary. Closely evaluate prices that differ widely from what your competition charges. They may be way off base and losing money just offering those services.

Continually modify your model until you achieve a price list based on sound cost analysis and savvy market research.

The High Price Myth

Some perceptions about your business are complimentary and can work to your advantage. If a competitor describes you as aggressive, your best response may be to simply thank them. If you're known as high priced, this can be bad. It can also be very good.

Being labeled as expensive is not bad as long as you provide plenty of value for what you do. If your fees are among the top in your area, you can only affect this perception by lowering your prices. However, if you do this, you risk suggesting a reduction in service or quality.

Actually, customers will grumble, but they'll pay more if you're perceived as providing the best products and services available. The best restaurants are expected to charge top rates. Yet, they don't lack for customers.

A printing industry rule of thumb is that if you don't get at least 20 percent of your customers complaining about your prices, you've probably set your rates too low.

Keeping your fees high means that competition can challenge you with lower rates, but they may not be able to survive the extremely low profit margins. After all, just like in retail, business success in desktop publishing and prepress is based on margin. We can purchase the same types of equipment and hire the same type of support. What makes us different is our operating location, how we perceive and apply customer service, and what margin of profit we are willing to accept.

Creative Pricing Strategies

There's pricing, and then there's pricing. As shown in Figure 3-2, there are many strategies being used by entrepreneurs around North America. In this section I'll share some of the creative ways that other business owners are pricing their products and services.

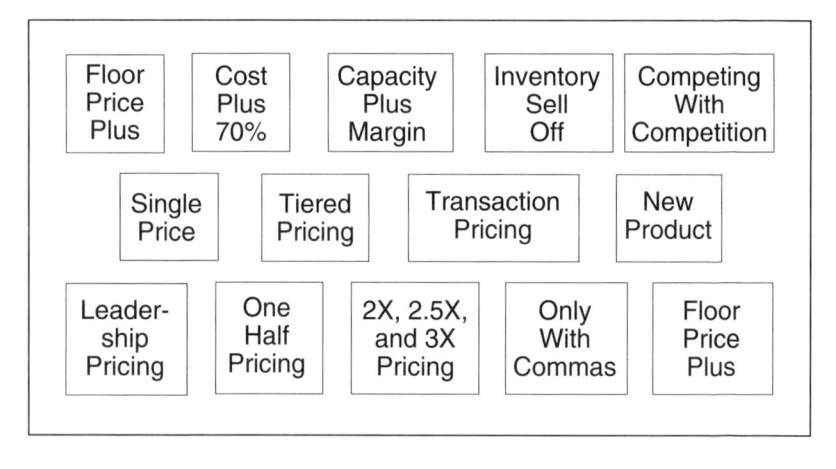

Floor Price Plus	Cost Plus 70%	Capacity Plus Margin	Inventory Sell Off	Competing With Competition
Single Price	Tiered Pricing	Transaction Pricing		New Product
Leadership Pricing	One Half Pricing	2X, 2.5X, and 3X Pricing	Only With Commas	Floor Price Plus

Figure 3-2. Various pricing strategies.

Floor Price Plus Some

Determine the minimum price at which you are willing to sell a product or service. This becomes the *floor price*. Then establish a target sales price. Any sale that is less than the floor price will result in a loss. So by clearly defining your "must-sell-at" and "want-to-sell-at" levels, you can determine how each sale impacts the profitability of your shop. This lets you sell at different price levels and still have a feel for profit per sale. You can accept lower margins on some sales and higher margins on those sales in which you enjoy a market niche.

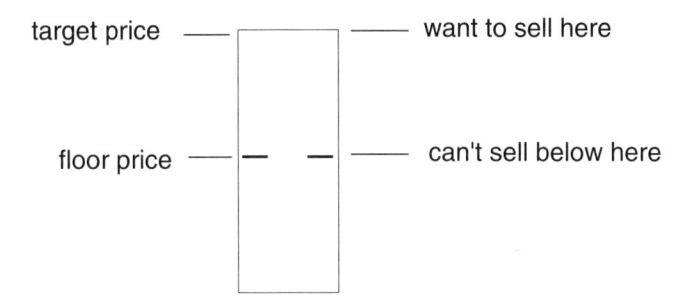

Figure 3-3. Floor price plus some strategy.

The trick is to avoid tying up valuable resources on jobs that contribute little to your bottom line. Each sale must be evaluated relative to your available capacity and where the sale income falls in your floor/target price range.

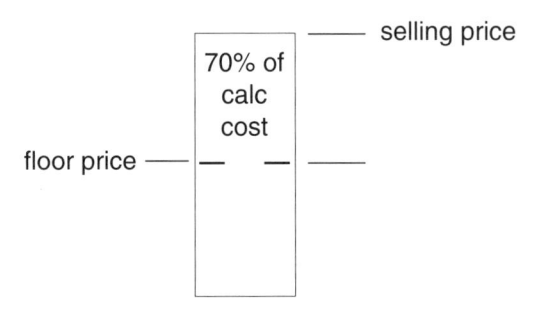

Figure 3-4. Calculated cost plus 70% strategy.

Calculated Cost Plus 70%

In this strategy, you calculate your job cost and add 70% more, disregarding any discount. This becomes your selling price—simple to calculate and simple to apply.

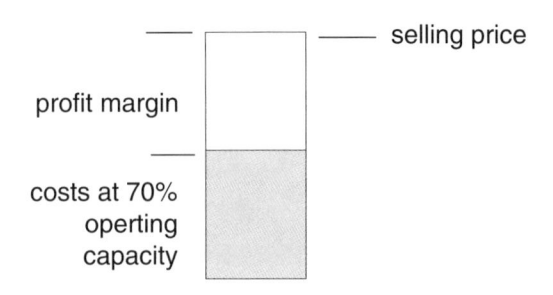

Figure 3-5. Percent capacity plus margin strategy.

Percent Capacity Plus Margin

Here you calculate your standard costs as if your shop is operating at 70% of capacity. Then you add a specific profit "margin" equal to your standard costs to arrive at a price.

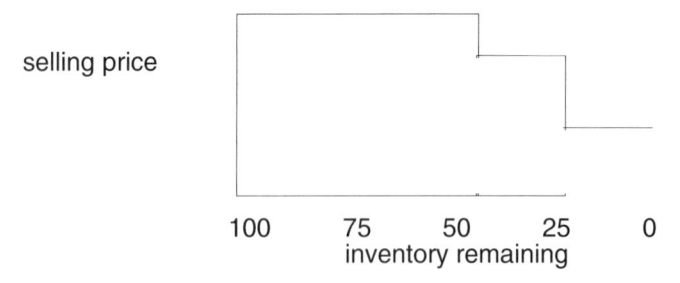

Figure 3-6. Net revenue, inventory sell-off strategy.

Net Revenue, Inventory Sell Off

Also called *net revenue marginal analysis*, this approach is used to determine when the last item in an inventory lot has been sold. It lets you reduce the selling price for remaining inventory so you can eliminate dated inventory.

This technique is typically used for retail products such as disks of clip art, toner cartridges, etc. It can also be used to meet aggressive sales tactics by your competition.

Competing with the Competition

Shop owners occasionally implement creative pricing techniques, such as adding a "fair" margin of profit to their costs to arrive at a selling price. Then they compare this price with that being charged by other shops to see if their prices are competitive.

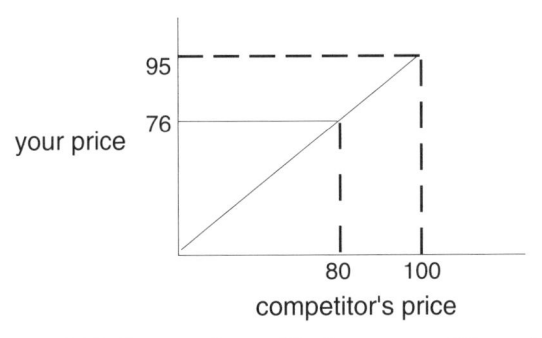

Figure 3-7. Competing with the competition strategy.

Another technique is to find out what a competitor is charging and then to charge five percent less.

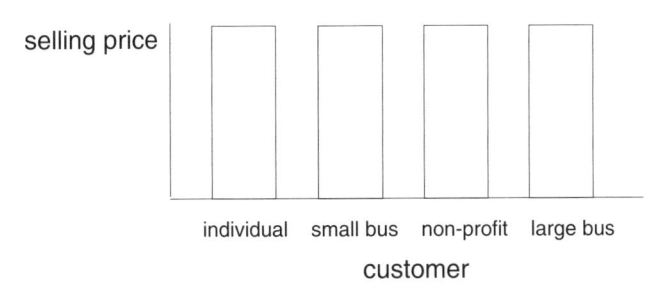

Figure 3-8. Single price, any customer strategy.

Single Price, Any Customer Pricing

In this strategy, you apply a fixed price schedule to every customer. No customer gets special treatment. The high-end corporate customer pays the same fee as the non-profit, low-budget customer.

Tiered Pricing

You've unbundled your products and services. You've tweaked all of your charges. You found discounting a fast way to eat into profits, so you minimize offering discounts and allowances. And still your margins continue to squeeze your bottom line.

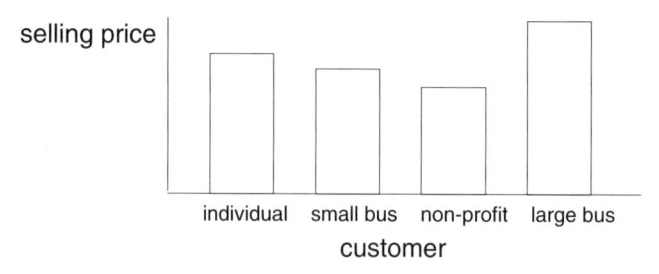

[Bar chart: selling price vs customer (individual, small bus, non-profit, large bus)]

Figure 3-9. Tiered pricing strategy.

Then you decide to go after the bigger accounts using a variable *(tiered)* pricing strategy. This means that you bill larger companies more for your products and services than you would charge a smaller business customer.

Your variable pricing strategy applies different prices to different customers. A high-end corporate client is charged a premium price while a non-profit organization or home-office entrepreneur is charged a much lower fee. There is a risk here for price discrimination, so be sure to work costs and margins carefully.

Research indicates that large companies are often less fazed by higher fees than the smaller companies. These larger organizations are more concerned with your survival, availability and service support than they are with what you charge. They take longer to get signed up to your products and services, but they don't dicker over "nickles and dimes." Therefore, the larger they are, the better your chance of increasing your fees on everything you offer. These customers appreciate the value your shop has to offer and are willing to pay more for your support.

Some shops find that business from the larger accounts gives a strong boost to their net profit. However, you must factor in the additional effort required to realize the sale. The after-the-sale support can also increase significantly.

Often, large accounts will pay a consulting fee up front, but your cost-of-sale can also be larger because they may insist on a lengthy multi-page proposal before any contract is signed and billable work can begin.

Then, there's the specter of discounting. It never really goes away. It looms on the horizon even with large companies. If they make a volume buy, they will likely expect a discount.

This means that your pricing strategy for larger accounts takes as much analysis as your strategy for the average accounts. You can't just pull a price out of thin air because your prospect is a large company. The buyer is usually quite sophisticated. They also talk to others in the business.

One form of tiered pricing is to unbundle all of your products and services so you can sell each item individually. It's much like Broadway performance pricing. An orchestra seat costs more than a seat in the balcony. This is a form of "yield management" in which you seek to maximize available revenues using price points for every market. This approach lets a customer pick and choose the amount of product or service that they want. It maximizes your ability to offer something for everyone.

When you consider tiering your products and services, carefully establish the size and scope for each pricing level. Some shops partition the prices of their products and services into essentially equal different levels—say 10 percent pricing packages. Each level of service and support includes a specific level of hand holding and type of support. For example, you could have one price for taking a document file and importing it into a "standard" style sheet layout. No alterations or other design changes can be made without incurring "extra" charges. There also will be no design consulting or suggestions for improvement. The input is simply converted into pages based on a fixed format.

For those who want a dialogue with the designer and who want to optimize the design, a different tier of prices will be applied. This means that those who have the most experience can get a job done for the least cost. It also means that you and your staff will be paid for the work you actually do. This minimizes the "giving" without "receiving" syndrome so prevalent in small shops today.

You could differentiating your customers by need level, then apply different service to each group. Divide your customer base into three classes. Class A customers have time sensitive projects and want high-quality service. They are willing to pay more. Class B customers are average customers who do business with you often and know you and your staff. They usually accept your rates. The Class C customers are price sensitive prospects who get multiple bids on every project, negotiate hard and buy low. They jump to the lowest bidder. Establish a pricing strategy for each group. Have a base price for Class B customers, a minimum price for price shoppers and a premium price for the quality buyer.

You can also use this tiered strategy as a form of flexible pricing for competitive and sensitive job opportunities. Flexible prices let you bill new work higher and more hand-holding is required, discourage additional work when you're at maximum capacity, encourage work when additional volume is needed, and add profit on more costly jobs.

Repackaging your products and services and then selling to a tiered market works. Software companies sell application programs without technical support and with abbreviated manuals. If a customer needs more detail or more support, they must pay for this information. Tiered support can be a wonderful cash cow and greatly enhance your business.

Transaction Pricing

In a *transaction pricing* strategy, a base price is set, which covers costs and adds profit and return. Then a target price is decided based on the size of order and the customer. The larger the order, the lower the price for each unit. Designing 25 book illustrations is priced at less per illustration than a job designing a single illustration. Likewise, laser typesetting 100 pages of a manual is billed out at less per page than a job involving just 10 pages.

selling price

| 1 - 5 | 6 - 10 | 11 - 25 | 25+ |

order size

Figure 3-10. Transaction quantity pricing strategy.

Transaction pricing lets you implement volume discounts, specific allowances, rebates, incentives, bonuses, and special terms on a deal-by-deal basis. If you have sales reps, transaction pricing gives them the flexibility to "deal." Everyone involved in setting the target price must understand that price is a tool. It reflects the value of what you're selling. Transaction pricing must be applied carefully. Look at the implications for both the customer and your own bottom line.

New Product or Service Pricing

Consider an early introduction pricing strategy that sets a relatively high price during the initial stages of the life of a product or service. This skimming strategy makes good sense when the demand for your service is uncertain, you've invested large sums of money in developing the capability, there isn't any known competition, and the service is expected to grow slowly.

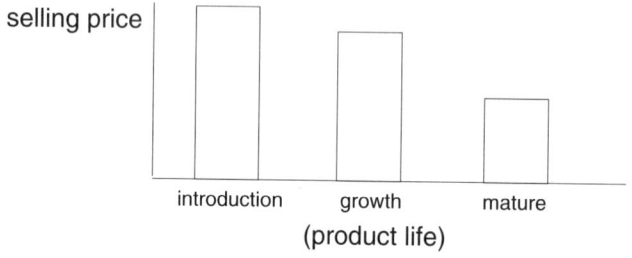

Figure 3-11. New product or service pricing strategy.

If you want to build market share rapidly, adopt a penetration pricing strategy that sets a relatively low price during the initial stages of the life of a product or service.

Leadership Pricing

A *price leader* is a company that is able to make a change in their pricing based on cost and demand conditions without starting a competitive price war. This company can make a price change announcement and others will follow (not undercut) the new price.

If you intend to become a price leader, your business must develop and possess certain characteristics. Your shop must service a large share of the market. You must

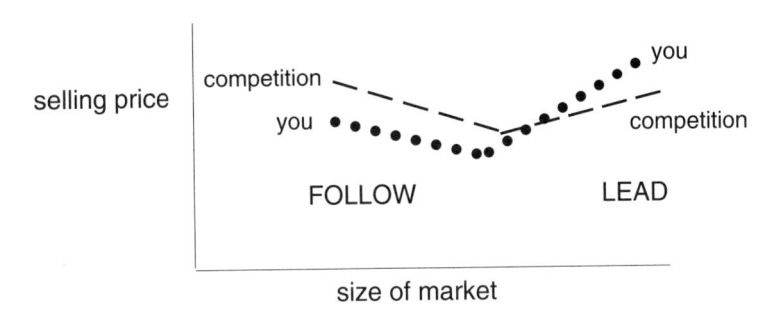

Figure 3-12. Leadership pricing strategy.

be committed to a particular product or service line and have a large share of the service capacity in your immediate area. You must have new, cost-effective equipment and support software. You need a closely controlled distribution system that can get price change information out quickly.

Be sensitive to the price and profit needs of your industry. Know pricing strategies intimately and have a sense of timing to correctly know when price changes are necessary. Good marketing research can help you forecast market response.

You must maintain good customer relations and gain a reputation for providing superior customer service. With effective project management controls in place (and operational), and clearly understanding the legal issues surrounding any pricing decision, you can position yourself to be a price leader.

Operating as a price leader is perfectly legal as long as you don't conspire with another firm in making your pricing decisions. A price leader sets rates independently of the competition, although the prices that competitors charge are certainly considered during strategic analysis.

Value-Based Pricing

In this pricing model, an analysis is made to determine how satisfied customers value the products and services that you sell. Instead of focusing on what price you need to charge to cover costs and earn a profit, this strategy focuses on what costs you can afford to incur to earn a suitable profit given prices for similar services in the market place.

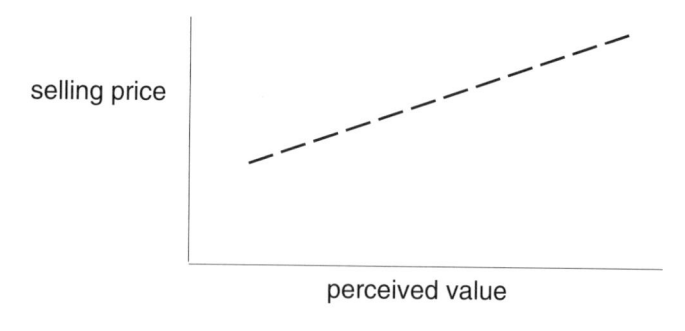

Figure 3-13. Value-based pricing strategy.

A good example is microwave popcorn. This product is priced almost six times higher than conventional "air-popper" or "pop-in-the-pan" popcorn. The marketing strategy is to equate "convenience" with the microwave popcorn. To save time and hassle, consumers pay a premium for the perceived value.

Supermarket pasta costs about one third the price for fresh pasta in a fast-food shop. According to John Mullins, former owner of Pasta Via International, "Customers are willing to pay a lot more for perceived value."

Value-based pricing is a reversal of traditional cost-plus pricing. It requires a clear understanding of how unit costs change as volume changes. As perceived value changes, so do the prices.

"One-Half" Pricing

Some small businesses have found a simple way to set rates. They adopt a modest pricing strategy in which they find out what the most expensive competitor charges and then cut these rates in half.

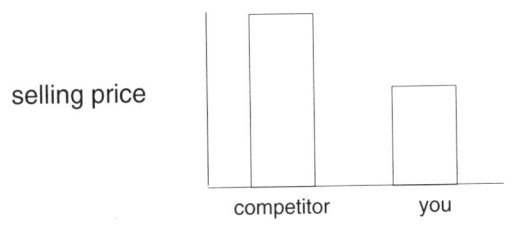

Figure 3-14. "One-half" pricing strategy.

This pricing strategy sometimes works in systems integration environments where the markup is extremely high. But this "Power of One-Half" strategy presents high risk for the desktop publisher and service bureau operator.

This simple solution may actually be no solution. In fact, it may convert all of your products and services into price loss leaders.

"2X" Pricing

Canadian desktop publisher, Don McCahill, uses a "two-times" (2X) rule to establish his fee. He takes what he wants to earn and then doubles this figure to come up with an hourly rate to charge.

Figure 3-15. "2X" pricing strategy.

If he wants to make $25 an hour after expenses, he'll mark up his services to $50 an hour.

"2.5X" Pricing

If you currently earn $50,000 a year, you're making about $24 an hour. Some shop owners apply a 2.5X multiplier to determine their hourly rate.

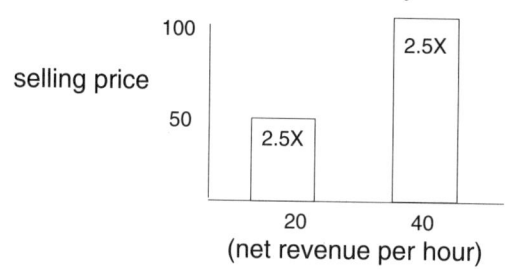

Figure 3-16. "2.5X" pricing strategy.

To net $24 an hour, they charge $60 an hour (24 x 2.5). This rule of thumb lets them earn what they desire while assuming the extra income covers overhead, fringes, administration, and marketing.

If you have a good handle on your overhead and capital investment, you can adopt a lower 2.1 multiplier. This reduces your fee basis to $50 an hour and still lets you net about $24 an hour after expenses.

"3X" Pricing

As a new kid on the block, many of your prospective customers wonder if you'll succeed and question why they should switch. They also question how your products and services will support their own operation better than the competitor they currently use.

Don Jones, president of four successful startups, was interviewed in *Success* magazine regarding his formula for taking on the large, entrenched market leaders.

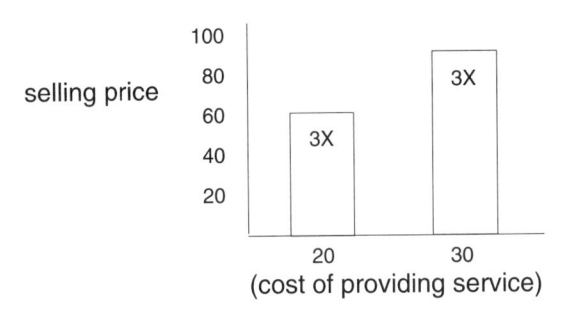

Figure 3-17. "3X" pricing strategy.

He feels that you first need a product or service that's unique. Then you need better resources and a significantly better product offering if you want to go after the business of an entrenched competitor. Jones says that you must provide products or services that are at least three times as good as the market leader.

This means that you must analyze your competition. Learn those qualities of the market leader that customers appreciate most. Understand what things make these customers take their business to that competitor?

There are two factors that you can address—product and price. You can take leadership away by developing a "goodness factor" of at least three. Sell a product or service that is three times better than anyone else. To address price, sell your products or services for one-third what the largest competitor charges. This can be difficult.

Another way to look at 3X pricing is that you must charge three times the cost for the employee doing the work. This covers their pay, support cost for them, sales costs, and profit.

Bottom Pricing

Another lower-price strategy is to offer unbeatable prices from the very start. Provide a product that is so strategically priced that no competitor can match it.

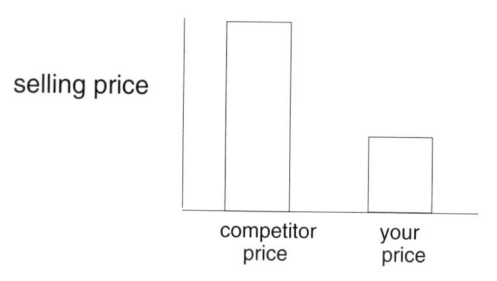

Figure 3-18. Bottom pricing strategy.

This is what Intuit did with their Quicken software product. They priced it at $39.99—a price so low, it locked up the market and blew all competing products out of the water. Microsoft has since offered to buy the company just to get control over the product. The rave reviews of Quicken quickly conveyed value and captured the market. The product is considered good, and word of mouth spread the news everywhere.

The key here is to avoid over-burdening your products and services with excessive overhead. If you price too low, you'll end up selling below your own costs. You must establish prices that yield a profit margin that you can live with.

Only Pricing With Commas Accepted

A recent article in *Home Office Computing* described.how a technical writing and desktop publishing business successfully adopted a pricing strategy that focuses only on high price jobs.

According to the article, if a job does not price out to over $1,000 (has a comma in the number), the job is declined or passed on to another shop.

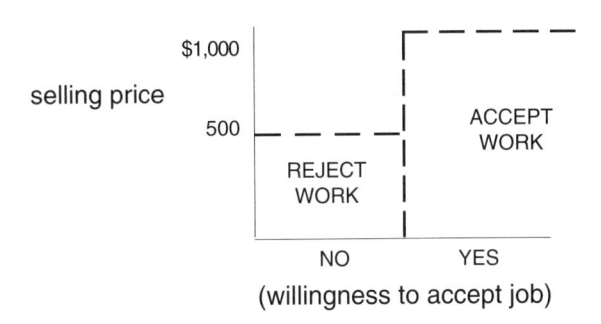

Figure 3-19. "Only jobs with commas" pricing.

The strategy here is that jobs with small income potential do not leave room for negotiation. They also don't provide the profit potential that a bigger project can. The idea is to pursue the big dollars and leave the scraps — the business job tailings —to the low price shops.

Selling Service Contracts

With a world suddenly awakening to the power of visual information—particularly printed and displayed graphics and innovative typography—hundreds of thousands of businesses are trying to market and sell in new ways. Often these customers just don't have the time or inclination to become experts on the process or technology to achieve visual effect.

So they look for service providers who are expert and can develop the affect and effect they desire. They compare shops by price, services offered, performance time and quality of work.

When you find that you have certain customers who bring repeat jobs, consider offering them an exclusive service contract at a lower overall price. You could also advertise this concept to new customers.

For example, ABC Industrial brings or sends work to you three or four times a month. The jobs average $500 each. Your analysis of them and of their competitors shows that their business will be growing over the next year. They will probably need more help. You decide to offer them a services contract in which they will pay less cost for a guaranteed number of hours of design or layout work each month. Twenty-five percent less is a good services contract discount rate.

You collect on the contract up front and guarantee to provide up to the agreed hours of support each month. You may choose not to carry forward hours not used. But your services contract specifies that they will pay a given rate for any time exceeding the contract hours specified. Say you agree to provide services for a flat $35 an hour. Your normal shop rate is $45 an hour. The annual contract is for 10 hours a month. Any time billed over 10 hours is based on a rate of $40 an hour. You collect $4,200 upon signing the contract ($350/month times 12 months) and you work to provide the 10 hours each month. On those months that the time expended exceeds 10 hours, you charge the excess at $40 an hour.

Each time you send the contract customer a statement, note on the form how much they would be paying if they were charged at the full price. This reaffirms the added value they receive by entering a services contract with you. It also keeps them from looking elsewhere for support and gives you a guaranteed income. At least for that year.

On Donating Your Services

Most shop owners occasionally donate time and services to charitable or religious organizations. There is a risk to being generous when people get professional services at little or no cost. Some people develop a perception that the value of your time and service equals the price they pay. Some also expect the same rapid response that you give to your "paying" customers.

There is another risk when you provide services

without charge for a particular group. Other groups may show up expecting similar free support.

You can easily spread the word about your business by doing volunteer work in community groups. But later, when you try to charge for additional services, many often turn away because they want your professional services at no cost and are not interested in paying for your support (even when the project is outside the interests of the nonprofit group).

A good strategy is to limit what you contribute freely, and make it very clear from the outset that you are donating your time for services that you normally charge a customer. Explain that you are in business to earn a living, and you cannot provide free services without detracting from your income. If people balk, ask them if they would ask an attorney or doctor for free advice. You may be amazed at how some people see nothing wrong with asking you, but accept that they must pay the lawyer or doctor. However, just asking the question helps to educate them that you are also a professional and are not there as a free commodity.

Some shop owners submit an invoice with each completed job, specifying what the work should cost. At the bottom of the invoice, they mark "Complimentary" or "No Charge to Non-Profit Organization."

But every job has a cost, and at the least, you should be reimbursed for the cost of materials.

Adding Products and Services

Members of the National Association of Quick Printers (NAQP), are rapidly adopting and offering desktop services. The number of printers introducing DTP as part of their business is dramatically increasing. This represents solid competition for independent DTP shop owners.

Quick print and copy shops are also renting DTP system time to their customers. The average charge for desktop publishing system use is $40 an hour. Most shops charge additional for each page of output produced and for each clip art graphic used.

You can establish an hourly system rental price by developing a profile of an average desktop publishing job. What hardware and software are required? How many hours are spent typesetting? How many hours are spent performing layout and design? How many pages are in the typical design job? How many pages are typically printed out on a laser printer? What supplies are consumed?

When you rent your hardware and software, bill more for the labor intensive activities than you do for those that consume machine time, because some users will expend more time using the hardware and software than others. Then, base your final price on costs, desired profit and what customers will pay.

The reference book *Pricing Tables for Desktop Services* contains details on the types of support provided by entrepreneurs across the country. In the pricing tables, each category has an associated percent value representing the relative number of shops offering that particular service. If you notice that few competitors offer a service for which you have expertise, consider being one of the few in your area to offer such service. Then advertise this uniqueness.

Even in large cities, there exist few businesses that offer particular services. For example, on one project I was co-authoring a VCR troubleshooting and repair book with a friend who runs a VCR repair shop. He has the technical knowledge. I provided the writing skills. A problem developed when he gave me his draft manuscript. It was written in a TRS-DOS format that my computers could not read. I quickly discovered that even in a city of several million residents, there was only one place where I could get a TRS-DOS file converted into

MS-DOS or MAC OS format. The price was steep, but I paid it. This company thrived on being unique.

Check the products and services being sold by other desktop shops and the quick print stores for ideas on new offerings that you can add to your business.

There are niche opportunities everywhere. Watch the business news. Identify and track trends. Then select those services that can make your shop unique.

Desktop services and support are becoming a lucrative sideline business. Typical charges are $1/page for 600 dpi laser printer output, $11/page for high-res output (1,000 dpi or better) and $1.25 for the use of each illustration or graphic clip art.

Ethics and the Desktop Professional

Ethics. The very term means different things to each of us. When I use the word "ethics," I'm referring to "fair play." There is an eternal order to life. This likely caused the adage: "What goes around, comes around."

If we want to be treated fairly in business as well as in other relationships, we must treat others the same way.

If your intent is to jump into business, make a quick buck and then jump out with the cash, you may be tempted to operate in the gray area of right and wrong and as close to the legal limits as possible. You may make money, but you'll not make a business.

As professionals, most of us are not in business solely for the money. Most of us are in it because we like our work. And if we want to continue doing work that we enjoy, we must perform in certain ways. Most of us have decided that our business behavior must be that of fairness, honesty, and integrity.

Although the line between right and wrong is not always clear—often skewed by government regulations and complex tax laws —we must define the guide-rails for society and for our profession.

When you meet a customer who will pay whatever you ask—who really doesn't understand the "going rate," hold to your published price standards. Don't gouge an unsuspecting client. That customer may tell someone else—someone who knows what they should have paid. They may even tell law enforcement officials.

But, more important, we know in our mind that what we are doing is "unethical." We must accept the premise that doing "right" is far better than "doing them in."

As professionals, we must do all we can to prevent the "bait-and-switch" tactics that give a black eye to some appliance stores and car dealerships. We should educate each other on the fact that it's illegal to offer one price and then suggest that no more of that product is in stock or that the advertised offer expired, so we can push the customer into some other more-expensive purchase. This is not only illegal, it's unethical—and to me, that's far worse.

In every country, ethical behavior is defined by the norms of that society. Ethics can be an exercise in gamesmanship. Even in North America, ethical behavior has certain accepted limits. Years ago, we as a society defined what was ethical in our conduct and the conduct of others. Some hold that right is right, and wrong is wrong. They don't accept a gray area where right may be partly wrong and wrong may be partly right.

Ethical conduct is particularly difficult when a small shop owner is both the check and the balance for proper business behavior. As business reversals occur, small shops are tempted to cut ethical corners because they sense minimal risk of detection. Their structure makes them extremely vulnerable to ethics violations. Without an attorney on their staff, many can be swayed into performance that pushes the bounds of legality and ethics.

My philosophy is simple— if we want to be treated fairly by those from whom we buy, then we should be an example and provide that same treatment to those to whom we sell.

Some people feel like Diogenes wandering through the streets of ancient Greece, holding up a lighted lantern in the bright sunlight and seeking an honest face. He couldn't find one. Perhaps we should consider his cynical philosophy and decide if we should be the example of what is right in business.

Take the Rosco Syndrome. Rosco was a small Midwest printer who offered a limited set of products and services. Each time a customer came in, Rosco would re-define the customer's job so it fit the operational constraints of his shop. He never turned away a job.

Many customers couldn't tell that he had altered their projects. Often, Rosco led them to believe that his solution was the best one possible given their requirements. Customers initially believed Rosco and paid him handsomely for their perceived value in his actions.

However, over time, the customers became more sophisticated. They learned that Rosco had been leading them into accepting his limited shop capability. They learned that he had changed their jobs and forced their requirements to fit his standard products and services. This awareness translated into a negative perception of Rosco and of his business.

Word spread quickly. His sales activity fell off, and soon Rosco was no longer in business. Perception and ethics run deep in the waters of commerce.

The early Roman sculpturers called their work "sine cera" when no cracks in the marble had been filled with a wax imitation of the stone. The words "sine cera" evolved into "sincere"—meaning honest and genuine In dealing with our employees and our customers, we should at all times demonstrate conduct that is sincere—without wax. Ethics and sincerity are synonymous.

Even though you'll encounter competitors who are at best unethical, someone needs to be the example of honest and professional conduct. Let's face it. When we look around for a leader—an example to follow—we're it. Be the leader. Others will follow.

Summary

A chapter on strategy is a book unto itself. However, strategy is only made good when implemented in a professional environment. In Chapter 4, you'll learn how to compete from the trenches and build a solid company image in any economic climate. In Chapter 4, you'll learn pricing tactics.

4

Pricing Tactics

"The only acceptable profit is the maximum profit."

Having a pricing strategy is a major part of your battle to gain market share and increase bottom line profits. But, you must still deal with the insistent telephone price-shopper. You must still deal with the new shop whose strategy is to undercut any and every price. And you must build and maintain your company's image in any economic climate. To do this, you'll need all the "street smart" guerrilla tactics that life and business have to offer. This chapter shows you how to wage economic war from the trenches of a desktop services business.

Tactical Pricing Actions

Armed with all the market intelligence you can collect, and both break-even and margin analysis, you can determine the tactical actions that will let you reach or exceed the strategic pricing objectives that you established earlier.

For example, if part of your strategic pricing objective is to achieve a 20 percent return-on-investment, you could implement tactical actions that identify those price levels that yield this desired return. A strategic pricing objective of surviving an economic downturn could mean that you set prices at a level that will keep business coming in while allowing your shop to scrape by with enough income to cover costs. A strategic objective of avoiding competition could include tactical actions that set prices to discourage competition.

Pricing Problems

There are three primary problems with the way that many businesses price products and services. First, they under-rate the real value of their products and services. They don't realize how much they freely give away. Second they don't understand how the marketplace perceives their products and services.

A perception of quality should command a higher price. The trick is to find a niche where your products and services are acceptable and perceived as valuable.

The third problem occurs when owners assume that all DTP and prepress products and services are alike. If you have a unique product or service, price it to what the market will bear—especially if you've invested time and money into its development.

Taking Time to Price Better

Pricing is one of the most important tasks you have in business. You should evaluate demand, determine all your costs, and then decide what profit is acceptable. These are not trivial issues. Actions by your competitors, the government, and technology all affect how you operate.

The value associated with your pricing also depends on the perception of the customer. This perception is based on what other options your customers feel are available and their expectation of added benefit by purchasing from you rather than a competitor. In this way, pricing can be used as a tool that reflects value.

Some customers have a feeling for what a price should be. This becomes their basis for acceptance.

They also have a threshold above which they simply won't buy. Above this point, they will accept lower quality or choose another option.

Your business will earn a reputation as it grows. This image has much to do with what a customer expects to pay. If your shop is perceived as providing good, high quality service, your prices can be higher. If your business is perceived as a cut-rate job shop, your prices should reflect this too. You must decide the image that you want to create. Then you must work hard to develop and maintain this image.

Consider the retail department stores. Some stores are perceived as expensive price leaders. Others are considered low-cost, low-price outlets. Yet the low-price store doesn't always have a lower product price than a high-price store.

Sometimes, a higher price stimulates demand because a customer perceives added value. Yet, on another occasion, the same product sold at a lower price can also stimulate sales demand.

Pricing is an art. There are too many fickle variables to make it a science. Yet we use as much science as possible to make the art of pricing easier to comprehend and apply.

When pricing products and services, some shops incorporate flexibility in their list prices so they can hold occasional sales. They add 15-25 percent to their initial prices, then lower the "retail" price by some percent while shouting "SALE" in their ads.

Real estate people recommend adding about 10 percent to the expected selling price of a house so you can negotiate down and arrive at a final price that seems a win for both buyer and seller. The negotiated final price is your original desired selling price.

Urgency also plays a factor in your pricing formula. If you have a product or service that suddenly comes into strong demand, apply the "WOW" formula and increase your prices to meet what the market will bear. Just remember, if you set your prices too high, competition will appear and challenge your sales success. Pricing takes skill, patience, and luck.

You must price for profit, and this means consistently evaluating the success of your strategy and readjusting your pricing as necessary. By taking the time to price right, you create the opportunity to profit more.

Pricing Service in a Competitive Market

Much of today's pricing is still done by the "seat of the pants." An acquaintance recently confessed, "I'm swamped with business designing one page flyers for $10 a pop, but I just can't seem to make any money at it." Of course not! This person didn't do a cost analysis and integrate a value for her own time and experience into her price formula. Intuitive and reactionary pricing decisions are dinosaurs in today's dynamic fast-paced world.

The same factors that you consider in arriving at a price for your products—costs, perceived value, market segment, and marketing objectives also apply to pricing your service. By systematically addressing each issue, you can clarify your own business goals and objectives and select a pricing strategy that best fits your situation. Only through logical, sound, and consistent decisions can you level the playing field and establish profitable prices.

The top factors determining your price are the competition that you face and the price your customers are willing to pay. Price is therefore strongly influenced by external forces, not strictly your own costs. Your customers don't care what it cost you to provide service. They care only what you charge them, the quality of your work, and how soon you can deliver.

This means that you'll have a tough up-hill struggle raising your prices unless you can develop a perceived difference in the mind's eye of your customers. If you can't, or you're the new kid on the block, you must adopt a "community standard" pricing strategy. This is essentially a *"going rate"* pricing format. It pays less attention to your costs or to marketplace demand and more to the prices that your competitors are charging.

Pricing can be both a challenge and a source for headaches. It is usually considered the main tool to gain new business. Often pricing strategies center around reactive formulas such as scurrying to match a competitor's price change.

There is a better way—combine cost-based pricing, competition-oriented pricing, and demand-pricing. Adding a desired margin to a cost basis to come up with a price is *"cost-based"* pricing. This is a no-strategy method to establish price.

When we set our price 10-15 percent lower than the competition to lure price-sensitive buyers into our fold, we are applying *"competition-oriented"* pricing. This method accepts a lower margin. But what do you do when your competition already has their prices set for minimum margin? You could sell yourself right out of business.

Basing your strategy primarily on competitive pricing can work in the short run. But it can also generate a downward spiral that causes competitors to match each other's lower price on the way down and out. This can also cause buyers to perceive your product or service as just another commodity.

By developing a marketing strategy, you make pricing a pro-active event and not a defensive activity. A typical marketing strategy addresses product, place, price, and promotion — what will be sold, where it will be sold, at what price, and how it will be promoted.

Solutions to these issues define the strategy of your business. Your marketing strategy becomes a plan that identifies the goals and objectives for the company. A pricing strategy is then developed to support the marketing plan.

Countless pricing formulas are hypothetically possible. You picture yourself as a shop owner who wants to be known as a high volume service-oriented operator, so you price your services 15 percent less than the leading service bureau in the area.

The price leader retaliates by selectively discounting its services to meet your lower price. This causes you to lose business.

You realize that you can't develop any lasting competitive advantage by price alone. You decide to reposition yourself away from a strategy based only on price. Analyzing your strengths and weaknesses, you decide that magazine and catalog publishing is where you are strongest. You develop a marketing strategy based on premier support to businesses that seek help designing and printing magazines and catalogs. You build on your expertise and offer experienced support, fast response time, and quality output. Your prices reflect the premier concept. You develop a promotional strategy that is consistent with your business focus. Sales build, and your shop thrives.

In another scenario, you envision yourself as a shop owner who wants to provide service to the city, county, state, and federal government customers in your area. You know that laws make government buyers very price sensitive, so you develop a low-price strategy based on product cost.

However, you discover that low price by itself won't guarantee sales and long term success. Your service product must be packaged so it exactly meets government specifications. It should provide nothing more, nor anything less. You redesign your service offering so it can be delivered at minimum cost in the exact form the buyer expects. You restructure your business to be profitable based on this service offering. You down play promotion and focus on getting on every qualified bidders list you can. You ignore the public market and limit your activity to government organizations. Your business grows.

A flash of insight later, you imagine yourself a service center owner with expertise in a unique field or in producing a unique product. For example, you have a particular expertise in working with prepress color. You invest in the equipment and software to exploit this expertise. Then you focus your promotion on those companies who use color documents. You build a capability to handle any type and form of color input and to produce any type and form of color output. You build a reputation for having every support and service tool available related to color work. By becoming the dominant provider of color services, you develop a business that is almost insensitive to price. You set your pricing based on perceived value. But you don't set your prices so high that others are tempted to enter your market niche. While providing high quality service, you set your prices moderately higher than your major competitors.

You conclude that market-driven pricing is the best way to go. You accept the hard work associated with gathering market intelligence. Rather than basing your price solely on historical production standards, experience, and on reference tables of standard costs, you decide to integrate all of these into a strategy unique to your particular market.

The amorphous mass of intelligence data that you gather begins to coagulate into a pricing strategy. You test the strategy against your estimated costs to see if the margins are acceptable for quoting a particular job. If the margins are too low, you pass on the job. Or, if you decide you still want the contract, you work even harder to improve the efficiency of your operation. You consider better equipment, better working techniques, and reduced overhead expenses. Combining cost and market-driven pricing fosters more efficient operation.

Through the preceding scenarios, the consistent theme is that a pricing strategy is based on a marketing plan. And the marketing plan is consistent with the objectives of the business. Just as a marketing plan shouldn't be established in a vacuum, your pricing strategy should have input from all aspects of the business. And it should reflect the goals and strategies of your company.

Use your marketing plan and pricing strategy to establish procedures for pricing new products and services, and for modifying existing prices as market conditions change.

Pricing actions are governed by state and federal laws. Besides the restrictions on collusion and price fixing, you must be concerned about perceived price discrimination. Competitive pricing is a key component in your business plan, but it should not conflict with law.

Income Versus Profit

Profit is not the same as the money that your shop makes and that you put into your pocket. There are cycles of activity in every business, and you need some reserve to pay the bills when job opportunities are slow. This lets you avoid borrowing from the bank (or your personal savings account) during economic down-turns.

Typically, a shop will factor in a business profit of 5-10 percent of total sales income. This profit should be considered a cost and should be factored into your prices.

When you analyze the cost factors associated with your shop, you'll probably find that your labor and direct expenses make up 30-40 percent of the total expense. Marketing will eat up another 20-30 percent. And non-marketing costs will chew up another 20-30 percent. Return on investment will fall between 5-10 percent, and expected gross profit should be between 10 and 20 percent. Each time one of these cost factors increases, you must take some action to reduce another cost factor to maintain your desired return on investment and profit percentage. Everything you do to reduce your overhead expense adds that much more to your bottom line profit.

Gross profit margin varies by industry and by company within an industry. High tech companies can achieve 55% gross margins. Distributors typically survive on 25 percent gross margins. Home desktop publishing businesses often have gross margins of 10 percent. Find out what your gross profit margin is and then try to increase it by five percent or more.

Productivity

For smaller shops, overhead is probably the best approach for tracking costs. But productivity plays a major part in the formula. Using overhead and expected productivity, you can calculate what you could charge per hour for your services.

Productivity impacts your shop billing rates because your calculated hourly rate must be divided by a productivity percentage to establish your actual budgeted hourly rate.

Buying bigger, better, more powerful hardware and software does not necessarily guarantee improved productivity. Productivity is only as effective as the use made of the resources that are available. Not all employees are as productive, and you yourself will not be as productive each day of the week. Besides working on income-producing tasks, you'll also be answering the telephone, sorting mail, making out invoices, performing maintenance, and a myriad of other non-billable tasks.

According to the so-called *"30-60-10 Rule"* for small business, you will spend 30 percent of your time marketing, 60 percent of your time actually performing billable work, and 10 percent of your time handling paperwork and chasing after payment. When you consider the time spent preparing for a job and cleaning up after a job, you will probably bill out only 50 percent of your available time. Your shop will be 50 percent productive at best.

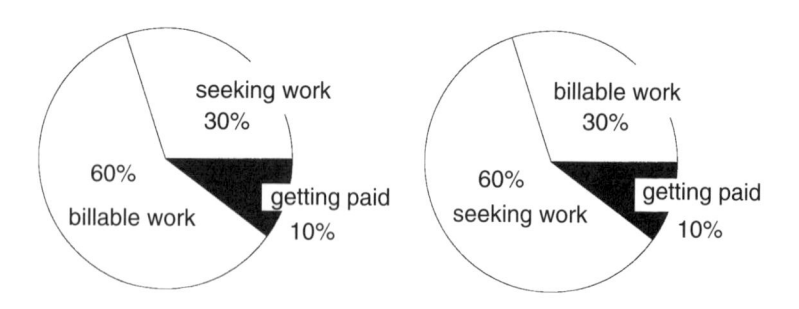

Figure 4-1. The 30-60-10 rule works two ways.

In reality, small shop owner-operators spend most of their time marketing and actively seeking new work. Only 30% of their time is available for billable work. This means that these small businesses are actually only 30% productive. The ratio of seeking work to actually working changes as more staff are added.

Calculating Shop Productivity

Productivity is directly affected by the number of employees in your shop. While productivity is usually between 30 and 60 percent, most shops seldom exceed 40 percent productivity. A "one-person operation" typically achieves no more than 30 percent productivity. Two or more people in a shop can achieve 40 percent at best. And it takes about five employees to reach a productivity level of 50 percent or more.

Productivity doesn't relate directly to costs. But if you establish a billable rate for service, you can determine how productive your shop is and then determine what hourly rate you need to charge to be profitable. If your shop is 50 percent productive, you can divide the income needed each hour of operation by a productivity factor to determine how much you really need to charge for each hour of service just to keep your doors open. For example, if you calculate that your hourly rate should be $15, at 50 percent productivity, you should actually charge $30 an hour to effectively make $15 for each hour that you work.

If you pay a designer $8 an hour, your overhead is $4 an hour, and you want to earn 10 percent ROI on your startup investment and 10 percent in profit, you may decide that you need $15 an hour coming in. Dividing the $15 by a 50 percent productivity factor (expressed as 0.50) yields a $30 per hour rate. This is what you must charge to realize the $15 an hour average net income that is actually desired.

A shop billing out at $25 an hour and 30 percent productive actually brings in $7.50 an hour—$300 in an average 40-hour week. It's critical that you know the productivity of your shop. The higher the productivity, the lower you can set your hourly rate to make the same return.

There are two ways to determine productivity. First, you can compare the labor billed by an employee each week with the hours worked and the hourly rate that the shop charged for those services that the employee provided. This productivity formula is shown below.

$$\text{Productivity} = \frac{(\text{Labor Income}) / (\text{Hours Worked})}{\text{Shop Hourly Rate}}$$

If one of your people earned $500 in labor charges for the shop, worked 40 hours that week with a shop hourly rate of $25, that person's productivity is 50 percent [(500/40) / 25 = 0.50].

A second way to structure the productivity formula is to multiply the shop's hourly rate by the number of hours worked and then divide this figure into the labor billed (the income) as shown below.

$$\text{Productivity} = \frac{(\text{Labor Income Produced})}{(\text{Shop Hourly Rate})(\text{Hours Worked})}$$

Thus $25 an hour for a 40 hour week yields $1,000. Dividing $1,000 into the $500 earned yields 0.5 or 50% shop productivity.

Some shop owners skew their productivity percentages by working 12 or more hours each day. If they were to work the numbers correctly, some of them could discover that they are actually paying their customers just so they can perform work for them. Productivity is a hidden hazard to profit.

Calculating Individual Productivity

If you measure the productivity of each employee, you can determine what each person contributes to the total required income. Based on this analysis you can compare the skill level and performance of employees who routinely perform the same tasks.

By combining the billable hours generated by all of your employees, you can derived a productivity figure for the shop. Many owners also calculate the productivity for each employee as a basis for pay and promotion opportunity. A basic rule of thumb is that each direct labor person should bring in about 2.5 times their wages. This works most of the time, but a better measurement is to compare the labor income for services rendered with the actual hours billed at the shop's hourly rate.

For example, assume that a designer worked 40 hours and brought in $400 in labor charges. Your shop rate is $35 an hour. But 40 hours at $35 an hour should have generated $1,400. Dividing $400 by $1,400 yields a productivity of 28.6%. If another designer could generate $500 in the same 40 hours, this person's productivity would be 35.7%. Assuming each spent an equal amount of time answering the telephone, filling out forms, and handling other administrative functions, the second designer would be worth more to your shop than the first. The pay that they earn should reflect this. Be willing to pay for performance.

However, any measurement of productivity should be balanced with factors that take time and effort away from income-generating tasks. Resolving a customer problem and improving customer satisfaction should be considered in providing a balance between productivity and adequate customer service.

Factors Affecting Productivity

Most of us have found ourselves assigning selective tasks to certain people. Consciously, or unconsciously, we've judged the ability and productivity of our staff. When we combine certain individuals, we can sometimes realize an increased productivity due to the effect of synergy—their joint efforts produce a result greater than what each individual could achieve if they worked alone.

As shown in Figure 4-2, there are many factors that can directly affect the productivity of an individual or a team. These can be partitioned into three basic areas: people, places and things. People are more productive when they're happy. A "down" day, when people are at the low ebb on their biorhythm curves, can also affect

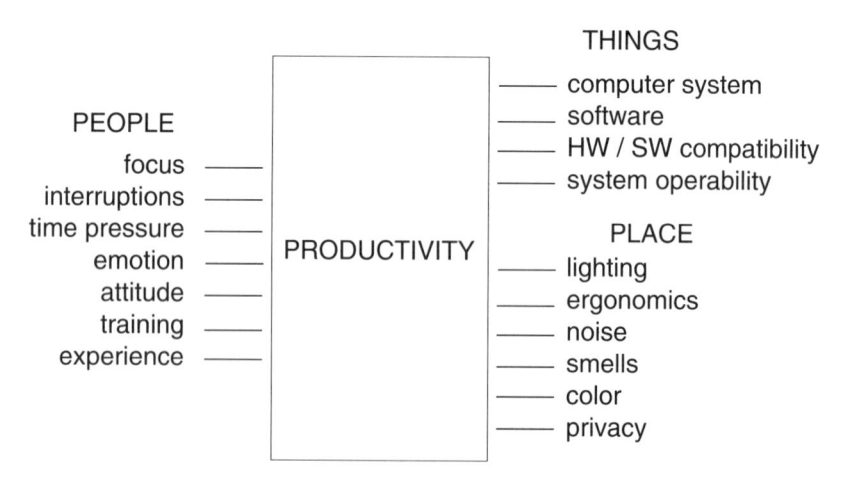

```
                                      THINGS
                                      ── computer system
      PEOPLE                          ── software
          focus ──                    ── HW / SW compatibility
   interruptions ──                   ── system operability
   time pressure ──   ┌───────────┐
        emotion  ──   │PRODUCTIVITY│    PLACE
       attitude  ──   │           │   ── lighting
       training  ──   │           │   ── ergonomics
     experience  ──   └───────────┘   ── noise
                                      ── smells
                                      ── color
                                      ── privacy
```

Figure 4-2. Factors affecting productivity.

productivity. A full 8-hour "person day" doesn't mean an 8-hour "productive day."

Interruptions play a significant role in productivity. It takes time to refocus on a job after unscheduled interruptions. In fact, studies suggest that refocusing after an interruption can take as long as 20 minutes. And this is for EACH interruption! If you get interrupted six times a day, you could lose two hours of productive time.

Four types of interruptions affect productivity—telephone calls, co-worker interruptions, visual interruptions, and sound interruptions. These interruptions directly affect job schedule and worker performance. A fully focused worker in a larger shop is typically 70-90 percent productive. This output is reduced by the number and severity of interruptions. Fortunately, you can affect how and when interruptive activities are handled.

If you can relieve your people of the need to hear and respond to customer telephone calls and spontaneous questions, their productive day will approach a full person day. A quiet and private working environment is the single, most effective thing you can provide to directly improve productivity.

Associated with these productivity factors is the impact of a request to "expedite" a job. As people are pushed, the risk of error increases. When you measure the actual time spent on a job, you must include the time needed to rework mistakes. You should mark up jobs that a customer wants "expedited."

You can affect each person's attitude quite subtly. For example, you can use color to stimulate or relax. You can cut a fresh lemon—Japanese businesses found that the aroma of fresh lemon can increase office productivity by over 10 percent.

How Costs Vary During a Project

There's no question that your cost basis changes during a project. As you use more time on the equipment, your electrical and telephone (and possibly water) use increases. You also incur additional costs in paying for part time help. Work pick up and delivery, and trips to buy materials add to your gas and vehicle expense. Then you'll use more paper, film, toner, chemicals, or other materials in conjunction with a project. This will increase your project materials costs. These variable costs should be charged directly to the appropriate project.

If you obtain new equipment or upgrades to software, be aware that installation and checkout costs average between 2.5 percent and 10 percent of a system's total cost. The actual costs depend on system complexity, the hardware and software mix required, and staff involvement.

These costs should be amortized over the life of your equipment and be charged to each job proportionately. Be aware that Congress is trying to extend the "useable life" of software so you'll have to amortize your expenses over several years rather than sooner, even when updates typically occur annually. Be certain to charge fixed costs associated with work on a particular project directly to that project. The more fixed costs that you can legitimately bill out to a project, the easier the pain when you evaluate your overhead costs.

Finding the Break-Even Point

One of the best ways to understand the relationships between cost, sales and profit is to perform break-even analysis. This business technique helps you identify the point at which cost equals income. It is the sales volume or quantity point where your costs are covered and profit begins.

There are two ways to approach break-even analysis—by comparing total sales volume with costs or by comparing total items (units) produced and sold with cost. In both methods, you must understand all expenses associated with your business.

Part of your costs are fixed and don't change with the volume of sales made—rent, utilities, salaries, insurance, and taxes. Other costs vary with the job—hourly wages, the costs of raw materials and additional utility expenses to produce the goods or services that you sell. To make a profit, you must pay both your fixed and variable expenses and then have some income left over. These residual dollars go into profit and return-on-investment or debt servicing (if you loaned money to your company).

The challenge is to find the point at which your costs are covered and profit can begin to accrue. This is *break-even analysis*. Your inspection can be made on a grand scale (looking at your total business sales and costs) or on a product-by-product basis.

Whether you choose a sales volume method or total units sold method of break-even analysis, your first step is to determine your fixed and variable expenses.

Sales Volume Method

This technique relates income to cost. First determine your total fixed costs. This becomes a reference baseline to both forms of break-even analysis. Then calculate your total variable costs. Divide the total variable costs by the total number of sales to get an *average variable cost per sale*. You can also determine your *average dollar per sale* by dividing the total revenue by the total number of sales. Then by dividing the average variable cost per sale by the average dollar income per sale, you can find the percentage of variable costs in each transaction.

An average variable cost of $9 with an average selling price of $14 yields 64.3% *variable cost percentage*. Each time you earn one dollar, 64 cents goes to pay for your variable costs and your business keeps about 36 cents. But this is not profit. Not yet. You need to apply this money to pay your fixed costs before you get to count your profit.

$$\text{Avg Variable Cost per Sale} = \frac{\text{Total Variable Costs}}{\text{Total Number of Sales}}$$

$$\text{Avg Dollars per Sale} = \frac{\text{Total Revenue}}{\text{Total Number of Sales}}$$

$$\text{Variable Cost Percentage} = \frac{\text{Avg Variable Cost per Sale}}{\text{Avg \$ per Sale}}$$

To determine how much sales volume you need before you get to keep the 36¢ earned on each dollar of sale, you need to find the break-even point. Express the percent as a decimal and subtract it from one (1 - 0.643 = 0.357, round off to 0.36, the 36¢ extra on each sale). Then divide this result into your total fixed costs. If your fixed costs are $36,000 annually, you will need $100,840 in sales income before all of your fixed and variable costs are covered (1-.643 = 0.357 and 36,000/ 0.357 = $100,840). Sales above this point will generate profit.

$$\text{Break-Even Point} = \frac{\text{Total Fixed Costs}}{1 - \frac{\text{(Average Variable Cost per Unit)}}{\text{(Average Selling Price per Unit)}}}$$

$$\text{Break-Even Point} = \frac{36{,}000}{1 - (9/14)} = \frac{\$36{,}000}{0.357} = \$100{,}840$$

If you assume that changes in sales volume don't affect your average selling price, that your fixed costs remain constant, and that your variable costs change in direct proportion to sales, you can plot costs versus sales volume as shown in Figure 4-3.

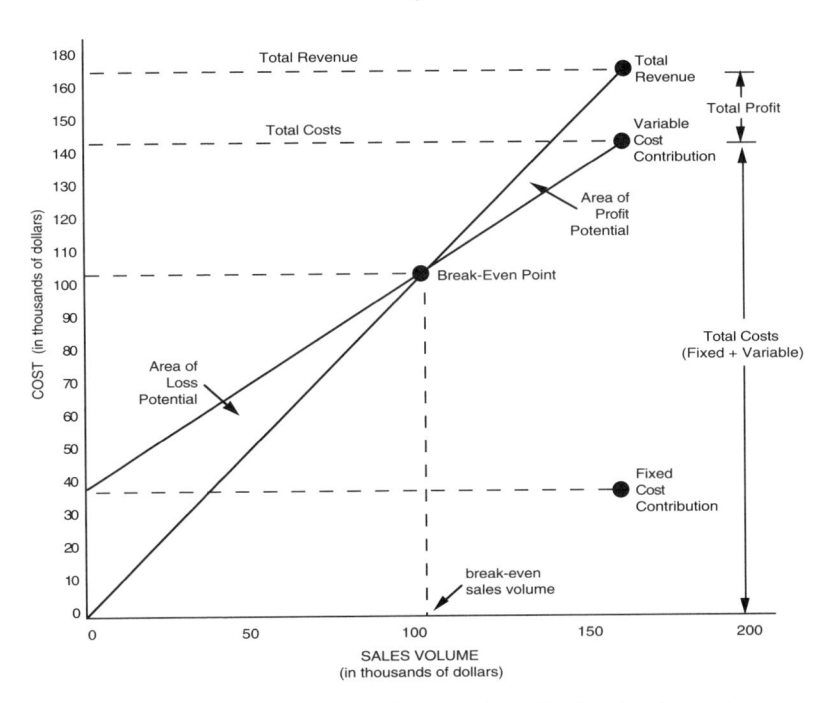

Figure 4-3. Break-even analysis based on the total sales volume.

In this case, the horizontal axis represents the volume of sales. The vertical axis represents dollars in costs and revenue. Break-even occurs at $103,000 dollars in sales.

Total Units Sold Method

Another way to perform break-even analysis is to determine how many sales are required before costs are covered and profit can accrue. To do this, you need to determine the margin of contribution made by the average sale and the average variable cost per sale. The *contribution margin* is the difference between the average price per sale and the average variable cost per sale.

$$\text{Break-Even Point} = \frac{\text{Total Fixed Costs}}{\text{Unit Selling Price - Unit Variable Cost}}$$

Dividing the total fixed cost by the contribution margin yields a break-even quantity. Using the same numbers in the previous method, we see that an average sale of $14, less an average variable cost of $9, yields a contribution margin of $5. Dividing our total fixed cost ($36,000) by the $5 contribution margin, we get 7,200 units of sale. This means that we must sell 7,200 units at an average price of $14 to cover our fixed and variable costs. Every unit sold beyond the 7,200 is full profit.

$$\text{Break-Even Point} = \frac{\text{Total Fixed Costs}}{\text{Contribution Margin}} = \frac{\$36,000}{5} = 7,200 \text{ units}$$

To get the break-even point in dollars, multiply the break-even point in units by the unit average selling price. This will check the arithmetic of the first method (7200 x $14 = $100,800).

By using the same assumptions as we did for the total sales volume method, we can plot costs versus units of sale to show graphically when break-even occurs. This is shown in Figure 4-4.

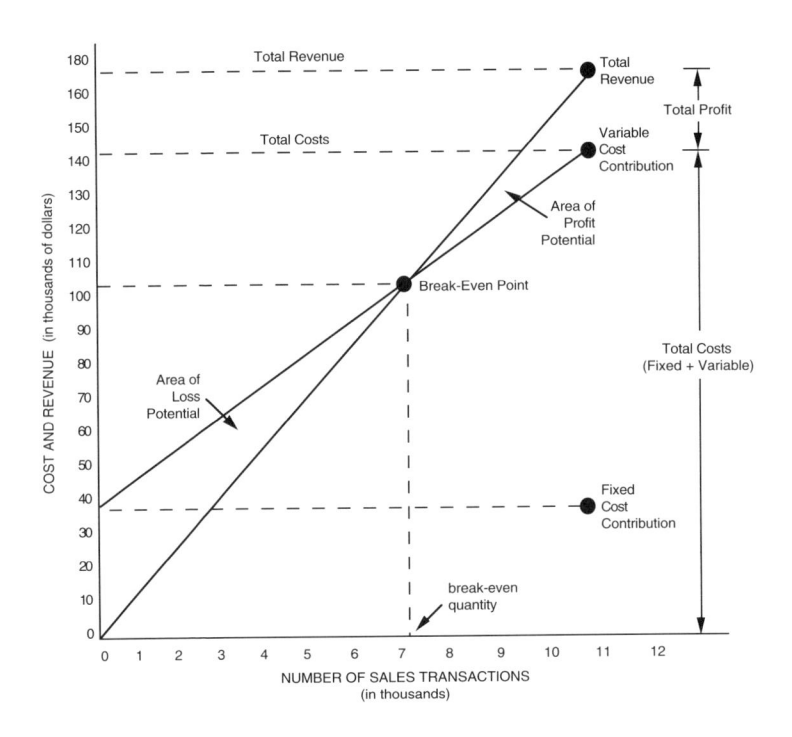

Figure 4-4. Break-even analysis based on the total sales volume.

The $5 made on each sale is applied first toward the fixed costs and then toward profit. If we lower our average sale price, we contribute less toward paying for fixed costs and less remains for profit. This also means that we push the break-even point further out to the right.

Typically, the smallest 20 percent of your orders account for less than 5 percent of your sales income. It may not be worth making these sales . There's a point at which your fixed costs exceed your income and you should decline the sale. The break-even chart shows you graphically why some sales just don't make financial sense. A pallet of low quantity sales may generate revenue that is consistently below your fixed costs with a small variable cost added. This suggests that you should decline these sales, or add a surcharge (charge a higher price) for low dollar sales. This is why many shops have a sliding scale of prices for laser printing and imagesetting output. A lower per unit price is charged for larger volume jobs.

Short-Cut to Find Break-Even Point

Suppose your shop has been in business for two years. You have historical data suggesting that your earnings average $5,000 a month and that you service 20 customers each month. Your fixed costs are running $2,150 a month. And your variable costs average $1,091 a month. With just these four data points, you can find the break-even customer quantity and the break-even revenue amount for your business.

First, break-even quantity:

$$Q_{BEP} = \frac{\text{Total Fixed Costs}}{\frac{\text{Budgeted Earnings}}{\text{\# Monthly Customers}} - \frac{\text{Avg. Variable Cost}}{\text{\# Monthly Customers}}}$$

$$= \frac{2150}{5000/20 - 1091/20} = \frac{2150}{250 - 54.55}$$

$$= \frac{2150}{250 - 54.55} = \frac{2150}{195.45} = 11 \text{ customers}$$

It takes 11 customers who pay for services to reach a point where your costs are covered and you can make a profit.

Likewise, you can calculate the revenue point when profit begins by applying the following formula.

$$\text{Revenue}_{BEP} = \frac{\text{Total Fixed Costs}}{1 - \dfrac{\text{Average Variable Cost / \# Customers}}{\text{Budgeted Revenue / \# Customers}}}$$

$$= \frac{2150}{1 - \dfrac{1091/20}{5000/20}}$$

$$= \frac{2150}{1 - 0.218}$$

$$\text{Revenue}_{BEP} = \$2{,}750.06$$

Break-Even, Overhead & Margin

Look at break-even from even another perspective. There is a direct relationship between break-even and overhead and margin, knowing two of the three can help you determine the third.

Gross margin ($) = Revenue ($) - Cost of Services Sold ($)

Cost of Services ($) = Overhead ($)

Gross margin ($) = Revenue ($) - Overhead ($)

Gross margin (%) = [Gross margin ($) / Revenue ($)] X 100

Gross margin ($) = Gross margin (%) X Revenue ($)

Revenue ($) = Gross margin ($) / Gross margin (%)

Revenue ($) = Gross margin ($) + Overhead ($)

Overhead ($) = Revenue ($) - [Gross margin (%) x Revenue ($)]

Overhead ($) = Revenue ($) x [1 - Gross margin (%)]

Gross margin (%) = {(1 - [Overhead ($) / Revenue ($)]} X 100

Suppose your gross margin is 50 percent and your overhead is running $50,000 a year. The break-even point for your shop is $100,000 in revenue. If your overhead remains the same, but your gross profit margin falls to 25 percent, you'll need to earn $200,000 just to break even. This is why business success is tied so closely to margin and overhead. An increase in overhead from $50,000 to just $60,000 will require revenues of $120,000 to maintain the same 50 percent gross margin. Notice that a $10,000 increase in overhead resulted in a break-even revenue requirement twice that amount ($20,000). It follows then that at a revenue level of $100,000, for every $1 decrease you can make in overhead costs, your gross profit can increase by twice that amount. For example, cutting overhead from $50,000 to $40,000 and keeping the same sales volume results in a gross profit margin increase to 60 percent as shown on the next page.

Gross profit margin (%) = {(1 - [Overhead ($) / Revenue ($)]}

Gross profit margin (%) = {(1 - [$40,000 / $100,000]) X 100}

Gross profit margin (%) = (1 - 0.4) X 100

Gross profit margin (%) = 60%

A decrease in overhead costs of $10,000 resulted in an increase in profit of $20,000. Not bad work for an afternoon.

The ideal way to perform break-even analysis is to develop a model using a computer spreadsheet. This lets you dynamically change the variables and determine new break-even points based on different selling prices and costs. It's particularly helpful when you begin changing the per item price.

Break-even analysis can help you decide the viability of a prospective new product. It can show you when it's too costly to produce and sell at a selected price. To increase the income generated, you may have to raise your prices. But this is not always possible. Competition may hold your prices too low to make this product or service worth selling. Your costs can also vary.

Break-even analysis isn't perfect. It doesn't consider discounting, customer demand (elasticity) and the actions of competitors. Nevertheless, it can help you quickly see the impact of various pricing strategies. It's one of the tools that you have for managing your business. By knowing the break-even point, you can determine which products or services to offer. It helps you decide if making an unprofitable sale to gain a long term customer is really worth the sacrifice. And it helps you highlight excessive fixed overhead expenses such as rent, leased equipment, and staff.

To succeed in this business, you must consider every analytical tool that might help you make better pricing decisions. Break-even analysis is one of the better tools.

Margin Analysis

Another management tool is a technique called *"margin analysis."* This tool evaluates the cost and expected income associated with producing and selling more of a product or service. It focuses on profit maximization rather than break even.

In margin analysis, the cost associated with producing "one more" unit of a product or service is called its *"marginal cost."* The added revenue associated with selling just one more unit of a product or service is called its *"marginal revenue."*

As shown in Figure 4-5, a margin curve can be constructed showing the relationship between price, quantity, cost, revenue and demand. As more units are produced and sold, the average cost decreases, pulling the marginal cost down. The marginal revenue also declines because the most recent sale becomes a comparatively smaller portion of the total income.

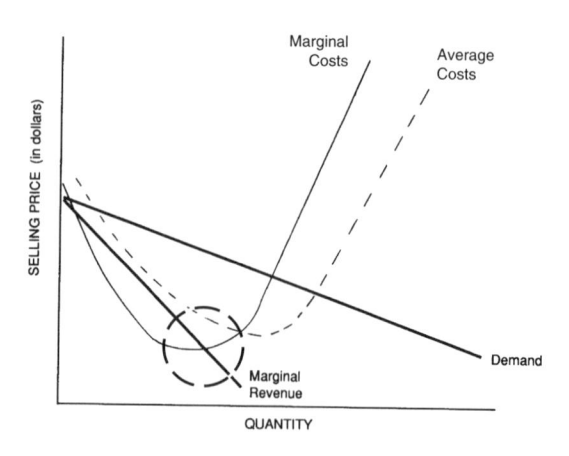

Figure 4-5. A margin curve showing the relationship between costs and revenues as demand and quantity increase.

A point is reached when you must expand your facilities and increase your equipment and staff to handle additional business. This added expense makes the marginal cost and average cost curves bend upward. The key here is that maximum profit is realized when you operate at the point where marginal cost exactly equals marginal revenue.

If we then focus on the area where marginal costs and marginal revenue intersect on the margin curve (Figure 4-6), we can identify a point where more business won't generate additional revenue for the company.

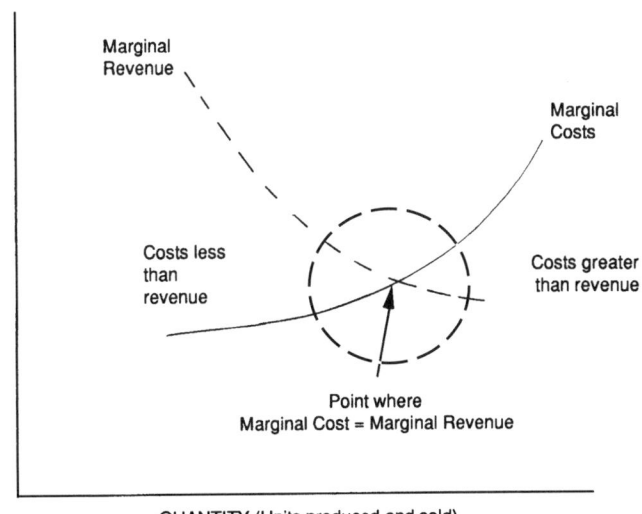

Figure 4-6. A margin curve showing the relationship between marginal costs and marginal revenue.

The idea is to find the margin crossover points for each product or service that you offer, and then strive to hold sales of each item at the point where marginal revenue exactly equals marginal cost.

Finding Optimum Order Size Using Margin Analysis

An interesting technique for determining if marginal orders are really worthwhile is to find your optimal order size. This requires knowing your cost per order and your *gross profit margin*. The process works like this:

First, find the spread of your orders by sales size. Some will be less than $25, others will be between $25 and $99, others $100 to $500, and so on.

Second, for each spread category, determine the total number of sales, the total sales dollar value, the percent these sales are of the total sales, and the average sales dollar per order.

Third, find your gross profit margin. Subtract the total cost of goods sold (all categories combined) from total sales (all categories combined) to get a *gross profit*. The *cost of goods sold* represents the total costs to produce the products or services that you sell. This includes inventory raw materials such as paper, toner, film, etc., and direct labor charged to the jobs.

By dividing the gross profit by the total sales, you can calculate your gross profit margin. Multiply the gross profit margin by 100 to get the *percent gross profit*. This is the percent of revenue left over to manage the business, sell the products and services, and provide profit and return on your investment.

Fourth, determine your *distribution costs*. These costs include order handling, billing, and salaries for everyone involved in fulfilling the order (but not directly involved in producing the order). A customer calls in. Someone handles the call, takes the order, places the order, adds the order to the job queue, receives the completed job, packages the order for delivery, delivers the order, bills the customer, and processes the payment.

The monies expended to do these things become your distribution costs.

Fifth, determine your *average distribution cost per order*. Divide the distribution costs incurred over a year with the number of orders handled. Even though some orders will be large and some small, this estimate provides a fair assessment of what it costs to fill an order.

Finally, calculate your *break-even order size*. Divide the distribution costs per order by the percent gross profit to find the order size needed to break even on the sale.

If it costs you $14 to handle an order and your gross profit margin is 35%, you need an average order size of $40 (14 /0.35 = 40) just to match your costs—to break even. On a $36 order, you can expect to earn $12.60. But if it cost you $14 just to handle the order, and you only earn $12.60, you would be losing money just by accepting the order. However, if you got a $250 order to design a newsletter, the cost to process and distribute the order is still $14, but your expected gross profit is $87.50. So after you subtract the $14 processing cost, you have $73.50 as a contribution to overhead and profit.

Break-even and margin analysis provide a valuable picture of your business and help you develop an optimum pricing strategy. Cost analysis gives you a clear picture of the margin possible, but your competitors' price lists still influence the price strategy that you eventually adopt. A good market-driven strategy considers both the internal cost issues and the external customer and competitor marketplace in setting price.

Selling at Reduced Prices

As shown in Figure 4-7, there are many ways to effectively reduce your prices. The key is to have a specific reason for taking this action—increase sales, or increase volume.

Cutting prices can be dangerous. Value—not price—sells products and services. Cutting your prices introduces a risk of encouraging cutthroat competition.

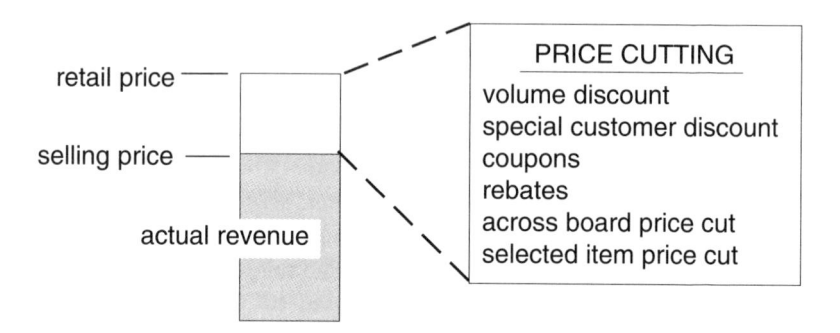

```
retail price  ─┐
               │            PRICE CUTTING
               │         volume discount
selling price ─┤         special customer discount
               │         coupons
               │         rebates
actual revenue │         across board price cut
               │         selected item price cut
```

Figure 4-7. Various forms of price cutting.

If you've claimed to provide high-quality service and then cut your prices, some customers will suspect that you've been gouging them. Customer want quality, but at a cheap price. This forces you to walk a "value-quality-efficiency" tightrope. Your pricing strategy requires special skills and a mindset that can relate clearly to the customer.

IBM and Compaq drastically cut the prices of their PCs in the summer of 1991. Normally, during a sluggish economy, price cuts would stir increased sales. However, the cuts by IBM and Compaq were not enough to stimulate demand in a recession when resellers were consolidating. Sales remained relatively flat and conservative buyers stuck with the clone computers, believing that clones still offered a better deal (perception). As sales stagnated, these two computer giants experienced huge losses in revenue.

Cutting your prices to a point that it costs you money to sell your products and services just so you can "build or regain market share" may be foolhardy. You'll attract the "el cheapo" bargain hunters, but when you must raise your prices to make a profit, you'll find them moving on to the next "cutthroat" vendor. Everybody loses except the low-price bargain buyers.

You must decide if your business should provide more than "mail order" service. Do you really want to target "customers" who aren't willing to pay for solutions and quality work? Perhaps you should let them go and focus on customers who appreciate value and are willing to pay for understanding, empathy, and solution performance.

A shop with excess capacity typically considers price cutting as a way to keep the equipment active. This occurs openly, or is disguised as discounting.

"Shotgun" price-cutting — making price reductions "across the board" — can seal a company's doom. In this strategy, the listed price for every product and service is reduced by a set percent. The owner uses experience and guesswork rather than surgically-precise analysis to re-define the selling price of goods and services.

Cost analysis is not a discretionary activity. It's critical. You must know the exact cost for each product or service that you sell. Improperly calculating your cost factors can drive you into liquidation or bankruptcy.

Never reduce prices across the board. If you cut prices, cut them surgically, cut them intentionally, and know the affect each action will have on your break-even profit point.

Coupons

An interesting tactic for converting a prospect into a customer is the implementation of coupons. Recently, I walked down the main street in Lahaina, Hawaii. As I passed a certain gift shop, a salesperson stepped out from the doorway and handed me a "10 percent Off" coupon.

"Everything in the store is 10 percent off today," he said. "And this is on top of the sale that we've been running all week."

Hawaii was in an economic downturn. Customers weren't spending freely. And shop owners were doing all they could to encourage people to spend.

```
┌─────────────────────────────────┐
│          COUPON                 │
│   10%        $      Today       │
│   Off!              Only!       │
└─────────────────────────────────┘
```

The concept of using coupons to attract business has been around a long time. Coupons are the reason some people buy newspapers on Thursday or Sunday. Coupons are also why many people purchase one product over another. And coupons are one of the most discussed subjects in some women's social group meetings. Women are the primary target for most coupon offers.

A friend, who owns a small shopping center and five retail stores, once told me that his best advertising tactic is to send a coupon book out to his local community. He tried flyers, display ads and many other advertising media. But the coupon booklet works best for him.

His booklet is produced three up on 11" x 17" paper. Printed two sides, folded, cut twice and then saddle stitched yields a booklet about 3.3" high and 8.5" wide. He puts one or two products on each page and typically designs it 16 to 24 pages long. For his particular retail businesses, women are his best customers. They carry his coupon book in their purse. They carry it in their car. And they buy what he advertises.

A recent article in the Wall Street Journal described a study by Drexel University, Ohio State University and Pennsylvania State University on the affect of coupons on consumers. Researchers found that of the 310 billion coupons distributed in the U.S. annually, only 7.7 billion were actually redeemed. But even though most (97.5%) go in the trash, coupons still influence what people buy.

The study revealed that coupons affect sales more than redemption rates indicate. It turns out that when consumers see coupons, even the noncoupon-clippers are more likely to buy a brand product advertised by coupon than they will a brand product not so advertised. In fact, purchases of a product advertised by coupon are just as strong with noncoupon users as they are for coupon redeemers. Just publishing a coupon offer can boost sales.

In addition, these researchers reported that people looking for specific coupons are affected by the messages conveyed by other coupons, too. Incremental sales by noncoupon users increase just by seeing the coupons. This helps offset a reduced profit margin caused by those consumers redeeming coupons.

Coupons work in retail. They may work in your business, too. Most DTP shops and service bureaus sell products as well as services. What if you offered laser printer output for 5¢ each during a "Get To Know You" sale? The idea is to get the prospects coming in. What if you gave 30 minutes free consulting if a customer comes in with a coupon?

I've not seen many service businesses using the coupon as a marketing tactic. Yet, coupons are worth consideration.

Rebates

Rebates are common in automobile, electronics and telecommunication sales. They're also common in video tape feature film sales. Why do these vendors offer rebates instead of just cutting prices?

The strategy behind rebates is that sellers want prospects to be attracted by the lower price (after rebate) but repelled by the bother of collecting. It's a fact that many people end up not asking for the rebate.

$ **REBATE** $

Return this!
Get $10 back
on your purchase

fine print, fine print, fine print

Marketing companies who study consumer preferences identify a "prospect theory" that drives rebate strategies. Thomas T. Nagle, of the Strategic Pricing Group in Boston was recently quoted in Fortune Magazine regarding the concept of rebates. "People judge the loss of any given amount as more painful than they judge the gain of an equal amount as pleasurable."

What sounds complex is simply that people view spending a few bucks more as more painful than if they have an opportunity to get a few bucks extra. This psychology pushes prospects into jumping on rebate deals. They view the rebate as a reduction in pain.

Yet, according to prospect theory, once they make the purchase, the actual rebate begins to look like a gain of minor importance. The small gain is less important to them once they've purchased the product. Thus they procrastinate and many don't bother to collect. A $5 rebate offer on a $14.95 product looks good and causes people to buy. But taking the time to fill out and send in a $5 rebate form just doesn't seem worth the effort. Many just don't want to take the time for only a five dollar gain.

Rebate deals are a very profitable form of price discrimination. Cutting prices will attract price-sensitive prospects and those who would pay the higher price anyway. If, instead of cutting price, you offer a rebate, many price-sensitive buyers will go for the deal and some will send in for the rebate. But less price-sensitive buyers will also go for the deal. They just won't be as eager to return the rebate form. In effect, they pay the higher price.

Think of it this way: If every buyer collected on the rebate offer, rebates would not be worth a seller's effort. A price cut would work just as well. But, exploiting the psychology of the prospect, you can make rebate offers quite profitable. This is a direct example where procrastination by others can make money for a small business owner. Rebate deals give the perception of price cutting without actually being the price cut they appear.

Discounting

Another way to reduce prices is to sell your products and services at discount.

The *list price* is that price that you quote when you get a call. This price can be adjusted based on a discount or allowance. A *discount* is a reduction from the list price that you apply to a customer's purchase when they meet certain conditions. These conditions include paying cash instead of using a credit card or asking for a net payment schedule, paying early, and buying a large quantity of work or service from you, buying during a seasonal promotion. It's called a *trade discount* if the customer is reselling the work to another client.

A customer may also qualify for a reduction from the list price for performing some activity. This is an *allowance.* It works like a discount. It can be a special markdown for including your promotional flyer in the customer's catalog. It can be a reduced price for participating in a community service project or becoming a member of a certain club or organization.

In some shops, the list price is really just a fictitious number—a wish price—from which to discount. In these businesses, products are rarely sold at list price. If this is how you operate, you're bound to encounter buyers who only care about the difference between what you list and what they actually pay.

In some businesses, list price is only important if you put it in your advertising. And publications like this that list comparative prices have no choice but to use each company's list price. It would be better if we had a "price tolerance" gauge that measures what a buyer will pay for a product or service. Then we could use this gauge to evaluate what shops are willing to charge.

The value of discounting is often overestimated. Research reported in *Entrepreneur Magazine* shows that some service providers must lower prices by 65 percent to substantially affect demand. This percentage may be lower in other fields. Pricing is specific to circumstance. And increasing demand is not as simple as just lowering price.

The risk here is that you must cover not only the cost of your goods and labor, but you must also account for basic selling expenses such as marketing, advertising, and commissions. And the results of discounting are often temporary.

In desktop publishing and prepress, price is often a tactic, not a strategy. If customers base their buying decision on price alone, you can always be late, as long as you offer the same quality and service as your competitor, but at a much lower price—20 percent is a much lower price.

Research shows that discounts tend to reduce customer loyalty. Discount buyers are easily lured away when another shop offers a deeper discount. And the risk exists that discounting can undermine your shop's credibility. Customers wonder what they would pay if they hadn't pressured you into a discount.

Immediate discounting from your list prices can make a buyer wonder it they're really getting the best deal. Customers who push for discounts can become suspicious of your pricing once you cave in. They wonder if lower prices cause comprises in quality.

According to Lawrence Steinmetz, author of *How to Sell at Prices Higher Than Your Competition*, "history shows no long-term successes that are discounters." He says that slipped profit margins always catch up with these companies. None of the top discount chains that were operating in 1962 are around today.

Discounting is a personal decision. Typically, as shop owners become more sophisticated in developing pricing strategies, their actual prices adhere closer to published prices. As we become better at pricing, the buyer will not be offered (and expect) discounts, and the confusion that arises between listed prices and actual prices will disappear.

However, there are situations when discounts are appropriate—promotions, markdown sales, and to reinforce your shop's position as an industry leader. In the service industry, you can offer special discounts to first-time buyers. And if you feel your customer is on the verge of growth, a discount may position you for a lot of future business.

To many, a better approach is to add value instead of cutting price by discounting. Including additional products or services creates a different dynamic than that produced by a price cut. When a prospect starts to focus on price, elevate the discussion to value and show them so much benefit in giving you the job that pricing becomes a minor issue.

Volume Discounts Frank Fox, Executive Director of the National Association of Secretarial Services (NASS) addressed sliding price scales for quantity discounts in a recent NASS Newsletter. In his article, he explained that it's good business to offer a discount to customers who purchase more than one of an item.

You start by identifying the lowest price that you can charge for a product. Then select the highest rate for the lowest quantity. Between the two quantity-price points, you assign a range of prices and quantities.

Some owner-operators establish a minimum price because it costs the same to open a file, generate an invoice and collect payment regardless of the quantity of prints desired. If you don't incorporate your costs into the lowest quantity, you will lose money taking the job.

Put your sliding scale into a table and make it available to your customers. Table 4-1 is an example of how sliding scale pricing is used.

Table 4-1. Example sliding scale (Seiko ColorPoint, 8.5 x 11)

	SEIKO COLORPOINT Wax Thermal Printer		
Quantity	8.5 x 11	8.5 x 14	11 x 17
1 - 5	$11.00	$12.00	$15.75
6 - 9	9.00	10.00	13.25
10 - 19	7.50	8.50	12.25
20 - 29	6.50	7.50	12.25
30 - 49	5.50	7.00	11.25
50 +	4.50	6.50	9.00

(Minimum charge $20)

Discounting and the Law Be careful if you're thinking of discounting your products or services. A deep discount may constitute unlawful price discrimination. Section 2(a) of the Robinson-Patman Act relates retailer pricing policies to distributors and resellers. It says that it's illegal for a retailer in commerce to sell commodities of like grade and quantity at different prices for use, consumption, or resale, where the effect of the discount difference will substantially lessen competition or will create a monopoly.

Software publishers sometimes get into trouble when they give their authorized dealers more discount than they do to other resellers. The differences must be "cost-justified" to the extent of the seller's actual cost savings incurred in making, selling, or delivering the product to a particular reseller.

Services are considered a product by some business people, but the Robinson-Patman Act only applies to retailers who sell a tangible product. Your product sales come under this Act, but your services do not.

The American Booksellers Association recently filed suit against five major publishers on behalf of small independent booksellers. They invoked the Robinson-Patman Act, and complained that these large publishers give big chain bookstores unjustly better prices and promotional allowances preventing equal competition by smaller publishers. The question is whether discriminatory volume discounts injured small independent book publisher competitors.

Robinson-Patman violations are difficult to prove. But it's safer if volume discounts are be equally applied. You can, however, discount to one customer more than another if that customer uses your output, but assumes a higher marketing cost.

Adding Loss Leader Jobs

Retail stores typically advertise loss leader products that have little or no profit, but entice customers to shop. Drive by a copy shop and notice the low price offer on the windows. Loss leaders can draw prospects in. The concept works in retail. It may or may not work when selling service.

The risk is that you'll sell lots of loss leader service, but realize little overall profit because you may not sell higher margin work. The key is cost. You must sell above break-even to make a profit. Selling at or below break-even can work for loss leaders, but you must sell higher margin products and services at the same time. I don't believe it's a good strategy to sell at or below cost.

I advice against accepting unprofitable business just to get more exposure in the market place. Unless you're a new business with deep advertising pockets, you need profit, not exposure. If you take a job at a loss, you pull valuable resources away from profit-making work.

When Price Cutting Works

Reducing prices to build market share often results in a short-term reduction in profits. You can minimize this effect by moving to increase market share only when one or more of the following conditions exist.

Customers only care about price. These customers will jump to another shop just to get the lower price. They have the least loyalty. To attract and keep these customers, offer a permanent price advantage. This is why some shops have a special price sheet for "corporate accounts" and a "counter" price sheet for walk-ins. You can make superficial changes in the style or brand of materials that you use, but you risk affecting the quality of your output product. You also risk upsetting current customers when the volume of added business increases, and they get less of your attention.

The total market is growing. Here, you don't have to "steal the sheep" from your competitors. Concentrate instead on inexperienced and new buyers. A lower price attracts this segment of the market as they cautiously buy document generation and printing. They will typically accept lower quality if the price is right. To them, the lower price is "right."

Your reputation for quality won't suffer. If buyers measure quality by your response time and how you communicate, or by some other criteria, cutting the price of your products and services can attract more business.

Your competition probably won't retaliate. When your competitors are preoccupied fighting "alligators"—funding deficits, cash flow, unmet regulations, less capable equipment, management and employee disputes—you can make a price move without their noticing, or being able to respond in like manner.

Your current market share is small. If you already have 50 percent of the market in your area, there's not much advantage in cutting prices. But, if you only hold 5 percent of the market, the potential for additional sales activity is significantly improved.

Your resources are under-utilized. There's an economy of scale when you can make every square foot of your shop and every piece of equipment work to generate money. Idle equipment and idle employees are costly.

The margin will remain high. If reducing prices to increase sales volume will reduce your variable cost per sale—the contribution margin (revenues less variable costs) should remain high.

If a majority of these conditions are present, it's likely that your price-cutting strategy will succeed.

How to Handle the Price Cut

There are always a myriad of factors that come into play when changing your price structure. Here are some suggestions on how to handle a price cut.

Look at past history. If you didn't raise your prices when your competitors did, determine if your sales volume and profit increased or decreased.

Offload excess capacity with "two-for-one" offers.

Consider occasional discounting, but watch the effect on positioning. You don't want a price cut to "cheapen the image" of your products or services.

Experiment with formal price cutting in just a few products or services. Don't make across-the-board cuts.

Cite the actual dollar savings rather than the percentage of savings in a price cut, so customers who know the prices will be attracted to your special offer.

Don't automatically follow the price moves of your competitors. They may not have done their homework.

Keep the new break-even point clearly in mind when you consider a lower price.

A Price Reduction Strategy That Worked

One company developed an effective strategy for holding market share while cutting prices.

Every time demand rose by 10-20%, the company cut prices. This increase in demand was not enough to attract competition into their market niche. Cutting prices slowly while demand increased slowly, but steadily, worked for them. They gained market share without facing challengers.

Raising Your Prices

Most shops are reluctant to increase prices. They feel that it's much harder to raise a price than it is to lower a price. This feeling is supported by studies suggesting that over 72 percent of all consumer buying decisions are based on price alone. With this in mind, be very careful when increasing prices. You probably shouldn't implement added features or time-saving devices if doing so will increase your list prices by 20 percent or more. This could exceed the "threshold of worth" held by your customer base. They'll find your actions unacceptable and seek other alternatives.

On the other hand, some owners literally "give away" services because they are afraid customers will balk if they increase their rates to a profitable level. You can only be generous if it doesn't curtail achievement of business goals. You are in business to make a profit. If not, close the doors and sell out. Otherwise, raise your prices so you can make a profit and get a decent return on any financial investment that you've made.

But be careful when considering a price increase. Besides alienating some customers, there is another risk to raising prices. The higher you raise your prices, the more you'll entice competitors to enter your type of business.

Keeping your prices high holds a "carrot" of temptation out to your competitors. If the temptation becomes too strong, they may add resources to compete in your market niche and unseat your leadership position. So when you consider a price increase, make each increase small.

A handy rule of thumb suggests that a one percent increase in price can produce a 10 percent increase in profit. This is usually a close approximation to reality because once you've developed your products or services, there's little added cost in raising your price. And any increase is applied immediately to the bottom line. Recall what pricing points can do for profit.

Your best approach is to conduct a product-by-product, service-by-service analysis. Then selectively raise those prices that warrant the action. Don't raise prices excessively, or you'll alert your competition to a potential opportunity.

How Some Shops Handle Price Increases

Dealing with new customers is relatively easy when you plan to implement a price increase. But for their current client base, many shops struggle with the mechanics of such a move.

Some owners send a warm, personal letter to each current customer reminding them of the successful projects that they've shared in the past. Then they tell them that they're upgrading several capital items (software, hardware, etc.) to provide better, faster service, that inflation is causing higher operating costs, or that they are experiencing higher materials costs from suppliers. Next, they hit them with a small (typically no more than $5 an hour) rate increase. They set the effective date for the price increase four weeks ahead to give their customers time to take advantage of the current low price. They reassure their customers that they will continue to bill at the old rate for any projects started before the price increase takes effect. Then they assure their customers that they value their business and look forward to new and challenging assignments in the future. Some shop owners include a paragraph that mentions projects that a client has talked about and may want to get initiated right away.

Another school of thought suggests that you avoid advising your clients of higher prices. This group feels that most shops give customers a quote based on more than just an hourly rate (including a flat fee for work paid up front or added charges for changes), so focusing on a higher hourly rate is unimportant.

They also suggest that you not worry about what NEW clients will think of your higher rates. Most will not be aware of the old rates (as long as you change the signs and paperwork properly). If they are referred by another client, then explain why your rate increase was necessary. Otherwise, don't say a thing.

Quoting your new rates in a price increase letter may turn away major clients who are not comfortable paying $70 an hour, but who can accept a flat-rate estimate or a daily or weekly rate. Quoting an hourly rate instead of a flat rate to these customers can scare them away. Some people are simply not comfortable working with professionals who charge by the hour. For these folks, it's better to put a job into perspective by expressing project costs as a total package price. You can quote a firm fixed price once you establish your machine standards, production standards, and budgeted hourly rates (covered in Chapter 5).

There are other advantages to quoting a flat rate. This approach lets you build in fees and charges that would stand out like a sore thumb on an hourly-rate price-breakdown sheet. If you quote a job 25 percent lower than what customers can find elsewhere, you can incorporate a price increase while still giving the impression that they are getting your services for "peanuts."

Some shops charge "by the line" for alterations and corrections rather than at an hourly rate. When customers insist on an hourly rate, you can offer a lower hourly rate for handling alterations and corrections. This gives your customer a feeling that they're getting a bargain (even though you still earn a good profit).

How Much Can You Raise Your Price?

Finding the customer's point of acceptance/resistance is a challenge. It involves knowing your market, your competitors, and your customer's price elasticity.

An increase of $5 an hour may be palatable. Raising rates by $10 an hour may be too much.

If you're new and your business is evolving rapidly, shift immediately to a well-researched solid rate regardless what increment you determine is appropriate. Just be certain that your customers still perceive sufficient value in your services.

If your analysis and calculations indicate a $15-an-hour increase is appropriate, move immediately to the new price. Most people recommend that you avoid step increases because these can cause confusion and word will spread rapidly that one client got a similar job done for a lower price. If you can justify the increase and give your customers advance warning, boldly move forward and increase your hourly rates. Be sure to replace your signs and price sheets.

Some shop owners say that the price is right when 20 percent of your customers complain that you're too expensive. Typically, 5-10 percent is average for a price increase.

Subtle Ways to Raise Your Prices

As shown in Figure 4-6, there are some subtle ways to increase a price without calling it a price increase. You can reduce the size of a product or service while keeping the price the same. For example, Pizza Hut reduced the size of its large pizza from 15 inches to 14 inches, keeping the price constant. This subtle act is actually a 15 percent price increase.

Software vendors who once offered 12 months telephone support, now offer only 90 days. This repre-

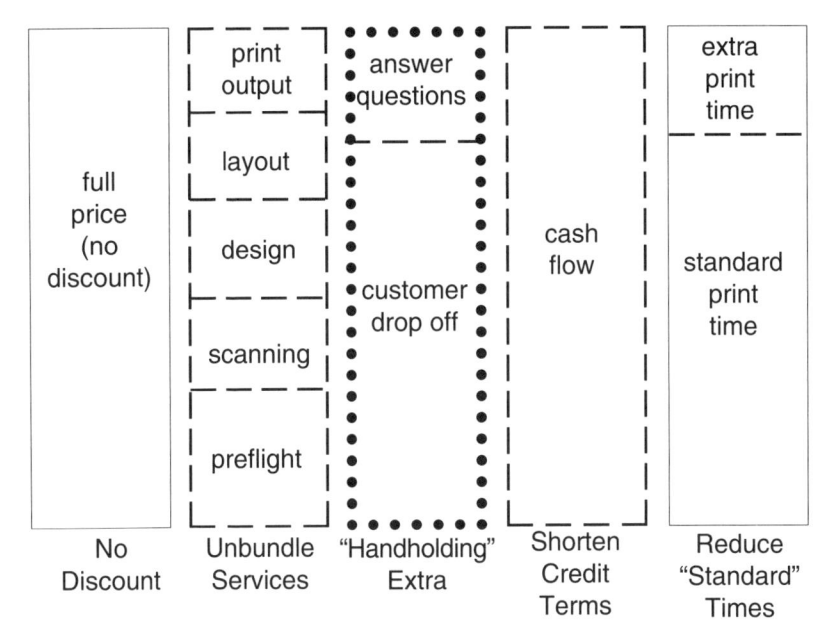

Figure 4-6. Various ways to raise prices.

sents a price increase to the customer (although most buyers don't perceive it as such).

You could unbundle services and reduce complimentary scan retouch from 30 minutes to 15 minutes. This is effectively a price increase. You could no longer provide free laser printer output on certain jobs. Again, it's a price increase.

You can also effectively raise prices by eliminating discounts and by reducing credit terms. Just reducing the payment terms from 30 days to two weeks will cause a noticeable increase in your cash flow position.

A Penny Here, A Penny There ... Adding Cents Makes Sense

The cents numbers appended to advertised prices is where added profit can be made with little or no added cost.

Advertising a price of $5.36 probably won't generate any more sales than you would get by advertising a price of $5.95. But the higher price can add 59¢ of pure profit to the sale. Natural price points occur in business. Using these points lets you increase your asking price without changing a customer's perception of worth.

These price points have enormous influence on the buying patterns of the public. Mathematically, they represent discontinuities in a price elasticity demand curve. You can sell much more product at $5.95 than you can at $6.05, but not much more at $5.85 than you can at $5.95. Customers consider the 10¢ difference between $5.95 and $6.05 a major hurdle but hardly notice the difference between $5.85 and $5.95. This difference represents 10¢ of direct profit. Making an additional 10¢ on high volume sales can add up fast. Supermarkets make a successful business working with pennies of profit.

Natural price points are more frequent at lower prices. Abrupt shifts in demand (price elasticity) are also more frequent at lower prices. Knowing these points of discontinuity can help you act to significantly affect your bottom line.

Eric Mitchell, publisher of *The Pricing Advisor* offers good advice on how you should use price points in your pricing strategy. He partitions product pricing into categories—less than $1, $1 to $10, $10 to $100, and more than $100. Each price category should be handled differently. Mitchell suggests that you can effectively add to your profit by pricing products less than a dollar at a value ending with nine — 39¢, 79¢, 99¢ etc. When most customers consider a product selling for "less than a dollar," they notice the tens value, but not the cents value. Therefore, rather than pricing your product at 96¢, make it 99¢ and your customer won't care. The extra 3¢ income passes directly to your bottom line profit.

Table 4-2. Use pricing points for more profit.

SELLING PRICE	TACTIC	EXAMPLE
<$1	price by 9s	39¢
$1 - !10	price by 5s or 9s	$1.55, $7.29
$10 - $100	price by 25s or dollars	$24.25 / $99
$100 +	dollars, no cents	$125 / $750

He further suggests that you avoid ending your product pricing with 1s, 2s, or 4s (e.g., 21¢, 42¢, 64¢), although ending in 5 is acceptable (e.g., 95¢). Just remember, you're trying to focus on profit. The more you can get for your product without changing the perception of value for cost, the better your profit picture.

For products priced between $1 and $10, Mitchell suggests ending the price with the digit 5 or 9 (e.g., $1.15, $1.39, etc.). Avoid using any other digit. A price presentation at $2.75 is equally as attractive as one at $2.79. And, a few cents here, a few cents there—pretty soon you've got real money. Especially if you're handling thousands of pages of data or graphics each week.

When the price exceeds $10, use increments of 25¢ or round off to a whole dollar value without cents (e.g., $11.50, $12, $24.25, $37.75, etc.). Between $10 and $100, he suggests that you avoid using the .99 digits (e.g., $11.99, $24.99, etc.). Mitchell feels that endings of $.25, $.50, and $.75 are preferable because they suggest fair pricing.

Above $100, Mitchell suggests that we stick with whole dollar amounts and never display the $.00 ending. A price of $110.00 looks much larger than a price of $110. It's all in the way we as customers view price.

This strategy is currently used in the pricing of trade and paperback books. Since 1965, publishers priced their books using a $.95 point level to distinguish them from other consumer goods. This has changed. The decimal point prices have been raised from $.95 to $.99. Some publishers now round off to the next highest dollar point. Hardcover books are being sold with prices rounded off to the nearest dollar or the $.50 price point. None of the publishers have reported consumer resistance to this new pricing strategy.

Many other products are also being introduced with prices that end with .99 rather than .95. Mass market prices are rapidly being converted to the .99 point over the .95 point.

Since most publishing and service bureaus charge a round number fee, you may be missing out on a lot of added profit. You can easily add profit by implementing pricing points in your pricing strategy.

Handling Staff Objections to a Price Increase

As you discuss a price increase with your team, you'll encounter some interesting objections from your own people.

Here are some typical comments.

"We'll lose customers."

"The customer buys on price alone."

"Our quality isn't high enough, so we need to discount our price."

"We'll lose long term business."

"The competition will eat us alive."

To help your staff understand why a price increase is necessary, hold a company meeting in which you openly and honestly explain your strategy.

Then conduct an "objection clinic" with your employees. Using role playing, have them counter objections that a customer might make. Often the employees can create objection scenarios that your customers haven't thought of. This role playing experience is helpful in getting both your staff and your customers comfortable with any price increase that is planned. The banking and financial services profession often conducts role playing sessions whenever adding or eliminating products, or changing fees. If it works for them, it just may work for you, too.

Easing Customer "Sticker Price" Shock

An article in *ThePage* described how to add clarity to a job and help customers overcome the shock of seeing a large project price. The article suggested that you generate an "Instructions to the Customer" sheet describing the things that the client can do to prepare and format text and graphics so your job is easier and faster, and their bill is lower. Consider providing a suggestion guide such at this prior to the start of a job.

The way a client prepares the work for delivery to you can directly save you time and your customer money. Explain to the customer that they can reduce job costs by carefully preparing the work before they bring it to you. Ask them to provide their input in the formats that your equipment can easily handle. Some shops provide clients the use of screen fonts so a customer can design their document in a form as close to final as possible.

If you must take raw text files and flow them into a page layout template, explain to your customer that they can reduce their costs substantially by giving you files in a form that makes your layout work easier and faster. Suggest that they provide text without any formatting. Have them use a tab or extra blank line to indicate new paragraphs. Ask them to use an agreed code such as [1],

[2], [3], etc. to designate different levels of heads and subheads. Ask them to provide hard copy art in a size that you can easily scan into the computer.

For art and photographs that you will strip into the document, explain that the cleaner they make their graphics, the less time you will spend cleaning them up for the stat process.

Explain how they can make the importing of text and graphics smoother and faster and directly affect the bottom line of their invoice. Show them how they can save project costs by considering a different paper or a lower resolution output. Suggest the use of clip art in place of custom art. Suggest different ways to handle color. Explain the cost implications of each approach. Describe your discount programs and how a customer can save by bundling work or purchasing work in quantity. Not only will they save project dollars, but you will be gaining a loyal return customer and likely several referrals in the process.

Hold Your Price!

According to Thomas J. Winninger, author of *Price Wars*, most customers can spend 20 percent more than they originally plan. This surely isn't evident by listening to some customers. Yet the reality is that people buy value, not price. If you can overwhelm them with value, price becomes minor in their buying decision.

Continue adding value to your service until you are convinced that the value you add far exceeds your price. You must sell yourself first.

Then when a customer complains that your prices are higher than the competition, agree. Tell them that this is part of your company's philosophy. Turn your high prices into a strength by showing them why your business offers the least risk to them. Give examples of how your services have directly benefited other companies.

As an aside, every time a customer calls and tells you how much benefit they gained or how great a job you did, ask them if you can use them as a reference. Ask if you can quote them—better yet, ask them to write a testimonial letter to your company. Then use these in flyers and brochures that you develop. You can hand a waffling prospect one of these and likely persuade them to become a customer.

Then, since your prices are higher, let your competitors reconfirm your strength philosophy by telling their prospects and customers how they are lower priced than you. Remember, lower price can be viewed as a more risky alternative.

If you're making a presentation to a prospect, start by telling them about the value of your products or services. The idea is to get them to view price through a mental filter—a value filter.

Don't "hem and haw" when you mention price. You could cause them to question the value of your services. They could feel they can negotiate a much lower price. Be direct. And state your price with conviction.

After they've accepted your price and paid for your services, tell them that they made a wise decision. Reinforce the value that they received for the price.

For customers who hold that your price is too high, explain how you can adjust the price if they will concede certain aspects of the job. You could let them do part of the work, you could use lower quality materials, change the delivery date or mode, or change some other aspect of the job that will pull costs out resulting in a lower project fee. You are essentially exchanging concessions for lower price without compromising value. They get less performance in the trade. And you hold firm on your shop's hourly rates.

Pricing in a Changing World

Recently Coopers & Lybrand completed a survey on how the fastest-growing companies in the U.S. set their prices. According to a write-up in *Inc Magazine*, these companies continually monitor and adjust prices. By increasing or decreasing prices these companies achieved 28 percent revenue growth. The companies that took no action—fixed pricers—achieved 8 percent less growth.

The study also found that few of these fast-growers consulted potential customers about price changes. Only 12 percent conducted end-user studies. Fully 65 percent based price changes on perceived value or perceived worth.

Over half of these companies base price on what the competition is doing and the uniqueness of their products or services. The cost-plus approach is used by 43 percent of them.

In this chaotic market, continual change is certain. To keep up and be competitive, you must change with conditions. It's not easy.

Determining the final prices for your products and services takes time and work. Your computer spreadsheet is a critical resource in this process.

Perform the analysis. Develop a draft set of prices. Compare these against the objectives and strategic and tactical pricing plan that you've developed. Work up a break-even analysis, and a margin curve analysis for each product or service. Obtain market intelligence on potential customers and existing competitors. Determine the likely reactions that your existing customers and competitors will take when you make your revised prices known. Include in your analysis the expected impact each price change will have on your other products and services. Be certain that you adhere to local, state, and federal regulations so you don't run into legal trouble.

Consider testing your prices. Marketing guru, Jay Abraham, described how one of his clients tested a $69 newsletter subscription price against $79 and found that the lower price pulled three times more subscribers. His $69 test price made 300% more money from the same effort and investment as the $79 price.

Abraham further reports that a $19 subscription price for his own newsletter out-produced a $15 price by two times and a $17 price by a factor of four.

There are unique dynamics in each business that cause different products and services to have different optimum price points. Testing your prices helps you find the optimum. The best price may be higher or lower than your initial set point. But you won't know until you experiment.

Once you feel that you have a good price list, develop a contingency plan on how to handle potential adverse consequences. If you know that a price increase will upset certain customers, develop a strategy to carefully work the increase into your operation.

Don't lock yourself into a price. Cast your pricing strategy in "Jello™"—a semi-rigid plan. There are always circumstances that require a slightly different approach to pricing—an opportunity, a threat, etc. When you bid jobs, price your work based on how much it will cost to perform on that particular project. Often the cost to perform on one job is greatly different than the cost to perform on another similar job.

Finally, develop a policy of periodically reviewing your pricing strategy. Don't be afraid to modify your prices as market conditions change. Pricing is an ongoing process. It doesn't end the moment you publish your counter price list.

Analyze Your Customer Base by Profit

Most of us categorize customers based on sales volume. But, there's much more to analyzing customers than this.

Customers generally fall into one of two categories — price-sensitive customers or service-sensitive customers. It's up to you to determine which they are. Price-sensitive customers still want service. In fact they often demand much more than they are willing to pay for.

As you analyze your customer base, note how much profit each client generates. Compare customers by sales or profit earned in a selected time period—say, annually. You could discover that small customers are more profitable than larger clients. In fact, the small jobs could be subsidizing those large contracts. This is why many shops don't go after the school and government markets. Hard negotiations and extended payments can make profiting in these markets tough and stressful.

For those customers who place service as top priority, make extra effort to develop a good relationship with these "cash cow" businesses. These customers bring repeat business. They can also be excellent referrals for long term business growth.

Other considerations involve resource utilization and spreading the source of your sales income. It may be better to have 100 customers each bringing you $500 in sales than five customers generating $10,000 each. Most of us prefer to spread our sales income over as many sources as possible to account for varying market conditions and to maximize resource utilization.

In this way, the loss of one major account won't put part of your staff out of work. Try to keep a single account from becoming 50 percent or more of your business.

What's the value of keeping customers? ADP recently stated that they found net earnings could increase by 20 percent if they could increase the retention of their existing customer base by just five percent. Since customers come and go, the extra effort to get repeat customers can be worth its weight in gold. Especially if they're customers who bring you high profit jobs. Be a discriminating entrepreneur. Focus on where the profit is maximum.

Don't Give Away the Store

I say again. Don't give away the store! At this point, you have the information necessary to get paid what you're worth. You have what it takes to reap larger profits. All that's needed is for you to build the courage to ask the prices that you deserve to earn.

One of the startling findings of our surveys, and of the hundreds of interviews that we've conducted, is that a large number of new business entrepreneurs don't value their own skills high enough to command the salaries that they should earn. In fact, statistically women pay themselves over 20 percent LESS than their male counterparts—even when they own and operate the business!

You CAN (and SHOULD) charge fees that are more in line with the education, skills, and experience that you have. But you must believe this statement before you will earn what you deserve.

Rather than giving free scanning services and free clip art use to customers who buy design support, unbundle these services and charge for these "freebies." You bought the hardware and software to generate income. You should receive a return on each business investment.

Rather than giving unlimited hand-holding and consulting to your customers (who won't complain about the free service), recognize that this information has value. Consider a consulting fee with a minimum charge based on 10 minutes of time. Not only will you make money from your knowledge, but you'll also reduce the repeated requests for free advice. This will let you put more time and energy into those activities that earn income.

Countering Cutthroat Competition

As Nathan Morton wrote in Computer Reseller News: "We are today in a 'take no prisoners' phase of weeding out the weak, the mundane, the imitators and the opportunist from the marketplace."

" We are going through maturation and the purification that comes from soul searching and a heavy dose of cutthroat competition for market share—both occurring at the same time."

" We are pushing, thinking, shoving, cutting, focusing, listening, and inventing like we have never done before."

Morton was describing the computer revolution. He may as well have been describing desktop publishing and prepress today. We truly are in the initial stages of an Information Revolution that will forever change the way we live and work.

Massive workplace restructuring is placing hundreds of thousands of jobs at risk. Over two million middle level managers are now out of work with the odds of someone over 40 finding a job and regaining equal pay work getting slimmer by the day. Many displaced workers are opting to start new companies.

People from all walks of life are establishing side jobs and starting part time businesses to give them some form of security as they worry about their primary employment. Many of these people are starting desktop publishing businesses in their homes.

This has made desktop publishing one of the fastest growing home businesses. The number of desktop service shops continues to grow at an exponential rate. Just examine the telephone yellow pages to see the rapid rise in businesses providing these services.

Most of these entrepreneurs are novices at operating and managing a business. Yet they jump in with both feet to provide desktop services. Often they sink in a quicksand of business mistakes.

Peel back the corner of a can containing failed businesses and much of the smell comes from undercutting on price without considering costs. By continuing to turn back the tin, we get a clearer picture of reality in the market place.

We just completed our fourth annual national survey on pricing. When the first survey was completed, we noted wide price ranges in our statistical data for almost every service associated with desktop publishing and prepress. We expected the bounds on this range to decrease as the industry matured and professionals became more experienced in the true costs of performing desktop services. This has not happened. Instead, we've seen price ranges widening—particularly for desktop publishing. Of most concern is the trend toward lower prices.

I believe there are three primary reasons for this phenomenon. First, there is a huge influx of new startups. With corporate-level jobs dissolving like snow on a hot, sunny day, many people are starting home businesses as primary or secondary sources of income. As I mentioned, many of these businesses are in desktop publishing.

Most of these shop owners understand the concepts of graphic design and page layout. Some have only the rudiments of training and skills. But many individuals in both groups fail to understand the realities of running a business.

Second, there is a relatively low entrance fee to starting a DTP business. Many people already own a computer and an inkjet or laser printer. This means that almost anyone can hang out a shingle and claim to be a desktop publisher.

Third, DTP shops can operate anywhere. Over 60 percent of them are located in the home. Home business entrepreneurs often fail to recognize many of their operating costs. Whether a shop is in a home office or in a strip center, rent and insurance still apply. This means that prices must be based on sound business basics. Novice shop owners often fail to look at the big picture. Many also start without knowing the value of their skills. A keyboard operator charging $1.25 a page for data entry does not understand the limitation they place themselves under. Eight or $10 an hour does not cover their cost of doing business.

Whatever the cause, the primary mistake many make is pricing poorly. Without a handle on personal professional value, break even, or true business costs, new entrepreneurs often look at competitors to decide what they should charge. Then they simply undercut every price they see.

Prepress shops are not immune to these pressures. Prices for a letter-size Matchprint integral color proof vary from $60 to as much as $140. The same price variation occurs when new printing technologies are introduced. Lee Cowan, Senior Editor of *Micro Publishing News* described in a recent article how vendors and providers of digital printing are attempting to sort out true costs so they can develop pricing models that work. Confusion results in unpredictable costs and prices that are not based on reality. Price sheets change often and prices vary widely. In a hot, competitive market, cut-throat pricing becomes rampant.

Undercutting prices puts tremendous pressure on successful shop owners who perceive cutthroat shops as sharks — scavengers who are willing to do any job at any price. The result is a reduction across the board in the perceived value of the services being offered. As some shops underbid everyone, they often incur costs that exceed income. Profit from the jobs slip away. Yet the jobs have also slipped through the fingers of the more professional shop owners. To compete they retaliate by lowering their prices. They stress service to the point that they often give away valuable information.

Jim Latham of Ink Spot Printing Services feels that the printing industry is in a "lamentable state of competition." He may as well have been describing desktop publishing and prepress. We seem to add value, but we don't charge for it. To be a professional business owner requires a tremendous investment in technical knowledge and skills. Why then do we spend so much time telling our customers how we do our job? This information represents trade secrets for our profession. This information is our "bread and butter."

As we educate our clients and customers on the desktop and prepress process—the hardware and software, the techniques to produce quality work—these people listen and learn. Often they learn enough to brow-beat us into price concessions on jobs that we should be paid much more to perform. By our intellectual indiscretion, we place our shops in the customer's vise and then help them turn down the screws to our own business survival. Sometimes these same clients become competitors against us.

Cutthroat behavior cheapens a proud and noble art. By not setting and holding to fair prices, the rest of us make ourselves participants in this tragedy. We go along with the crowd and lower our own prices leading each other down into Chapter 11 bankruptcy.

Savvy buyers know how to sniff out and exploit weakness within the ranks. They suck the financial energy out of a low-price cutthroater until that shop sinks into oblivion. Then these "leeches" move on to the next unsuspecting price-undercutter and begin the process all over.

As prices fall, many desktop publishing products and services become mere commodities. Take the price of 300 dpi laser print output. It has fallen from over a dollar a page to less than 10¢ a page in many areas. This puts laser printing at the level of desktop copying—a commodity service.

Recently, a reseller won a contract with the U.S. Postal Service to provide computer equipment at extremely low prices. This company bid 10 percent BELOW cost and was willing to forgo profit to increase cash flow. "It's the most ludicrous thing I ever heard of," said Terry Theye, CEO of The Future Now Inc., one of the bidders.

An increasingly competitive environment is forcing some businesses to win contracts regardless of cost. The name of their game is cash flow. In the short term, their desperate acts may keep their doors open. But in the long run, all bets are against them. And there's little doubt that the company winning the Post Office contract will provide anything other than boxes and definitely no hand holding or solution support. They are acting as a catalog mail order dealer (although some catalog direct mailers offer good support). The strategy of this company is cutthroat. And it's a loser.

So how do we counter cutthroat pricing? Jeff Hayzlett, former owner of several printing shops and now a public relations expert, suggests that we jostle "lowballers" by inundating them with jobs.

According to Hayzlett, "If a competitor bids well below cost, I'd send them as many jobs as possible."

"That increases my profit margin since they're doing the job for less money than I can." He can also then focus on higher margin projects.

Hayzlett feels that subcontracting more business to the low-price competitor eventually crushes them in their own losses. As you'll see in Chapter 7, there is a way to evaluate project bids to estimate how much profit a competing shop will realize if they win a job. Sometimes by winning a project award, a shop can lose thousands of dollars just by performing the work. Thus, passing jobs to them while they consistently sell below costs eventually puts their business under. Hayzlett suggests that you become their worst nightmare.

When buyers pursue the lowest price, their strategy is subject to the law of diminishing returns. The benefit of a lower price has limits. If buyers base purchase decisions solely on price, negative experiences will eventually dampen their approach. Selecting is much more complex than choosing the shop that has the lowest price. Buyers who always chase the lowest price are usually from poorly operated businesses that seldom amount to much and generally are not worth your sales effort.

I feel that the way out of a "price-only" situation is to build value in the customer's eyes. As cutthroat prices produce razor-thin margins, keep a tight lid on your costs and specialize. As a business banker once shared: "Stick to the basics. Stick to what you do well, and the money will follow." She was right. By keeping a focus on a specialized product (or a specialized industry) you heighten your efficiency and increase your ability to respond positively to price pressures. Become known as the best in your area of expertise. Then price accordingly.

Charlotte Taylor, small business advisor for *Entrepreneur* magazine says the key is your *unique selling proposition (USP)*. Pinpoint what makes your business unique. Then target your advertising, promotion and sales efforts accordingly. The USP of digital color printing is that it's a digital process—it delivers capabilities new to the marketplace. Find your unique selling proposition by putting yourself "in your customer's shoes." Learn what motivates them and why they buy from you rather than from competitors with lower prices. Then focus on this difference. By using USP, you can make your products and services stand out—even in a market saturated with similar things.

Because desktop service providers operate at the "bleeding edge of technology," don't get discouraged. Aggressive competitors will come and go. But by using smart value-pricing techniques, you can cause rays of brilliant sunlight to shine on your business and your bank account. Focus on value and keep costs constantly in mind. Then price for whatever the market will bear. Don't become known as the "cheapest price in town." Become known as the "highest value producer in town."

How to Break Out Top Profits

Thousands of small shops are struggling with plunging profits. The triple whammy—recession, diminishing margins, and tougher competition—is hitting everyone hard. Yet, some shops are not just holding their own in this economic climate, they are realizing profit margins of 30 and 40 percent! Why? How? What do they know that many others don't?

Interestingly, what they know works best, both in good times and in bad, is to focus on the basics. This means that they apply common sense to their business practices. They develop close customer relationships. They form partnerships with their customers, their vendors, and even their competitors, and they offer flexible products and services. But more important, they understand that they are in business to make money. They charge for their time and their equipment and materials.

These people succeed regardless of what business niche they're in, regardless of their size, and regardless of their location. They can operate out of a barn on the plains of Kansas. They can operate out of a studio apartment in a congested metropolitan area. They can operate from a store front in a small town. And they can operate from shared offices in a busy industrial park. More important, they can generate a six figure income in all of these places.

Meanwhile, other shops offer products and services based solely on what they think everyone else is charging. They lose money on their service because they underestimate the time and energy required. They fail to use the business expertise and contact base of their suppliers. And they leave dollars on the table each time they negotiate a job.

High-margin shops implement good business methods. They charge separately for each service, or they bundle all the tasks into a composite job with a keen eye toward break-even and maximum profit. The successful shops offer different packages, hourly rates, and support services to their customer base. When the economy slows, they don't change their service. They just change how it's packaged. They make pay schedules and contracts flexible and work to ease the cash flow problems of their customers.

Other highly successful shops achieve a 30 percent profit margin by staying within a small business niche, improving performance, and carefully watching their checking account. They regularly talk themselves out of accepting certain jobs if the work will spread them too thin. They won't promise quality or response times that they can't deliver. Thus, they keep customers coming back.

Some hire part time professionals and work hard to develop a cadre of experts who have the broad overall knowledge and business skills needed. By forming partnerships with their customers, their vendors, and other shops, they keep their own personnel costs down and maximize their individual profit potential.

The consistent advice from high-profit shop owners is to be a business person first and then work to make your customers successful. View profit, return on investment, and margins as more important than having the latest equipment and the newest version of software.

Instead of getting caught up in the technology of desktop, get caught up in business planning and sound implementation. Be business and profit oriented. Everything else follows.

Successful shop owners suggest that you work to reduce your fixed costs. Forecast cash flow. Find better ways to manage your variable costs. And take the time to do a better job defining the market.

Focus on the kind of business that you want to be, and then gear all of your time and energy toward that vision. Yet, you should be sensitive to change. Know your limits, but don't be afraid to adapt as conditions change. Recognize that your business is constantly evolving. In this Information Age, you can't afford to remain static. To do so will cause your company to be left behind in the dust of competition.

Instead of pricing at what the competition charges, high margin people use cost-plus pricing techniques and build in plenty of profit. Rather than chasing volume, these shops chase profit. And, they control their growth. They turn their backs on deals that don't offer the profit they want. They're convinced that they can't recover lost profit through volume sales.

And they cultivate customer relationships like horticulturists cultivate fine roses. They learn their customer's needs and maintain an attitude that the customer is always right. They also work hard to learn the business issues that potential customers face. The more they know, the more value they offer to their customer base.

These entrepreneurs realize that once they get a client, they can substantially increase profit by getting repeat business. Once the marketing and advertising has converted a prospect to a customer, all repeat jobs generate residual income. The net profit is higher on repeat and referral jobs.

Rather than taking a short term view of their business, they look and plan long range. They are willing to invest money now to build their business so they can earn more later.

They are also alert for new opportunities. For example, one shop eagerly collects "junk mail." Each time they spot a poorly designed flyer, they re-design it. They correct the warts and moles, and then return a copyrighted re-design to the company that originally sent the advertisement. They offer to support them on future endeavors. This shop doesn't make money on the initial re-design, but this approach generates substantial follow-on jobs. Their strategy is simple. Give more value than the customer expects. View each customer as a 20-year client. Expect follow-on jobs, and consistently work as part of a customer-vendor team. These are the keys to success.

Summary

Pricing tactics are how you keep ahead of the competition. They are the actions you take to make your business succeed. In Chapter 5, you'll learn how to develop baselines and standards so you can optimize your pricing structure and be able to bid a flat rate for your products and services, knowing how much you'll make or can negotiate on every job. You'll also discover that there are many ways to price your work and some ways are more suitable than others depending of the characteristics of the job.

5

Baselines, Standards and Budgeted Hourly Rates

"Intuitive pricing is a fool's folly in today's highly competitive world."

As Roger Dickeson, production productivity specialist and one of my favorite writers has said, "Until you measure, you can't control." You cannot begin to price, or to estimate a job until you have a reference, a point of origin on which to base your rates. This chapter helps you establish the baselines for your business. It shows you how to develop production standards and how to use these to calculate budgeted hourly rates on which you can build a bid.

Generating a Cost Baseline

Developing a reference point for pricing requires a clear understanding of costs. And there are a variety of costs associated with operating a business. These include marketing, selling, administrative, labor, and materials. Sometimes understanding and defining these costs can be one of the toughest jobs that you'll tackle. Yet, your price can only be as accurate as the information used to generate it.

The best way to baseline costs is to clearly identify all the tasks associated with a job. Each task represents a cost to your business. Some tasks are billable. Others are part of your overhead. By developing a historical record of costs, you can use this to estimate future work.

Essentially, your costs of doing business must be partitioned into fixed costs, variable costs, direct costs, indirect costs, and overhead. These terms are related and are often confused.

Fixed Costs

Fixed costs are those expenses that you must pay whether you have little or lots of business. Fixed costs don't vary with the volume of sales. They exists just because you're in business. Fixed costs include:

- rent
- parking
- taxes
- most utilities
- salaries
- depreciation
- grounds keeping
- insurance
- etc.

For example, you must pay someone to produce billable services. It doesn't matter if you perform design and layout or another person does the work. One or both have to perform billable work to generate income. Some shop owners fool themselves by not considering their own direct labor in calculating project costs. Since most shop owners are also designers and technicians, they should charge their time to the business and be paid for their efforts.

Variable Costs

Variable costs are those expenses that change with the level of business activity. They include:

- cost of goods sold
- supplies

- fringe benefits
- commissions
- marketing
- advertising
- wages (part-time and freelance help)

If you take on more projects, you'll use more paper, more toner, and more electricity. Part of your utility bill is a fixed cost. But, the additional electricity required for each project is a variable cost. Thus, some expenses are part fixed, part variable. You should separate these into the fixed and variable components for good cost analysis.

Direct Costs

Direct costs can be directly related to a job or project. These costs can be associated with a unique project number or work order. Direct costs include:

- salaries of employees who directly work on a project (direct labor)
- equipment leased or rented to do a job
- materials used on a specific project
- consultants hired to support a project
- job-specific computer and software purchases
- job-specific documentation purchases

Anything that can be charged directly to a job work order (direct labor, direct materials, etc.) is a direct cost. Commissions or finders fees paid for activities that result in a job can also be considered a direct cost.

Indirect and Overhead Costs

Indirect costs are those expenses that can not be directly charged to a specific job or project. These costs become overhead expenses to your business. Indirect costs can include both fixed and variable costs.

We collect the indirect expenses that we must pay whether or not we sell a product or service and call these our *overhead costs*. Indirect or overhead costs include:

- rent
- marketing
- insurance
- supplies
- maintenance
- utilities
- advertising
- taxes
- depreciation
- management salaries
- secretary/clerk pay
- vacation expenses
- vehicle expense

Overhead costs do not include designer and technician wages. The overhead for a shop is pro-rated—partitioned into a cost per hour and then allocated to each service that the shop performs. Typically, you calculate your annual overhead costs and then allocate a portion of your overhead costs to the total hours worked during a year. The total hours worked depends on your staffing and how many hours each person actually worked. One person working 40 hours a week with two weeks vacation equals 2,000 hours of work a year. A full year of 40-hour weeks is considered 2080 hours.

A DTP shop or service bureau will typically have overhead costs that equal 40-50 percent of the shop's income. A reasonable amount of your overhead costs should be allocated to each job or hour of billable time.

If the more expensive hardware and software are typically used by the higher paid employees, your overhead costs closely track your labor costs. If everyone uses all the equipment and software, your overhead costs will track with the shop's billable labor rate.

Therefore, overhead can be expressed as a percentage or as an hourly rate. In shops where pay can be directly associated with the equipment used, overhead is expressed as a percent.

$$\text{Overhead (\%)} = \frac{\text{Total Overhead Costs}}{\text{Total Direct Labor COSTS}}$$

For example, a business with a total overhead of $65,000 a year and direct labor cost of $130,000, will have an overhead of 50 percent.

Conversely, in shops where there's little difference between the hourly wages for the employees, and everyone works on all the equipment, you can calculate an overhead rate based on the actual costs and hours billed.

$$\text{Overhead (Hourly Rate)} = \frac{\text{Total Overhead Costs}}{\text{Total Direct Labor HOURS}}$$

A business with a total overhead of $65,000 and 2000 hours of direct labor will have an overhead of $32.50 an hour.

General & Administrative (G&A) Expenses

Figure 5-1 on the next page is a composite drawing showing the various components that comprise total costs. General and administrative costs are often called *"G&A."* These costs include secretarial support, clerical help, and any cost not covered under direct and indirect labor or manufacturing costs.

Some companies group selling costs with general and administrative costs, calling the composite benchmark selling, general and administrative *(SG&A)*. Controlling these expenses can differentiate winners from losers in a competitive environment. G&A or SG&A is a catchall category that varies from company to company and from industry to industry. It can include travel expenses,

Direct material costs	Direct labor costs	Shop overhead costs		
Shop costs			Selling expense	
Total shop and sales costs				G & A costs
Total costs				

Figure 5-1. The components of total cost.

copying services, consumable supplies, and possibly sales overhead costs. Because what is included can vary, it's difficult to compare SG&A values among companies.

Accountants are curiously silent about what specific costs should or should not be assigned to SG&A. This may change in the future. If every portion of your company's value chain are benchmarked and managed, curtailing SG&A growth can have a significant impact on your bottom line. According to *CFO Magazine*, SG&A "is the soft underbelly of a company's spending."

Computer Retailer Week projected CompUSA's SG&A to be just under 11 percent—retail stores usually have SG&A under 20 percent. They've got to be cost conscious since they measure profit by the pennies per product.

Desktop publishers and prepress service bureaus have fewer employees with higher expenses per employee. As a rough benchmark, publishing and printing SG&A typically runs 30 to 35 percent of revenues. The point is to compare G&A or SG&A within your own industry. If SG&A comparables for your industry are

30 percent and your shop comes out at 35%, you certainly can't boast about being lean and mean. Entrepreneurs with an eye to the future need to watch G&A/SG&A carefully.

Overhead Factor

The monthly hours that you bill vary based on many factors. For example, a freelance desktop publisher working out of a home office will bill about 150 days a year—100 hours a month. The rest of the month is spent on marketing and non-earning follow-up. This will affect the daily labor rate and the fees that are charged.

A monthly $6,000 overhead expense and a 22 days-a-month billing factor results in a daily overhead cost of $272.73— $34.09 an hour ($6,000 a month divided by 22 days a month divided by 8 hours a day equals $34.09 an hour).

If you earn $100,000 a year and bill 264 days each year, your daily labor rate is $378.78 [100,000 / (22 x 12) = $378.78]. This equates to $47.35 hourly income.

Dividing the hourly overhead by your hourly income yields an *overhead factor* of 72% (34.09/47.35 = .72). This is how much of your hourly labor rate is allocated to paying for overhead.

Obviously, overhead costs can be significant. They can easily eat up more than 70 percent of your gross income. An overhead of 40-50 percent of your gross income is typical. The *labor rate* that you establish must cover your overhead expenses.

Some shops calculate overhead by combining both direct and indirect costs (total annual expense). Then they convert this overhead into a *burden rate* by subtracting direct labor from the total annual expense and dividing this result by the direct labor expense.

Burden rates can exceed 200%. The burden rate is added to the hourly fee to generate a *burdened hourly rate*. This means that each employee has a portion of overhead allocated to their billable work whenever they bid a job. A graphic designer making $15 an hour with an overhead load of 125% ($18.75) will have a labor rate of $33.75. This means that bids that include that person's support on a job will be at the $33.75 rate. Large companies often use accounting systems that apply the burden rate concept.

Project Cost Analysis

Not only do you need a good understanding of how much time each task takes to perform, but you must be careful to cost out every action and activity associated with performing on a job. Don't forget any. These tasks include the time spent on indirect cost activities:

- meeting with a client
- corresponding
- answering questions
- communicating on the telephone
- communicating by fax or modem
- scheduling work
- recording actions and times

And they include the time spent on direct cost activities:

- system power up
- program execution
- converting files to a useable form
- converting data for importing
- job preparation and setup
- downloading project data
- proofreading and spell checking
- editing
- text generation
- other keyboarding
- typography
- innovating a design concept

- developing a style sheet
- designing illustrations and artwork
- designing a logo
- designing clip art
- scanning art and photographs
- image manipulation and retouch
- developing a thumbnail layout
- creating a design
- implementing a design
- importing text and graphics
- importing clip art
- importing CD-ROM photographs
- more keyboarding
- dropping illustrations into the design
- adjusting the layout
- revising the draft design
- paste-up
- producing color proofs
- producing color separations
- typesetting/imagesetting
- generating camera ready output
- printing
- post printing
- etc.

Anything that takes you away from income-generating activities becomes an indirect cost or overhead expense. When you meet with an illustrator or photographer, or when you meet with a client to present draft copies or to deliver the final output, you are not available for other billable activities. Thus, when you estimate how long a job should take, you should include a block of time to cover these activities.

When you break out your machine and labor costs, remember the overhead allocated to the costs of your equipment. If you're making payments on hardware, you should allocate this cost over the hours that the hardware will be used. (Making payments on a loan to buy equipment is called *debt servicing*.)

It's also wise to include a cost factor for future replacement at the end of the equipment's useful life. Replacement cost can be determined by taking the total cost of the current hardware (including finance charges), factoring in inflation over its useful life, subtracting the expected trade-in value, and then dividing by the estimated life of the machine to get an annual replacement rate. Dividing again by 12 months and then again by approximately 168 hours a month will give you an estimated hourly replacement cost factor to use in your calculations.

Let's say you want to lease an imagesetter. It costs $100,000 and has a 5-year useful life. You can lease it for $1,274.82 a month on a 5-year contract at 10%. Inflation is expected to average 3 percent for the next five years. Your ownership costs is equal to the $100,000 purchase price, plus $1,274.82 times 60 months ($16,489), plus 3% inflation on $100,000 over five years ($15,930) less the residual trade in of $40,000. The total cost is $92,419. Dividing by five years useful life, dividing by 12 months per year and dividing by 168 hours per month, you calculate $9.17 as the hourly replacement cost for having this system. By estimating how many copies of RC paper or film you can output each hour, you can incorporate a portion of the $9.17 hourly replacement cost into your per copy charge.

Next, you should consider your "out-of-pocket" expenses to do the job. These include raw materials and various actions necessary to perform the job. Consider:

- laser printer paper
- toner
- file conversion costs
- special typefaces and fonts
- stats
- illustrations

- film
- resin-coated paper
- telephone calls
- travel
- postage
- facsimile

Within your materials costs are hidden charges that you should also consider. It takes time (and hence costs your shop money) to order, receive, and pay for materials. Credit card purchases mean possible interest payments. Don't forget waste and spoilage. Not all of the paper that you buy will be converted into a final product. You'll use paper producing drafts; you may find some damaged paper when you open the packages, and some will be used in setting up the machine to produce acceptable output pages.

About five percent of your materials costs should be added to handle accounting functions. Another 20 percent in expenses should be added to cover waste and spoilage.

Some of the tasks involved in completing a job will not be within the scope of your capabilities. These will be subcontracted out as *"buy-outs" or "job-outs."* If you farm portions of a job out to an outside vendor, the costs to you should be marked up to cover working through them, and to cover your accounting and transportation costs. Many shops mark up subcontractor charges 30-50 percent to arrive at the selling price to quote their customers.

Standard Benchmarks

Quoting confidently on a fixed price project is possible only when you have a clear understanding of your shop's capabilities. When you know how long it takes to perform each task in a job, you can apply budgeted hourly rates to each function and calculate a flat rate for a job. This is invaluable in competitive bidding.

To be able to quote a flat rate, you need baselines. And to get baselines, you must benchmark tasks and capabilities to get standard operating times.

There are three "standards" on which you can base prices—a machine standard, a worker performance production standard, and a baseline production standard that fits your business. All three are interrelated.

Machine Standard

The *machine standard* is based on the capability of your hardware and software. It takes a finite time for a scanner to move the lamp over the page (or to rotate the page past the lamp). And it takes a finite time for a laser printer to print a sheet. These times are directly related to the performance capability of the system that you're using.

Whether you can print six, eight, or more pages each minute with a particular laser printer depends on the printer. The best use for a machine standard is to establish an upper limit on how long it takes to do a particular machine-oriented task. You can't push hardware or software faster than its design capability. The slowest device in a computer establishes the maximum speed that the computer can run. Having a "screamer" PC with minimum RAM and a slow hard disk drive causes the computer performance to be limited by the number of hard disk accesses that occur during a task. Adding RAM can significantly improve performance — particularly when working with graphics.

You generate machine standards by listing the capabilities of your equipment. Input or output speed depends on the type of computer and peripheral that you are using, the organization of hard disk resources (fragmented files take longer to access) and the clock speed of each system. The slowest device determines the best speed possible in your electronic factory.

Developing A Machine Standard Model

This section will give you an idea how to develop your own machine standards. Two examples will be provided. The first covers scanning. The second covers laser printing.

What information should you collect to generate a benchmark for scanning? Besides the computer and scanner hardware configuration, you'll need the scanning software used (including the version). You'll also need the set-up time to get ready to scan. Then you'll need the type of scan (black and white line art, gray scale, color photograph, etc.), image size, time to get the first scan, and time to get the subsequent scans.

Figure 5-2, on the next page, shows a format that you can adopt for developing a machine standard for scanning black and white line art.

```
SCANNING, B&W LINE ART:
                                          Effective Date: _____
System Configuration:
    Computer: (type) (clock speed) (RAM installed) (size HD)
             (interface connection to scanner)

    Scanner:  (type) (scan rate) (resolution)      Software Used: (name) (version)

    Start-up/Set-up Time: (minutes)    Scan Rate Per Page (first page):_____
                                                        (subsequent page): _____

    Start-up/Set-up Time: (minutes)    Scan Rate Per Page (first page):_____
                                                        (subsequent page): _____

    Start-up/Set-up Time: (minutes)    Scan Rate Per Page (first page):_____
                                                        (subsequent page): _____

    Start-up/Set-up Time: (minutes)    Scan Rate Per Page (first page):_____
                                                        (subsequent page): _____

    Start-up/Set-up Time: (minutes)    Scan Rate Per Page (first page):_____
                                                        (subsequent page): _____

    Start-up/Set-up Time: (minutes)    Scan Rate Per Page (first page):_____
                                                        (subsequent page): _____

    Start-up/Set-up Time: (minutes)    Scan Rate Per Page (first page):_____
                                                        (subsequent page): _____
```

Figure 5-2. Model for benchmarking scanning times.

A second form can be used for scanning black and white gray scale. A third form design can be used for halftone photographs. Two more forms can be generated to cover color illustrations and color photographs.

After enough data samples have been collected, averaging the set-up time, and the scan time for the first page and then the time to scan subsequent pages will yield machine standards for scanning each type of image—standards that are custom to your business!

A similar process is used to record laser printing times. Figure 5-3 shows a format that you can adopt for developing machine standards for laser printing.

LASER PRINTING:

Effective Date: _____

System Configuration:
    Computer: (type) (clock speed) (RAM installed) ___
        (size HD) (interface connection to printer) ___

    Laser Printer: (type) (print output page rate) (resolution) ___

    Start-up/Set-up Time: (minutes)   File Type: (text, PICT, EPS, WP1, etc)
        Complexity: (text) (30% art) (70% art) ___   Printing Time First Page: ___
        Complexity: (text) (30% art) (70% art) ___   Subsequent Page: ___
        Complexity: (text) (30% art) (70% art) ___   Subsequent Page: ___

    Start-up/Set-up Time: (minutes)   File Type: (text, PICT, EPS, WP1, etc)
        Complexity: (text) (30% art) (70% art) ___   Printing Time First Page: ___
        Complexity: (text) (30% art) (70% art) ___   Subsequent Page: ___
        Complexity: (text) (30% art) (70% art) ___   Subsequent Page: ___

300 dpi Resolution - First Page

Total Pages Text Only: ___	Total Printing Time: ___	Average Pages/Min ___
Total Pages 30% Art: ___	Total Printing Time: ___	Average Pages/Min ___
Total Pages 70% Art: ___	Total Printing Time: ___	Average Pages/Min ___

600 dpi Resolution - First Page

Total Pages Text Only: ___	Total Printing Time: ___	Average Pages/Min ___
Total Pages 30% Art: ___	Total Printing Time: ___	Average Pages/Min ___
Total Pages 70% Art: ___	Total Printing Time: ___	Average Pages/Min ___

1000 dpi Resolution - First Page

Total Pages Text Only: ___	Total Printing Time: ___	Average Pages/Min ___
Total Pages 30% Art: ___	Total Printing Time: ___	Average Pages/Min ___
Total Pages 70% Art: ___	Total Printing Time: ___	Average Pages/Min ___

300 dpi Resolution - Subsequent Page

Total Pages Text Only: ___	Total Printing Time: ___	Average Pages/Min ___
Total Pages 30% Art: ___	Total Printing Time: ___	Average Pages/Min ___
Total Pages 70% Art: ___	Total Printing Time: ___	Average Pages/Min ___

600 dpi Resolution - Subsequent Page

Total Pages Text Only: ___	Total Printing Time: ___	Average Pages/Min ___
Total Pages 30% Art: ___	Total Printing Time: ___	Average Pages/Min ___
Total Pages 70% Art: ___	Total Printing Time: ___	Average Pages/Min ___

1000 dpi Resolution - Subsequent Page

Total Pages Text Only: ___	Total Printing Time: ___	Average Pages/Min ___
Total Pages 30% Art: ___	Total Printing Time: ___	Average Pages/Min ___
Total Pages 70% Art: ___	Total Printing Time: ___	Average Pages/Min ___

Figure 5-3. Model for benchmarking laser printing times.

Just as with machine standards for scanning, the laser printing model in Figure 4-3 helps you generate machine standards by collecting and averaging a number of sample points. The averages become the laser printing machine standards for your shop.

A similar form can be generated and used to collect timing data for copying services—both black and white and color, depending on the equipment that you have.

This process of collecting machine output times works for each input or output device in your business.

Machine standards are covered in detail in our reference book, Desktop Production Standards (see descrption before tear out card at the back of this book)

Worker Performance Production Standards

A *production standard* describes how much time it takes to complete a task or to produce a product. The worker production standard incorporates the human aspect of a job. It helps you determine the typical times to perform billable shop activities.

Some professional groups such as the National Association of Quick Printers (NAPL) and the National Association of Secretarial Services (NASS) have developed *industry production standards* that you can obtain. These standards can be used as indicators to help you recognize deficiencies in your own organizational and operational structure.

Table 5-1 lists some common measurement units for defining desktop production rates.

Table 5-1. Worker performance production rate measurement units for desktop services.

FUNCTION	MEASUREMENT
Keyboarding	Characters per time unit Words per minute
Editing	1,000 characters per minute
Proofreading	1,000 characters per minute
Scanning	Minutes per scan
Scan retouch on various scan	Minutes per image (based sizes and complexities)
Color editing on various scan	Minutes per image (based sizes and complexities)
Typography	Characters per time unit
Design	Minutes/hours per page (based on size and complexity)
Layout	Minutes/hours per page (based on size and complexity)

On the following pages are samplings of "accepted industry standards" for various functions based on research by associations, professional groups and our own extensive survey.

NAPL Standards The National Association of Printers and Lithographers developed a *Cost Study on Desktop/Electronic Publishing Operations*. Non-members can purchase this study from the NAPL for $100. (Members pay $50).

Table 5-2 is a synopsis of their analysis for individual (first time) operations. Subsequent operations can take slightly less time.

Table 5-2. NAPL standards.

Operation	Measurement	Comments
Keyboarding	4.8 min/1000 char	12,500/hr - Straight text
Proofreading	2 min/1000 char	30/hr - non-technical text
B&W Scanning (halftones)	14 min/scan	4.3 scans/hr - up to 8 x 10 incl setup, scan, preview, adjustments, name & save file
B&W Scanning (line art)	10 min/scan	6 scans/hr - up to 8 x 10 incl setup, scan, preview, adjustments, name & save file
Color Scanning	33 min/scan	1.8 scans/hr - up to 8 x 10 incl setup, scan, preview, adjustments, name & save file
Color Editing	25 min/image	2.4 images/hr - med quality incl setup, scan, preview, adjustments, name & save file
Composition/ Layout (text) (non-process)	15 min/pg	4 pg/hr - setup, importing text, composition, pagination, adjust for non-process color
Composition/ Layout (text & graphics) (non-process)	26 min/pg	2.3 pg/hr - setup, import txt & graphics, add tints, composition, pagination, adjustments for non-process color pages
Composition/ Layout (text & graphics) (process color)	42 min/pg	1.4 pg/hr - setup, import txt & graphics, add tints, composition, pagination, adjustments for process color pages

Trapping	26 min/pg	2.3/hr - setup, EPS file, display pg, check color traps, adjust
Laser Print B&W Proof	1.5 min/pg	40 pg/hr - downloading text fonts & graphics, RIPing, and imaging
Color Proofs Proof	3 min/pg	20 pg/hr - downloading text fonts & graphics, low res color RIPing, imaging
Imagesetting Final output	4 min/film	15 films/hr - text & graphics. Incl download fonts, RIPing, imaging, developing film
Blueline & Dyluxes final proof	9 min/flat	6.7 flats/hr - setup, vacuum frame, exposing, development trimming
Matchprint & Chromalin final proof (color)	36 min/flat	1.7 flats/hr - setup, vacuum frame, exposing, development laminating, trimming

A complete copy of the NAPL industry standards can be purchased by contacting them at 780 Palisade Avenue, Teaneck, NJ 07666 (201/342-0700).

NASS Standards The National Association of Secretarial Services also developed a timing standard for their industry. They call their special report: *Industry Production Standards - Guidelines for Business Support Providers.*

Table 5-3 is a sampling of their timing standards for individual (first time) operations. Subsequent operations can take slightly less time.

Table 5-3. NASS industry production standards.

Operation	Measurement
General Keyboarding	70 words/min
Word Processing Single-space	15 minutes/page
Word Processing Double-space	7.5 minutes/page
Type names & addresses from list	100 addresses/hr
Print merged letters (1 page)	1 minute/letter
Print 3" x 15/16" labels	500 labels/hr
Desktop Publishing	12 minutes/page plus attributes
Attributes:	Add for each occurrence:
Each column	6 minutes/page
Each font over 3 fonts/pg	6 minutes/page
Each tab setting	6 minutes/page
Each type of bullet	6 minutes/page
Each type of line	6 minutes/page
Each type of Dingbat	6 minutes/page
Each boxed element	6 minutes/page
Each reverse	6 minutes/page
Each Shaded area	6 minutes/page
Each line art placed	6 minutes/page
Each color illustration	6 minutes/page
Each photo placed	6 minutes/page

A complete copy of the NASS industry standards can be purchased by contacting them at 3637 Fourth Street North, Suite 330, St. Petersburg, FL 33704 (813/823-3646).

BIG Survey Analysis "Standards" Each year, our company conducts an extensive survey to collect pricing information covering desktop publishing and prepress operations. Over 20,000 businesses are invited to participate in the confidential survey.

Some owners respond by listing hourly rates. Others list prices by the job, by the piece, or by the page. When both hourly rates and project prices are provided, we can calculate a rough time expectation for each operation. While these unit measurements are subject to the responses in the survey, these numbers do provide a good relative representation of how long it takes to perform specific tasks. We were fascinated to confirm how close our numbers came to industry production standards published by others.

Table 5-4 is a sampling of survey responses. Assume that the values represent an average complexity of page or difficulty of job performed by an average employee.

Table 5-4. BIG survey responses.

Operation	Survey Measurement
Keyboarding, general	10.7 minutes/page
Copy Editing, general	10.6 minutes/page
Proofreading, general	6.8 minutes/page
Typography, general	25.1 minutes/page
Typography, tables	33.3 minutes/page

Design & Layout (Product)	Survey Measurement Text Only	Text with Graphics
Announcements	43.8 minutes/each add 0.1 hrs/graphic	1.08 hours/each
Annual Reports, 1C	54 minutes/page add 0.1 hrs/graphic	1.05 hours/page
Annual Reports, 2C	1.01 hours/page	2.29 hours/page
Annual Reports, 4C	1.70 hours/page	3.42 hours/page
Book Covers	5.00 hours/page	7.14 hours/page

Booklets, 1C	36 minutes/page	1.06 hours/page
Booklets, 2C	1.05 hours/page	2.34 hours/page
Book Interior, 1C	12.51 min/page	20.95 min/page
Brochure, 1C	1.05 hours/page	1.43 hours/page
Brochure, 4C	1.48 hours/page	2.49 hours/page
Bulletin	0.95 hours/page add 0.1 hrs/graphic	1.55 hours/page
Business Cards (Custom)	0.81 hours/each	1.39 hours/each
Cards, Fold Over	1.11 hours/each	1.26 hours/each
Catalogs	0.66 hours/page	1.01 hours/page
Certificates	0.61 hours/page add 0.1 hrs/graphic	1.18 hours/page
Directories	0.43 hours/page	1.02 hours/page
Display Advertising	1.23 hours/ad	2.43 hours/ad
Door Hanger Ad	0.81 hours/ad	1.42 hours/ad
Flyers (Letter Size)	0.98 hours/page add 0.1 hrs/graphic	1.69 hours/page
Handbooks	0.63 hours/pg	0.79 hours/pg
Invitations	0.81 hours/each	1.44 hours/each
Logos	10.04 hours/each	
Logotype	2.96 hours/each	
Magazines	0.56 hours/pg	1.79 hours/pg
Menu - Page	0.94 hours/pg	1.16 hours/pg
Menu - Each	2.20 hours/each	3.69 hours/each
Newsletter, 1C	1.14 hours/pg	1.74 hours/pg
Post Card (1C, Custom)	0.97 hours/each	1.52 hours/each

Poster, 1C	1.49 hours/each	2.48 hours/each
Print Ad, 1C	1.60 hours/each	3.04 hours/each
Programs	0.58 hours/pg	1.48 hours/pg
Tabloid	1.11 hours/pg	1.29 hours/pg

Scanning Operation	**Survey Measurement**
B&W (Line Art)	4.92 scans/hour
B&W (Gray Scale)	4.76 scans/hour
B&W (Photographs)	4.62 scans/hour
Color (Illustrations)	2.97 scans/hour
Color Photographs)	2.56 scans/hour
OCR Text	16.71 pages/hour

To tie the three industry standards together, consider page layout of a 3-column newsletter comprised of two typefaces, two fonts, a single tab setting, two types of lines, one boxed element, one line art graphic, and a single photo on the page. According to the NAPL study, this should take 125% of 42 minutes (text plus 30% graphics) or 52.5 minutes total. According to the NASS, this should take one hour and six minutes (1.1 hours). By our survey analysis, the time should be one hour and 8.4 minutes (1.14 hours). There is a strong correlation, especially between the last two "standards."

Performance production standards are covered in greater detail in our reference *Desktop Production Standards.* A complete copy of this special report can be purchased by contacting our offices at P.O. Box 721000, San Diego, CA 92172-1000 (800) 811-4337.

Generating Function-Time History

Once you've obtained production standards developed by others, generate timing standards unique to your own shop. Start by making a historical log of how long it takes each person to perform the functions associated with producing billable work. This act of measuring time to perform requires discipline and habit. Ask each person to log the time that they spend performing various tasks. This will take about 10 minutes a day—an acceptable investment in time to get useful data. Follow-up to be certain that times are actually being recorded.

The times listed for each task will vary based on job complexity, equipment used and individual involved. Not only will one person take less time to perform the same task than another, but you yourself will take more time one day to do a task than you will on another day. This is a reality when people are involved in the process. The goal is to find the average time for performing each task at several levels of complexity.

Since both time and costs are critical in pricing, you can develop an Activity Time Worksheet for each job. On this form you can estimate the time spent on indirect project activities. Figure 5-4 shows a project time tracking form that you could adopt for your business.

As you collect time-motion data, don't reveal the individual time results to others on your staff. Keep this to yourself and the originator of the data. Employees can get concerned that you'll use this information to evaluate performance for a salary review. Show by example that you do use time-function information to assign workers to their best tasks. And show by example that you also use the information to plan training and skill sessions.

If you intend to apply pay for performance, understand that if you tell employees that they'll be paid based on their productivity, most will focus on the easy

Time Tracking Sheet

NAME: _____   DATE_____

PROJECT	TIME IN	TIME OUT	ACTIVITY	TOTAL MINUTES

Figure 5-4. Sample project activity time tracking form.

jobs to keep their productivity figure high. The detail to which you partition jobs into functional tasks will help keep the evaluation even. Just be certain to consider ALL work associated with a task. Productivity should include direct labor and the rework resulting from pushing so hard that errors occur. Corrections can take as long as doing it right the first time.

After tracking time-to-perform over a period such as a month, a pattern will develop that shows the best, worst, and most likely times that each direct labor employee will take to complete specific functional tasks.

Baseline Production Standards

Combine the production time-study information with rules of thumb, historical records, and published industry standards to develop *baseline production standards* unique to your company.

As mentioned earlier, published industry standards are a helpful guide for comparison, and most standards organizations point out that your particular cost rates and production speeds may be higher or lower than their "standard" published rates. That's why we call your own time rates baseline production standards. They're unique to your business.

Baseline production standards represent the typical for your shop. They combine machine and personnel operating capabilities and compensate for differences between an industry standard and your particular shop. They're based on all the information you collect. They not only establish standard performance times unique to your business (so you can quote flat rates on jobs), they are also useful for evaluating the performance of individual employees. Finally, baseline production standards are your best source for estimating project costs.

A helpful feature is that baseline standards establish all work at an average level. This means that efficient workers who finish faster and actually spend less time on a job don't cause a project to generate less revenue. The billing is based on standard times, not the actual performance times of individual workers.

Actually, you can realize a marketing advantage by advertising that your prices are based on "published industry standards." Many storefront shops display a statement near the work input counter indicating the basis for their pricing. By basing rates on the average time to perform tasks, you demonstrate that customers are consistently charged the same price for the same service. Figure 5-5 is an example of such a statement.

Baseline production standards are extremely useful in billing for work because you can price at a consistent level while managing your resources to take advantage of available efficiencies. For example, suppose you get a request to provide 600 dpi printouts of several different manuals. To complete the job, you must power up and prepare the computer and the laser printer. Then you must execute the application program from which the manuals will be printed, open the correct file, go into the print mode, command a printout—possibly wait for Postscript conversion—and then wait for the output printer to produce each page of the manual.

FOR YOUR PROTECTION

(Company Name) uses a common pricing system for desktop publishing and prepress services based on industry production standards published by (name the source).

The basis for these standards is the average time required to perform specific duties related to project production by professional DTP and prepress operators.

As such, they protect you from being overcharged for work by a slower operator. Through consistent and equal task billing, all customers are charged the same price for the same service performed.

Figure 5-5. Sample production standard pricing statement.

Your baseline standards (incorporating the machine and production standards) establish a time basis for the job in your own shop. The machine standard says your printer can output eight sheets a minute. However, your system has a print spooler and multitasking capability. Thus you can command the computer to print this job in the background while you work on another job in the foreground.

Rather than charging each job for a portion of the time to warm-up, checkout, and execute the layout print actions, you bill out each job at the baseline standard full production rate. It's important to present consistent pricing to your customers.

Consider this case. A computer operator has several jobs to perform. After the first job is designed and page layout is complete, the operator commands a print output. Printing takes about 20 minutes, so while the printer is chugging out the first job, the operator begins work on the next job. This time-leveraging lets one person perform several tasks simultaneously. Yet you bill each job as if each were unique and had a dedicated person attending to the job during the full time of performance. This provides a cushion for rework caused by inadvertent errors or system breakdown.

Baseline production standards enable flat rate pricing, and more important, they prevent improvements in efficiency from reducing income by completing projects faster. Let's say that at some point, you decide to upgrade your hardware and software. You had been charging $40 an hour based on your cost using the old system configuration. When you install and place the new system into operation, you recalculate your costs basis and determine that you must now charge $55 an hour. This looks good until you realize that now you can perform the same job in half the time. Should the customer be charged only $67.50 for a job that previously they were paying you $90 to do?

You raised your rates, but could bring in less income for the same job. If you charge by the hour, rather than by the job, you could pass a production efficiency to your customer and earn less in the process. Owning the best equipment and current software is good, but shop owners tend to pass the time savings on to their clients. Pricing by the job can be better in several ways. You can keep your income stream high, yet when competition appears, you can bid a lower price making you more competitive. You can also handle more jobs each work day.

There are risks in setting price on baseline production standards alone. Take this scenario. You get an order to print camera ready copy of a 20-page catalog. You have several different computers and printers available for the job. Each machine operates at a different clock speed so the actual time to perform depends on the configuration that you use. The actual production time using the slower equipment can be much longer than the time to do the job with the newest and fastest hardware. If you base your estimate on production standards alone, you'll end up with two different prices for the same job.

You choose the longer time basis for your estimate to ensure that you cover costs and earn a profit regardless which machine configuration you use. The risk here is that your equipment may be so old that basing your bid on its slowest performance time could put your estimates outside the ballpark of customer acceptance. A competitor with new hardware and current software could out-produce and under-bid you.

Watch your use of historical information in timing jobs. History doesn't always repeat itself. Be careful that production inefficiencies aren't reflected in old time data. You may have developed your old standards using slower equipment and slower operators. You could have collected your historical data using a very skilled employee. Whenever you consider historical job-time data, clearly understand how it was developed. It helps if you convert historical data into baseline standards by extrapolating older machine capabilities to current configurations and comparing your task performance times with published production information. Keep current on evolving industry production standards since they will reflect new technologies and refined operating efficiencies.

By maintaining historical baseline standards you can identify trends and monitor shop efficiency and productivity based on actual averages custom to your business.

Developing Baseline Production Standards

The concept is simple. The implementation is time-intensive. You establish machine standards for your system configurations. Then you collect timing information and establish a baseline production standard for each function performed in the services that you provide.

Here's how. Partition the operations in your shop into cost categories (e.g., keyboarding, layout and design, graphics, typesetting, prepress, bindery, etc.) The National Association of Printers and Lithographers (NAPL) identified 13 different production areas in desktop—six single color functions and seven process color functions. These include keyboarding, scanning, page composition, proofreading, black and white or color proofing, final output, and final proofs.

Make your own list of functions. Then generate a data collection form for each function similar to what you did for your machine standards.

Each time you do a job, keep a detailed log of the activities and time spent on each task. A range of times-per-task will develop. From these you can determine the average time it takes to perform. Assuming that you are at least as motivated as the most productive person in your shop, you can use your results to compare with those of your other workers. This process lets you generate average performance times for your shop.

For example, what information should you collect to generate a benchmark for keyboarding? What measurement criteria should you use? Most people select 1,000 characters and a set time period as their yardstick. Therefore, you want to determine how long it takes an average typist to keyboard 1,000 characters. Figure 5-6 shows a format that you can adopt for developing a production standard for keyboard data entry. The start time does not include set-up time. Assume the hardware and software are ready for operation.

```
┌─────────────────────────────────────────────────────────────────────┐
│                          KEYBOARDING:                               │
│                                                                     │
│ System Configuration:   Computer: (type) (clock speed) (RAM installed) (size HD) │
│                                                                     │
│ Software Application Used: (name) (version)"    Project: _____  │
│                                                                     │
│   Date: _____       Start Time: _____    Stop Time: _____   │
│                                                                     │
│   Difficulty        # Words   # Char   #       Characters  Total Minutes  1,000 Characters │
│   Low Moderate High Entered   Entered  Pages   per Page    Expended       per Minute       │
│                                                                     │
│ Software Application Used: (name) (version)"    Project: _____  │
│                                                                     │
│   Date: _____       Start Time: _____    Stop Time: _____   │
│                                                                     │
│   Difficulty        # Words   # Char   #       Characters  Total Minutes  1,000 Characters │
│   Low Moderate High Entered   Entered  Pages   per Page    Expended       per Minute       │
│                                                                     │
└─────────────────────────────────────────────────────────────────────┘
```

Figure 5-6. Model for benchmarking keyboarding production times.

Generate a separate set of forms for each computer system used to keyboard data. Look for the best, worst, and typical times based on the resources available. You can establish a baseline production model after collecting a number of sample points. The averages become the standard keyboarding times for your shop.

Likewise, a production standard can be developed for page layout. In this case, develop a template for each size page—letter, legal, and tabloid—and for each complexity—text only, 30% art, and 70% art.

Figure 5-7 is a sample form that you can adopt to collect data on letter size page layout. Figure 5-8 covers legal size, and Figure 5-9 covers tabloid size. Again, the start time does not include set-up. Assume the system is ready for the page layout function.

FUNCTION: PAGE LAYOUT (LETTER SIZE)

System Configuration: Computer: (type) (clock speed) (RAM installed) (size HD)

Software Application Used: (name) (version)"   Project: _____

Date: _____   Start Time: _____   Stop Time: _____

Difficulty Low Moderate High	# Words Entered	# Char Entered	# Pages	Characters per Page	Total Minutes Expended	1,000 Characters per Minute
___ ___ ___	___	___	___	___	___	___

Page Number	Complexity Text 30% 70% Only Art Art	Start Time	Stop Time	Total Time Expended
___	___ ___ ___	___	___	___
1				
2				
3				
4				
5				
6				
7				
8				
9				
.				
.				
.				

Total Pages Completed (Text Only): _____ Total Time: _____ Average Pages/Hour: _____
Total Pages Completed (30% Art): _____ Total Time: _____ Average Pages/Hour: _____
Total Pages Completed (70% Art): _____ Total Time: _____ Average Pages/Hour: _____

Figure 5-7. Model for benchmarking page layout production times.

Baselines, Standards & Budgeted Hourly Rates - 181

FUNCTION: PAGE LAYOUT (LEGAL SIZE)

System Configuration: Computer: <u>(type) (clock speed) (RAM installed) (size HD)</u>

Software Application Used: <u>(name) (version)"</u>   Project: _____

Date: _____   Start Time: _____   Stop Time: _____

Difficulty Low Moderate High	# Words Entered	# Char Entered	# Pages	Characters per Page	Total Minutes Expended	1,000 Characters per Minute
___ ___ ___	_____	_____	____	_____	_____	_____

Page Number	Complexity Text 30% 70% Only Art Art	Start Time	Stop Time	Total Time Expended
_____	___ ___ ___	_____	_____	_____
1				
2				
3				
4				
5				
6				
7				
8				
9				
.				
.				
.				

Total Pages Completed (Text Only): _____ Total Time: _____ Average Pages/Hour: _____
Total Pages Completed (30% Art): _____   Total Time: _____ Average Pages/Hour: _____
Total Pages Completed (70% Art): _____   Total Time: _____ Average Pages/Hour: _____

Figure 5-8. Model for benchmarking page layout production times.

```
┌─────────────────────────────────────────────────────────────────┐
│  FUNCTION:  PAGE LAYOUT                    (TABLOID SIZE)        │
│                                                                  │
│  System Configuration:  Computer: (type) (clock speed) (RAM installed) (size HD)
│  Software Application Used: (name) (version)"    Project: _____
│   Date: _____    Start Time: _____  Stop Time: _____
│                                                                  │
│      Difficulty      # Words   # Char    #    Characters  Total Minutes  1,000 Characters
│   Low Moderate High  Entered   Entered  Pages  per Page    Expended       per Minute
│   ___  ___  ___      _____   _____  ____  _____   _____       _____
│                                                                  │
│   Page        Complexity            Start    Stop       Total Time
│   Number   Text  30%   70%          Time     Time       Expended
│            Only  Art   Art
│   ____     ___   ___   ___         _____    _____       _____
│                                                                  │
│    1                                                             │
│                                                                  │
│    2                                                             │
│                                                                  │
│    3                                                             │
│                                                                  │
│    4                                                             │
│                                                                  │
│    5                                                             │
│    .                                                             │
│    .                                                             │
│    .                                                             │
│                                                                  │
│  Total Pages Completed (Text Only): _____  Total Time: _____  Average Pages/Hour: _____
│  Total Pages Completed (30% Art):   _____  Total Time: _____  Average Pages/Hour: _____
│  Total Pages Completed (70% Art):   _____  Total Time: _____  Average Pages/Hour: _____
└─────────────────────────────────────────────────────────────────┘
```

Figure 5-9. Model for benchmarking page layout production times.

The key is to generate all three templates. After sufficient data collection, and after enough projects, averaging the data will show you what production standard to apply for each function.

Similar templates can be developed and used to collect data on proofreading, scanning, scan retouch, color editing, typography, and even design.

The best production standards are those that you develop yourself. But be aware that changes in hardware, software, or production procedures can significantly alter the time baselines. You must keep on top of your standard times. (A spreadsheet program works well for this.)

As you upgrade your hardware and software, you'll find certain jobs take less time to perform. We upgraded our OCR scanning software and discovered that scanning and interpretation of text took less than half the original time. This translates directly into production cost benefits for you.

Budgeted Hourly Rates

Every service that your shop performs can be partitioned into unique activities or functions. Every function has a cost to the company. By breaking out the individual labor and materials costs, you can generate a *budgeted hourly rate* for each activity.

By multiplying the baseline production time associated with each function by its budgeted hourly cost, you can calculate a budgeted cost for each task in a job. Then, by adding up the budgeted hourly costs for each activity, and adding material costs such as film and special paper, you can calculate a project cost to which profit, return on investment, and intangibles such as job turn-around time, design skill, and competitive advantage are added to achieve a final selling price. Partitioning any project into functional tasks and applying budgeted hourly rates to each task lets you bid a flat rate for any job.

You start by partitioning all of your shop's services into individual operations. For example, producing a newsletter could involve receiving text on a disk and converting the file into a usable form (file conversion), correcting typographical or grammar mistakes in the text (editing), designing a style sheet (design), importing graphics and text into an electronic page (layout), and generating a laser printout (print out). Each of these operations can have an associated budgeted hourly rate.

Once all of your operations are identified — keyboarding, file conversion, typography, scanning,, design, layout, print output, and so on—you specify the labor skills and equipment required for each operation. Consider every resource in your business — people, equipment, software, facility, and investment capital.

Then identify the annual costs of these resources as allocated to each operation. These costs will be fixed or variable. Then, determine an hourly overhead cost for the shop.

Each operation or function can be considered a cost category to be budgeted. You determine the number of chargeable hours that each cost category generates. Then, divide the total annual costs for each function by an estimate of the annual billable hours for that operation to get its budgeted hourly cost rate. Using these, you can price a job based on the combination of the individual hourly rates for each operation.

The more detailed you make your cost breakdown, the easier it is to define tasks and build budgeted hourly rates. The idea is to have the total shop's operating costs partitioned into chargeable activities. Each function is analyzed and production times established. These times are converted to costs that you budget or allocate to each task. A job will be comprised of several specific tasks. Each task activity has an associated cost category and a budgeted hourly cost rate.

Once you have your budgeted hourly cost rates, you factor in productivity, return on investment, and markup to generate a "straw-man" price that you can quote. Then look at your marketplace and your competition to establish hourly billing rates for each functional activity. These are the rates that you publish on your counter price sheets.

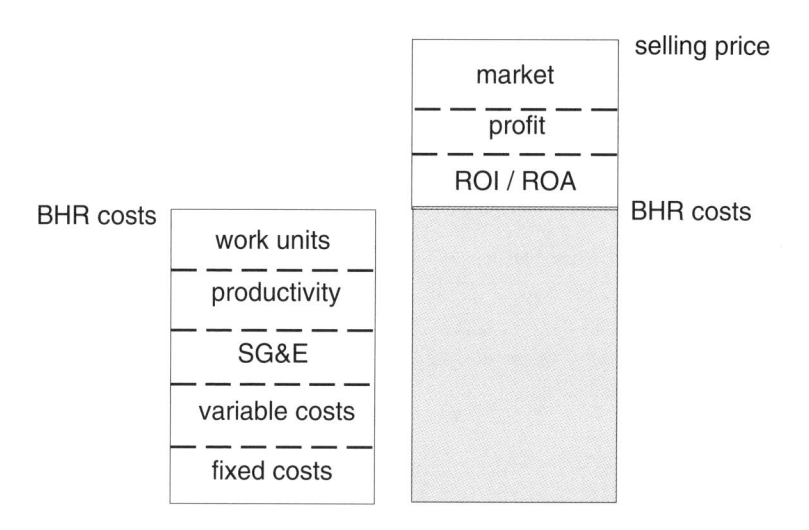

Figure 5-10. Components of a budgeted hourly rate and the BHR relationshp to selling price.

A recent International Prepress Association survey concluded that the best approach for pricing desktop services is to establish a budgeted hourly rate for each piece or group of equipment worked on. This allocates (budgets) pricing to the hardware and software used to perform a job. Good time assessments on each type of project can help you apply proper markup and establish budgeted hourly prices that work.

So how do you use a budgeted hourly rate to establish selling price? Use your baseline production standards for each specific task.

Suppose you want to set a price on providing typography services. Based on your analysis, the function "typography" has a baseline production rating of 13.2 minutes per page. This means that it takes 13.2 minutes for an average employee to change the typeface, font, point size, leading, or kerning of a single column 8.5" x 11" page of 12 point type.

To determine your selling price for this service, multiply your baseline production standard by the budgeted hourly rate that you calculated for this function. Add the costs of materials and your desired profit. Then add any costs for outside services. The sum of these factors yields a total cost plus profit factor to use as the selling price.

[(BHR x Prod Std x units) + Material Cost + Other Costs + Profit] = Selling Price

Take another example. You have a job typesetting 10 pages of text in 12 point type, and you're to produce 300 dpi laser printed sheets for the customer. If your budgeted hourly rate for typesetting is $40 an hour, multiply 40 times the production standard (say 13.2 minutes/page), times the 10 pages all divided by 60 minutes/hour to get $88 [(40 x 13.2 x 10)/60 = 88].

Then add the costs for 10 pages of 300 dpi laser output (10 times $0.75 = $7.50) and a profit of 10 percent on both the labor and materials [(0.1 x 88) + (0.1 x 7.50) = $9.55) to yield $105.05 (88 + 7.450 + 9.55 = 105.05) for the job. Assuming there are no other costs to recover, this is what you could charge your customer.

As work proceeds, keep a list or record of the average times to perform each task. Use these to update your baseline production standard. Don't forget "system start-up" and "modified start-up" (re-start) times. Many shops call this *"set up"* time. They often charge a flat rate for setting a system up to perform a specific service. This is where many *"minimum charge"* prices come from.

Incorporate start-up and re-start in your final bill. It can take about three minutes for your computer system to initialize, run an application program and open in the job that you will be working. The first effort on a job includes page setup time. Once the page format is established, then each time that you go back to the job, you must re-start the system—boot up the application program and open the job that were working on. The total job time should incorporate these re-start actions.

With budgeted hourly cost rates, you can factor in productivity, return on investment, profit, expected sales, the marketplace and your competition to generate a price basis for each task. Then when you price a job, you can separate out the activities and quote a job by tasks with unique rates for each task. Budgeted hourly rates vary from $15 to $150 an hour.

If each individual shop function is considered a *profit center*, then the budgeted hourly rate concept can be used successfully to allocate specific hourly rates to each center. This approach is covered in *Desktop Dividends: Managing Electronic Prepress for Profit* by Philip K. Ruggles.

It's important to understand that both fixed and variable costs are used in determining your budgeted hourly rate for a particular service or profit center. If you vary the number of hours each day that the service is provided or the profit center is active, fixed costs can have a major impact on the budgeted hourly rate that you calculate. Essentially this means that the more utilization you have, the lower the budgeted hourly rate because you spread the fixed costs out over more hours.

Likewise an under-utilized function or profit center can have a higher budgeted hourly rate. This can prevent your shop from being competitive in certain service areas.

Because they depend on an industry or custom production standard, the budgeted hourly rate method can provide an easy way to quickly price a job. A shop's billing baseline depends on the type of job and the customer. Many new owner-operators initially apply a fixed hourly rate to every service (shop rate). With experience, some develop a unique hourly rate for each service that they provide. Then they fine tune these hourly rates and establish page or word count baselines for pricing.

Budgeted Hourly Rate Example: Home Business

The following is an example of how to calculate budgeted hourly rates for a small desktop publishing business. This hypothetical shop operates out of a home office and earns $70,000 a year in revenue. To make the example as basic as possible, assume this business has a single employee, the owner-operator. This owner-operator uses 20 percent of the home (about 200 square feet) strictly for the business.

The business has been operating for one year. The owner takes no vacation and works 2,080 hours a year (52 weeks, 40 hours a week). The sources of income for the business can be partitioned into:

Keyboarding	10%	$7,000
Scanning	10%	7,000
Creative Design	20%	14,000
Layout	50%	35,000
Laser Printing	10%	7,000
		$70,000

To perform these functions, the owner purchased a computer, a laser printer and a scanner with word processing, scanning and page layout software. Total investment was $10,000 ($5,000 in purchases depreciated over five years and $5,000 in purchases written off this year).

The objective is to determine a budgeted hourly rate for each activity listed above. This involves identifying fixed and variable costs for labor and materials, and specifying and allocating a baseline production standard to each activity.

Figure 5-11 shows the fixed and variable costs associated with this business.

FIXED COSTS
Rent (Indirect/Overhead)	6,000
Basic Utilities (Indirect/Overhead)	272
Property Insurance (Indirect/Overhead)	240
Taxes (Indirect/Overhead)	7,500
Depreciation (Indirect/Overhead)	1,000
Hardware Not Depreciated (Indirect)	5,000
Software to Run Business (Indirect/Overhead)	500
Documentation to Operate Business (Indirect/Overhead)	100
Office Cleaning (Indirect/Overhead)	360
Grounds Keeping (Indirect/Overhead)	48
Vehicle Insurance (Indirect/Overhead)	1,200
Vehicle Purchase Loan (Indirect/Overhead)	4,800
Total Fixed Cost:	$31,080

VARIABLE COSTS
Marketing Expenses (Indirect/Overhead)	$2,100
Advertising Expenses (Indirect/Overhead)	2,100
Salaries — Owner-Operator (Indirect/Overhead)	21,840
Salaries — Owner-Operator Working on Jobs (Direct)	9,360
Wages - Part Time Help (Direct)	1,000
Cost of Goods Sold (Direct)	100
Supplies Used to Do Job (Direct)	100
Fringe Benefits (Indirect)	936
Vehicle Operation (Indirect)	500
Total Variable Cost:	$38,036
TOTAL FIXED & VARIABLE COSTS	$68,116

Figure 5-11. Fixed and variable costs for a home desktop services business.

Notice in our example, this home business made a profit of $1,884 on the $70,000 income—about three percent. Not bad, but the owner-operator is paying $6,000 in rent each year for using the owner-operator's own home. This is additional income (although taxable) to the home business owner.

At first blush, you'd think that salaries should be a fixed cost. But many entrepreneurs defer salary while building their business. And, once they're operating well, if the work load decreases during economic declines, independent business owners usually reduce their own salaries first to keep things going. This places salaries in a variable category.

Now, based on this cost breakdown, let's calculate a budgeted hourly rate for each activity performed by this home desktop publishing business. The following budgeted hourly cost analysis forms cover keyboarding, scanning, creative design, layout, and laser printing.

The details for each form are covered in *Desktop Production Standards*. At this point, just get a feel for the process. The allocation of costs and assignment of productivity levels depends on the capabilities of your own shop. These forms are provided to give you an idea how to proceed. All numbers are rounded up to the nearest dollar.

BUDGETED HOURLY RATES
Home Office
(KEYBOARDING)

INVESTMENT - Computer with word processing software:　　$2,500
SPACE needed to perform function:　　20 square feet
PEOPLE - Percent of time that a person is involved in activity:　　100%

NOTE: The typical pay for keyboarding is $7 an hour. Since this is a one-person business, both the pre-defined $15/hour and $7/hour rates are used for calculating a budgeted hourly rate.

ONE PERSON SHOP
Annual hours worked   2,080

FIXED (NON VARIABLE) COSTS	@$15/hr	@$7/hr
Depreciation (computer system)	500	500
Space Rent	600	600
Basic Utilities	27	27
System Insurance	8	8
TOTAL FIXED COSTS	1,135	1,135

VARIABLE COSTS	@$15/hr	@$7/hr
Labor	31,200	14,560
Pension Fund	624	291
Health/Medical insurance	2,340	2,340
Payroll Taxes	2,964	1,383
Workers Comp Insurance	468	218
Direct Supplies	200	200
Repairs, Maint & SW upgrades	375	375
TOTAL VARIABLE COSTS	38,171	19,367
Other misc costs	3,817	1,937
TOTAL FIXED & VARIABLE COSTS	43,123	21,304
Sales, General & Administrative Costs	12,936	6,391
TOTAL COSTS	$56,060	27,695
TOTAL HOURLY COSTS	26.95/hr	13.32/hr

COST/HOUR		
50% Productive	53.90	26.63
30% Productive	89.84	44.38

UNIT OF WORK OUTPUT PER HOUR:
50 wpm, 250 char/minute, 15,000 char/hr, 1500 char/pg ==> 10 pages/hr

COST PER 1000 CHARACTERS	@ $15/hr	@ $7/hr
50% Productive	3.59/M	1.78/M
30% Productive	5.99/M	2.96/M

COST PER PAGE	@ $15/hr	@ $7/hr
50% Productive	$5.39/pg	$2.66/pg
30% Productive	8.98/pg	4.44/pg

Figure 5-12. Budgeted hourly rates for keyboarding.

If we were to use the typical $7 an hour wage price, the effect on the budgeted prices will be startling. Keyboarding would budget out at $2.66 a page (50 percent productivity) and $4.44 a page (30 percent productivity). A page consisting of 60 percent text and 40 percent graphics would budget out at $3.23/page at $15 and hour and $1.60/page at $7 an hour.

In Figure 5-12, the "other misc cost" value is sometimes called a *"margin of safety"* or *MOS*. This amount is used to compensate for costs that were forgotten in the budget, or to cover unforeseen events and conditions. It's an arbitrary value. In Figure 5-12, I used 10 percent of the fixed and variable costs for the number to plug into the calculation. Some owners use 10 percent of revenue as the MOS. It's in the budget because experienced operators know that you'll always need "just a little more" the next time you calculate budgeted hourly costs.

Remember, these are budgeted prices. To this you add profit and return on any initial investment to start the company. This gives you a reference price. Then set the actual price to what the market will bear.

BUDGETED HOURLY RATES
Home Office
(SCANNING)

INVESTMENT - Computer, scanner and software: $5,000
SPACE needed to perform function: 20 square feet
PEOPLE - Percent of time that a person is involved in activity: 100%

NOTE: The typical pay for a scanner operator is about $8 an hour. Although this is a one-person business, both the predefined $15/hour and typical $8/hour rates wages are used for calculating the budgeted hourly rate for scanning.

```
ONE PERSON SHOP
Annual hours worked - 2,080
```

FIXED (NON VARIABLE) COSTS	@$15/hr	@$7/hr
Depreciation (computer system)	1,000	1,000
Space Rent	600	600
Basic Utilities	27	27
System Insurance	8	8
TOTAL FIXED COSTS	1,642	1,642

NON VARIABLE COSTS	@$15/hr	@$7/hr
Labor	31,200	16,640
Pension Fund	624	333
Health/Medical insurance	2,340	2,340
Payroll Taxes	2,964	1,581
Workers Comp Insurance	468	250
Direct Supplies	200	200
Repairs, Maint & SW upgrades	750	750
TOTAL VARIABLE COSTS	39,638	21,794
Other misc costs	4,128	2,344
TOTAL FIXED &VARIABLE COSTS	45,408	25,780
Sales, General & Administrative Costs	13,623	7,734
TOTAL COSTS	$59,030	33,514
TOTAL HOURLY COSTS	28.38/hr	16.11/hr

COST/HOUR		
50% Productive	56.76/hr	32.23/hr
30% Productive	94.60/hr	53.71/hr

UNIT OF WORK OUTPUT PER HOUR:
  Line Art ==> 4.92 scans/hr (includes minor cleanup and saving on disk)

COST PER SCAN (Line Art)	@ $15/hr	@ $7/hr
50% Productive	$11.54/scan	$6.55/scan
30% Productive	19.23/scan	10.92/scan

Figure 5-13. Budgeted hourly rates for scanning.

If you add profit and return on any initial investment to this you come up with a target price for scanning. In North America, the going rate for line art scanning is about $10 a scan.

BUDGETED HOURLY RATES
Home Office
(CREATIVE DESIGN)

INVESTMENT - Computer and draw-illustration software: $3,000
SPACE needed to perform function: 20 square feet
PEOPLE - Percent of time that a person is involved in activity: 100%

ONE PERSON SHOP
Annual hours worked   2,080

FIXED (NON VARIABLE) COSTS
Depreciation	600
Space Rent	600
Basic Utilities	27
System Insurance	9
TOTAL FIXED COSTS	1,236

VARIABLE COSTS
Labor (@ $15/hr)	31,200
Pension Fund	624
Health/Medical insurance	2,340
Payroll Taxes	2,964
Workers Comp Insurance	468
Direct Supplies	200
Repairs, Maint & SW upgrades	450
TOTAL VARIABLE COSTS	38,246

Other misc costs	3,825
TOTAL FIXED &VARIABLE COSTS	43,307

Sales, General & Administrative Costs	12,992
TOTAL COSTS	$56,299

TOTAL HOURLY COSTS	27.07/hr

COST/HOUR
50% Productive	54.13/hr
30% Productive	90.22/hr

UNIT OF WORK OUTPUT PER HOUR:
Depends on creativity level of designer. Assume one page per hour.

COST PER DESIGN
50% Productive	$54.13/design
30% Productive	90.22/design

Figure 5-14. Budgeted hourly rates for creative design.

BUDGETED HOURLY RATES
Home Office
(PAGE LAYOUT)

INVESTMENT - Computer and page layout software:	$3,000
SPACE needed to perform function:	20 square feet
PEOPLE - Percent of time that a person is involved in activity:	100%

ONE PERSON SHOP
Annual hours worked   2,080

FIXED (NON VARIABLE) COSTS
Depreciation	600
Space Rent	600
Basic Utilities	27
System Insurance	9
TOTAL FIXED COSTS	1.236

VARIABLE COSTS
Labor (@$15/hr)	31,200
Pension Fund	624
Health/Medical insurance	2,340
Payroll Taxes	2,964
Workers Comp Insurance	468
Direct Supplies	200
Repairs, Maint & SW upgrades	450
TOTAL VARIABLE COSTS	38,246
Other misc costs	3,825
TOTAL FIXED &VARIABLE COSTS	43,307
Sales, General & Administrative Costs	12,992
TOTAL COSTS	$56,299

TOTAL HOURLY COSTS
27.07/hr

COST/HOUR
50% Productive	54.13/hr
30% Productive	90.22/hr

UNIT OF WORK OUTPUT PER HOUR:
Flyer:	0.4 hours/page
Newsletter:	0.52 hours/page

COST PER PAGE (NEWSLETTER)
50% Productive	$28.15/pg
30% Productive	46.91/pg

Figure 5-15. Budgeted hourly rates for page layout.

BUDGETED HOURLY RATES
Home Office
(LASER PRINTING)

INVESTMENT - Computer, laser printer and software: $4,000
SPACE needed to perform function: 20 square feet
PEOPLE - Percent of time that a person is involved in activity: 20%

> NOTE: The typical pay for a computer operator is $7 an hour. Since this is a one-person business with a pre-defined $15/hour owner-operator pay, both wage rates are used for calculating a budgeted hourly rate.

ONE PERSON SHOP
Annual hours worked (40 hrs/wk, 52 wks)   2,080

FIXED (NON VARIABLE) COSTS	@$15/hr	@$7/hr
Depreciation (computer system)	800	800
Space Rent	600	600
Basic Utilities	27	27
System Insurance	12	12
TOTAL FIXED COSTS	1,439	1,439

VARIABLE COSTS	@$15/hr	@$7/hr
Labor	6,240	2,912
Pension Fund	125	58
Health/Medical insurance	468	468
Payroll Taxes	593	277
Workers Comp Insurance	94	44
Direct Supplies	1,000	1,000
Repairs, Maint & SW upgrades	600	600
TOTAL VARIABLE COSTS	9,120	5,359

Other misc costs	1,056	680
TOTAL FIXED &VARIABLE COSTS	11,615	7,478
Sales, General & Administrative Costs	3,485	2,243
TOTAL COSTS	$15,099	9,722

TOTAL HOURLY COSTS	7.26/hr	4.67/hr

COST/HOUR		
50% Productive	14.52/hr	9.35/hr
30% Productive	24.20/hr	15.57/hr

UNIT OF WORK OUTPUT PER HOUR:
6 pages/minute, 360 pages/hour

COST PER PAGE	@ $15/hr	@ $7/hr
50% Productive	0.040/pg	0.026/pg
30% Productive	0.067/pg	0.043/pg

Figure 5-16. Budgeted hourly rates for laser printing.

Perhaps this is why laser printer output prices are coming down to less than 10¢ a page. The next section deals with the same activities. But this time, the operations are performed out of a storefront.

Budgeted Hourly Rate Example: Store Front

In this scenario, the same business is assumed, but it operates out of a 400 square foot storefront office with several employees. The owner-operator is paid $15 an hour. The computer operator is paid $7 an hour. This hypothetical shop earns $150,000 a year in revenue.

The business has been operating for one year. Both employees take one week vacation and get paid for five holidays when the shop is closed. The shop has 2,000 annual productive hours each year at 100 percent productivity (2,080 hours less 40 hours vacation less 40 hours holiday = 2,000 hours). The sources of income for the business can be partitioned into:

Keyboarding	10%	$15,000
Scanning	10%	15,000
Creative Design	20%	30,000
Layout	50%	75,000
Laser Printing	10%	15,000
		$150,000

To operate, the owner purchased a computer, a laser printer and a scanner with word processing, scanning and page layout software. Total investment was $10,000

($5,000 in purchases depreciated over five years and $5,000 in purchases written off this year).

The objective is to determine a budgeted hourly rate for each activity listed above just as we did for the home business. Figure 5-17 shows the fixed and variable costs associated with this storefront business.

FIXED COSTS

Rent (Indirect/Overhead) $1,000/month	12,000
Basic Utilities (Indirect/Overhead)	2,460
Insurance (Indirect/Overhead)	1,200
Taxes (Indirect/Overhead)	
Federal	28,500
State	16,500
Local	1,000
Payroll	4,348
Depreciation (Indirect/Overhead)	1,000
Hardware Not Depreciated (Indirect)	5,000
Software to Run Business (Indirect/Overhead)	500
Documentation to Operate Business (Indirect/Overhead)	100
Office Cleaning (Indirect/Overhead)	1,800
Grounds Keeping (Indirect/Overhead)	960
Vehicle Insurance (Indirect/Overhead)	1,200
Vehicle Purchase Loan (Indirect/Overhead)	4,800
Total Fixed Cost:	$81,368

VARIABLE COSTS

Marketing Expenses (Indirect/Overhead)	$4,500
Advertising Expenses (Indirect/Overhead)	4,500
Salaries — Owner-Operator	31,200
Salaries — Computer Operator	14,560
Wages - Part Time Help (Direct)	1,000
Cost of Goods Sold (Direct)	100
Supplies Used to Do Job (Direct)	1,000
Fringe Benefits (Indirect)	1,372
Vehicle Operation (Indirect)	500
New Software Required for Job (Direct)	1,500
Documentation Purchased to Support Job (Direct)	100
Total Variable Cost:	$60,332
TOTAL FIXED & VARIABLE COSTS	$141,700

Figure 5-17. Fixed and variable costs for storefront business.

Based on this cost breakdown, the following shows a budgeted hourly rate calculation for each activity performed by this storefront desktop publishing business. As in the last example, figures are provided covering keyboarding, scanning, creative design, layout and laser printing.

```
                BUDGETED HOURLY RATES
                      Storefront
                    (KEYBOARDING)
```

INVESTMENT - Computer with word processing software: $2,500
SPACE needed to perform function: 20 square feet
PEOPLE - Percent of time that a person is involved in activity: 100%

TWO PERSON SHOP
   Annual hours worked   2,000

FIXED (NON VARIABLE) COSTS
Depreciation	500
Space Rent	600
Basic Utilities	123
System Insurance	8
TOTAL FIXED COSTS	1,231

VARIABLE COSTS
Direct Labor	14,560
Indirect Labor	6,240
Pension Fund	416
Health/Medical insurance	2,340
Payroll Taxes	1,976
Workers Comp Insurance	312
Direct Supplies	200
Repairs, Maint & SW upgrades	375
TOTAL VARIABLE COSTS	26,419
Other misc costs	2,642
TOTAL FIXED & VARIABLE COSTS	30,292
Sales, General & Administrative Costs	9,088
TOTAL COSTS	$39,380

Figure 5-18. Budgeted hourly rates for keyboarding.
(more on next page)

TOTAL HOURLY COSTS	19.69
COST/HOUR	
50% Productive	39.38
30% Productive	65.63

UNIT OF WORK OUTPUT PER HOUR:
50 wpm, 250 char/minute, 15,000 char/hr, 1500 char/pg ==> 10 pages/hr

COST PER 1000 CHARACTERS	
50% Productive	2.63/M
30% Productive	4.38/M
COST PER PAGE	
50% Productive	$3.94/pg
30% Productive	6.56/pg

KEYBOARDING COST PER PAGE (60% text, 40% graphics)
1500 characters per page X 60% = 1500 X.6 = 900 characters/pg
15,000 char/hr divided by 900 char/pg = 16.67 pages/hr

50% Productive	$2.36/pg
30% Productive	3.94/pg

Figure 5-18. Budgeted hourly rates for keyboarding.

BUDGETED HOURLY RATES
Storefront
(SCANNING)

INVESTMENT - Computer, scanner and software: $5,000
SPACE needed to perform function: 20 square feet
PEOPLE - Percent of time that a person is involved in activity: 100%

TWO PERSON SHOP
Annual hours worked   2,000

FIXED (NON VARIABLE) COSTS
Depreciation (computer system)	1000
Space Rent	600
Basic Utilities	123
System Insurance	8
TOTAL FIXED COSTS	1,731

VARIABLE COSTS
Direct Labor ($8/hr)	16,000
Indirect Labor (supv)	6,240
Pension Fund	445
Health/Medical insurance	2,340
Payroll Taxes	2,113
Workers Comp Insurance	334
Direct Supplies	200
Repairs, Maint & SW upgrades	750
TOTAL VARIABLE COSTS	28,422

Other misc costs	2,642
TOTAL FIXED & VARIABLE COSTS	32,995
Sales, General & Administrative Costs	9,899
TOTAL COSTS	$42,894

TOTAL HOURLY COSTS   21.45

COST/HOUR
50% Productive	42.89
30% Productive	71.49

UNIT OF WORK OUTPUT PER HOUR:
Line Art ==> 4.92 scans/hr (includes minor cleanup and saving on disk)

COST PER SCAN - LINE ART
50% Productive	$8.72/scan
30% Productive	14.53/scan

Figure 5-19. Budgeted hourly rates for scanning line art.

BUDGETED HOURLY RATES
Storefront
(CREATIVE DESIGN)

INVESTMENT - Computer and draw-illustration software: $3,000
SPACE needed to perform function: 20 square feet
PEOPLE - Percent of time that a person is involved in activity: 100%

    TWO PERSON SHOP
    Annual hours worked (40 hrs/wk, 52 wks)   2,000

FIXED (NON VARIABLE) COSTS

Depreciation (computer)	600
Space Rent	600
Basic Utilities	123
System Insurance	9
TOTAL FIXED COSTS	1,332

VARIABLE COSTS

Direct Labor	30,000
Indirect Labor	1,200
Pension Fund	624
Health/Medical insurance	2,340
Payroll Taxes	2,964
Workers Comp Insurance	468
Direct Supplies	200
Repairs, Maint & SW upgrades	450
TOTAL VARIABLE COSTS	38,246
Other misc costs	3,958
TOTAL FIXED &VARIABLE COSTS	43,536
Sales, General & Administrative Costs	13,061
TOTAL COSTS	$56,597

TOTAL HOURLY COSTS   28.30

COST/HOUR
50% Productive	$56.60/hr
30% Productive	94.33/hr

UNIT OF WORK OUTPUT PER HOUR:
Depends on creativity level of designer. Assume one page per hour.

COST PER DESIGN
50% Productive	$56.60/design
30% Productive	94.33/design

Figure 5-20. Budgeted hourly rates for creative design.

BUDGETED HOURLY RATES
Storefront
(PAGE LAYOUT)

INVESTMENT - Computer and page layout software: $3,000
SPACE needed to perform function: 20 square feet
PEOPLE - Percent of time that a person is involved in activity: 100%

ONE PERSON SHOP
Annual hours worked (40 hrs/wk, 52 wks)   2,000

FIXED (NON VARIABLE) COSTS
Depreciation (computer)	600
Space Rent	600
Basic Utilities	123
System Insurance	9
TOTAL FIXED COSTS	1,332

VARIABLE COSTS
Direct Labor	30,000
Indirect Labor	1,200
Pension Fund	624
Health/Medical insurance	2,340
Payroll Taxes	2,964
Workers Comp Insurance	468
Direct Supplies	200
Repairs, Maint & SW upgrades	450
TOTAL VARIABLE COSTS	38,246

Other misc costs	3,958
TOTAL FIXED &VARIABLE COSTS	43,536

Sales, General & Administrative Costs	13,061
TOTAL COSTS	$56,597

TOTAL HOURLY COSTS   28.30

COST/HOUR
50% Productive	$56.60/hr
30% Productive	94.33/hr

UNIT OF WORK OUTPUT PER HOUR:
Flyer:	0.40 hours/page
Newsletter:	0.52 hours/page

COST PER PAGE (NEWSLETTER)
50% Productive	$29.43/pg
30% Productive	49.05/pg

Figure 5-21. Budgeted hourly rates for page layout.

BUDGETED HOURLY RATES
Storefront
(LASER PRINTING)

INVESTMENT - Computer, laser printer and software: $4,000
SPACE needed to perform function: 20 square feet
PEOPLE - Percent of time that a person is involved in activity: 20%

TWO PERSON SHOP
Annual hours worked (40 hrs/wk, 50 wks)   2,000

FIXED (NON VARIABLE) COSTS
Depreciation (computer system)	800
Space Rent)	600
Basic Utilities	123
System Insurance	12
TOTAL FIXED COSTS	1,439

VARIABLE COSTS
Direct Labor	2,800
Indirect Labor	1,248
Pension Fund	81
Health/Medical insurance	2,340
Payroll Taxes	385
Workers Comp Insurance	61
Direct Supplies	1,000
Repairs, Maint & SW upgrades	600
TOTAL VARIABLE COSTS	8,515

Other misc costs	995
TOTAL FIXED &VARIABLE COSTS	10,949

Sales, General & Administrative Costs	3,285
TOTAL COSTS	$14,234

TOTAL HOURLY COSTS (2,000 hours)   7.12

COST/HOUR
50% Productive	14.23/hour
30% Productive	23.72/hour

UNIT OF WORK OUTPUT PER HOUR:
6 pages/minute, 360 pages/hour

COST PER PAGE
50% Productive	$0.066/pg
30% Productive	0.040/pg

Figure 5-22. Budgeted hourly rates for laser printing.

Table 5-5 compares the cost baseline for a home office and a storefront business based on various productivity factors.

Table 5-5. Budgeted hourly rate comparisons for home office and storefront.

OPERATION	HOME OFFICE $15/hr 50%	30%	$7/hr 50%	30%	STOREFRONT 50%	30%
Keyboarding (per page)	$5.39	$8.98	$2.66	$4.44	$2.36	$3.94
Scanning (per scan)	11.54	19.23	6.55	10.92	8.72	14.53
Design (per design)	54.13	90.22	-	-	56.60	94.33
Layout (per page)	28.15	46.91	-	-	29.43	49.05
Laser Printing (per pg)	0.040	0.067	0.026	0.043	0.066	0.040

Table 5-6 is a snapshot of the retail prices for keyboarding, scanning, design, layout and laser printer output based on a recent survey. Remember that these reflect the asking price —profit and return are already factored in.

Table 5-6. Snapshot of survey prices for various services.

REGION	KEYBOARDING (per page)	SCANNING (ea line art image)	DESIGN (per hour)	LAYOUT (per page)	LASER PRINTING (page)
New England	$8	$10	$60	$40	$0.75
Mid Atlantic	3.60	10	60	35	1.50
South Atlantic	6	10	60	50	1.00
North Central	8	6	95	30	1.00
South Central	10	10	50	45	1.00
Mountain	12	10	55	45	1.00
Pacific	20	8	50	35	1.00
California	9	10	50	48	0.75
Canada	8	10	45	40	3.00

When you compare Table 5-5 with Table 5-6, you get an idea which jobs pay how much and how productive the typical shop really is.

Summary

Baselines, benchmarks, and standards give you yardsticks with which to measure and bid new work. Baseline production standards and budgeted hourly rates are key factors in establishing a flat rate for any job. These factors let you respond quickly to customers who'd go elsewhere if you quoted them your hourly rates but who don't resist a flat price for a job even when increased budgeted hourly rates are incorporated. What they see is what they buy.

Knowing what you must charge lets you decide for yourself what you CAN charge based on market conditions. In the next chapter, you'll discover how to estimate jobs using baseline production standards and budgeted hourly rates.

6

Charging For Products & Services

"There is no such thing as a free lunch."

Pricing products is straightforward—you charge by the unit—page, piece, sheet, item, and so on. Pricing services can be more complicated. Like a product, we can charge by the page, by the kilobit (Kb), kilobyte (KB), megabit (Mb) or megabyte (MB),or by some other unit of measure. We could also charge by the character, by the word, by the scan, by the minute, by the hour, or by the job. The challenge is to determine which pricing method is appropriate for each activity and each job that your business performs.

Ready, Set, Charge!

The functions of desktop publishing and prepress are merging. And printing companies are rapidly incorporating desktop publishing and prepress into their core business. Secretarial services and word processing businesses are also moving into desktop publishing following significant improvements in word processing software and demand by customers for more graphics integration into their documents. Yet, these businesses typically charge differently for products and services.

Designers usually charge by the hour, by the project, or by the page. Typesetters and typing services typically charge by the number of lines or keystrokes. Desktop publishers and typographers estimate and bill a job based on the number of expected pages, the amount of conceptual layout, the complexity of the design needed, and the costs for photography, illustrations, and actual printing. Laser printer and imagesetter output can be billed by output media (paper or film), by resolution required, by the inches (or square inches) of output, or by the standard page. Scanning can be billed by the scan or by the hour and may or may not include touch-up (also called "retouch").

Today, word processing software forms the basis for the text in most desktop-generated documents. Therefore, page costs should be based on the time it takes to format the text, design the page, and then import the text into the layout program to produce the final document. Both design and typographic functions are involved.

With so many diverse ways to figure composition, design and production costs, the specific method of charging depends on the work, the volume, the customer, your resources, and the marketplace.

Frank Fox, Executive Director of NASS suggests that labor intensive activities such as word processing, copy writing, and layout, be priced by the hour. The driving function is the time of a computer operator to complete each task. Labor hour is the pricing metric.

Machine intensive activities such as laser printing and photocopying should be priced by the page or sheet. Production depends on the capabilities of the hardware and software. And a person need not be attending the task all the time. Billing for machine intensive production is typically added to the labor charges.

Charging by the Character and by the Line

In our pricing surveys, we are interested in how many shops price keyboarding and typography work by the character. Of those that used this billing method, most quoted prices by the thousand characters (1,000 or 1M keystrokes).

They used their software to calculate the total character count in a document. Or they count the characters in 10 lines of text and take this as a basis for counting the number of lines of text. By multiplying the average number of characters in a line by the total number of lines typeset, they achieve a value approximating the total number of characters in the document.

This method works well with text material. It works better when the software can count the characters. You can get an accurate count. The software will also account for condensed or expanded fonts and varying typefaces.

We've heard about, but didn't note any shop owners billing by square inch for composition services. The square inch method is fast, but it doesn't compensate for the time it takes to set special typefaces or varying type widths.

Charging by the Page

Pricing a job by the page can be tricky. The time and energy spent on each customer can vary significantly. Per-page pricing requires that you know exactly how each page will be designed. It depends on the total number of pages in the job, the complexity of each page, the volume of work this client brings to you, and the type of tasks that you'll be performing (data editing, grammar checking, spell-checking, illustrations, etc.).

Changing the style can affect the page count in the total package and cause significant re-design.

Without a page layout specification and a good count of the number of pages of each layout complexity, you must estimate a job based on many possible design configurations.

You could establish a "base page" price and then adjust this price depending on job difficulty, the customer, the turnaround time desired, the amount of skill required, and special conditions related to the job (e.g., comparable costs of mechanical art production, competitor pricing for similar work, and the hardware and software resources required). The key is to know your costs, then add in profit and return on any investment to get an idea of what to charge per page.

There is a simple way to track average page costs for desktop publishing. Make notes on the job folder associated with each project that you complete. Your notes should include page count, page complexity, the units of time spent and the total costs involved.

Maintain a running record of all of your projects over a period of time. Then perform a cumulative analysis on this information. A computer spreadsheet program is an invaluable tool for this.

In your analysis, make a list of each multiple page job, the number of pages, the total costs (less out-of-pocket expenses), and any special things that should be considered. Delete the charges for alterations and corrections so you normalize your analysis on just the basic project cost. Also note special shortcuts that you found and used.

Divide the costs for each project by the number of pages to get a basic cost-per-page value. You'll find that larger projects typically have a lower cost-per-page, and you'll find that alterations and corrections can dramatically affect the final cost to the client.

Some people group pages and go for an average page complexity. They look primarily at projects involving 16 pages or more and exclude small projects involving fewer than 16 pages. They feel that the effort varies substantially with short page-count projects and can skew the data for larger projects such as books and manuals. In addition, complex jobs with multiple columns, lots of graphics and wrap-around text can increase the time spent on each page.

Other estimators partition a page layout into simple, moderate, or complex. A simple page has a single column and simple headings. They establish a base rate for the simple page layout. As the design becomes increasingly complex, they add a percentage to the base price.

For example, two columns adds 50 percent more to the base rate. Three columns adds another 50 percent to the base rate. Thus, a three column design would have an estimate of 100 percent base rate plus 50 percent for a second column, plus 50 percent for the third column or an estimate that is 200 percent of the base page rate. A $12 base charge and a three column design would equate to a $24 charge for each three-column page ($12 + $6 + $6 = $24).

These estimators typically charge another 25 percent of the base rate for each special feature such as drop caps, pull quotes, photos, etc., and 10 percent more for each instance of kerning, drop ins, large type, and graphic sizing required.

This means that a page with two columns, a drop cap, a graphic illustration, and a photo would price out at $12 base, plus $6 for the second column, plus $3 for the drop cap, plus $1.20 for sizing the graphic, plus $3 for adding a photograph. The total bill comes to $25.20 for this page. Charts or graphs can add additional charges to the job.

Add up all the costs for each page and total the package. Then factor in the cost to stat (or scan) photographs, imageset the pages, and deliver the final product. This becomes the cost basis for the project. Then add overhead and the other associated expenses and profit to derive your final quote.

Before you establish a per-page rate, do some testing. Develop a style sheet and lay out some pages. This will give you a feel for the size of the project.

Costs will probably vary from $20 to $125 for each page in the project. David Doty, Editor and Publisher of *ThePage* found that the costs for his magazine averaged just over $50 per page. Be certain that your price incorporates all of your pro-rated costs — labor, materials, and overhead.

I find that using custom production standards and budgeted hourly rates with complexity ratings for each activity works the best. This technique partitions a project into byte-sized chunks (pun intended) and causes my per page cost estimates to come in quite close to reality.

Knowing your typical per page cost can be extremely helpful when you bid on future jobs.

When customers new to desktop publishing and prepress bring you work, don't offer per-page billing. Instead, opt for an hourly rate. Inexperienced customers often require significant hand-holding and make many design changes before a final product emerges. Every time you think you're done, you're probably not. Changes in the layout, text, graphics, or output form will occur, so plan extra time to handle these. And plan to charge for all of the work that is actually performed.

Charging by the Hour

In this technique, an owner calculates all the labor and materials costs associated with a particular job. Each piece of hardware and software required to complete the job is included in the cost basis. Even software and hardware maintenance contracts are amortized over each job and added in as part of the hourly rate. Software maintenance usually costs between $300 and $1,000 a year. Hardware maintenance will cost between 10 and 15 percent of the purchase price.

Next add in overhead, profit, and return on any investments to reach the final target price.

The quote that you make can be an overall figure that includes all tasks and all hardware and software components required, or it can be a set of prices partitioned into separate rates for each task and each piece of hardware or software used on a job. The budgeted hourly rate method for pricing each activity (Chapter 5) is useful when bidding by the hour or by the job.

Depending on who is doing the work and how alert they are each time they approach the job, you can average the time to perform each task—check a document file for spelling and format, import a file, layout and typeset a certain number of characters each minute, and so on. You can also establish an average time for handling graphics and photographs. Include the time to input each graphic, manipulate and re-size images, retouch photos and proof and print the final job.

Add up all the associated times for each task and multiply by the budgeted hourly rate for each specific task. Then add up the hourly rate charges for each task to get a total job estimate. Add profit and return and this becomes the price for the job—based on charges for increments of time in specific activities.

Once you have a job estimate, you can used it to estimate future jobs that are similar and based on the same budgeted hourly rates.

Charging by the Shop's Hourly Rate

The hourly rate that you use to develop your bids and that you use as a basis for your pricing considerations can be based on costs and return information for the shop as a whole or on individual functions within the shop.

Your *shop's hourly rate* is calculated using the total wages paid each hour, your overhead costs per hour, and the amount of return on investment, debt servicing and profit you need to earn each hour to achieve the results that you expect. This is an overall shop hourly rate. Unlike the budgeted hourly rate, a shop hourly rate does not allocate a separate hourly charge to each individual activity.

Typically, profit is calculated using the sum of hourly pay plus hourly overhead costs. Profit planning is based on these two costs outlays.

Let's assume that you operate a sole proprietorship with a single employee—you. You put $10,000 into your business and find your overhead running at 50 percent of what you make each month — your gross income. You don't need new equipment yet so you don't have any loan debt to service (amortize and pay back monthly). You plan to keep the $10,000 in the business and be paid a return for the investment.

Your income has been running $6,000 a month, but overhead will eat up $3,000 of it. Based on $6,000 per month of income, your shop should bring in $72,000 a year. You pay yourself $15 an hour and work 52 weeks (2080 hours) a year. (You defer vacations during these startup years). You'd like to earn 10 percent return on your investment and another 10 percent profit on expenses. What should you charge?

First, realize that a one-person shop will likely be 30 percent productive at best. This means that you will bill out for only 30 percent of the time that you work. Also, even though you are alone, you have certain overhead costs that must be covered. Overhead costs are often around 50 percent of income. Your profit is based on how much you spend for wages and overhead.

Table 6-1 shows how to calculate your hourly shop billing rate.

Table 6-1. Hourly rate calculation for a representative one-person DTP shop.

Hourly Wage (one person, $15/hr))	$15.00
Hours worked per year (40 hrs/wk x 52 wks = 2080 hrs)	
Hourly Overhead expense [(72,000*.5) / 2,080]	17.31
Hourly Return on investment (10,000 * .1) / 2,080	0.48
Hourly Business Profit Desired [(15 + 17.31) * .1]	3.23
Total hourly income needed each week (one employee) (100% productivity)	$36.02
Total hourly income needed if 30% productive	$120.07 SHOP BILLING RATE

Quite a shock! You should be charging $120.07 an hour just to make this operation profitable! What can you do? You decide to modify your spreadsheet to show that you work 60 hours a week and calculate costs and profit based on working 40 hours. (You go on salary.) This makes each day appear more productive. By working more hours, you double your effective productivity. You redo your calculations. (See Table 6-2.)

Table 6-2. Hourly rate calculation for a one-person DTP shop operating 60 hours each week.

Hourly Wage ($15 - effectively $10/hr @60 hrs)	$15.00
Hours shop operated each year (60 hrs/wk x 52 wks = 3120 hrs)	
Hourly Overhead expense [(72,000*.5) / 3120]	11.54
Hourly Return on investment (10,000 * .1) / 3120	0.32
Hourly Business Profit Desired [(15 + 11.54) * .1]	2.65
Total hourly income needed each week (100% productivity)	$29.51
Total hourly income needed if 60% productive	$49.19 SHOP BILLING RATE

Well this is better. But $49.19 an hour still exceeds the average $40/hr fee in North America. Backing into the numbers, it turns out that you need to earn over $92,000 just to pay your costs. What else can you do?

You could work 80 or more hours a week, but what would happen if you simply added staff? Adding an employee means that you share the shop's non-earning tasks such as answering the telephone, mailing, and certain administrative functions. Naturally, there must be enough work to keep both of you fully occupied (at maximum productivity).

If you pay this person $7 an hour, you both work 40 hours a week, and neither of you take paid vacations, you can achieve a better hourly rate as shown in Table 6-3 below.

Table 6-3. Hourly rate calculation for a two-person DTP shop open 40 hours each week.

Hourly Wage $7 +15)	$22.00
Hours shop operated each year (40 hrs/wk x 52 wks = 2080 hrs)	
Hourly Overhead expense [(72,000*.5) /2080]	7.30
Hourly Return on investment (10,000 * .1) / 2080	0.48
Hourly Business Profit Desired [(22+ 17.30) * .1]	3.93
Total hourly income needed each week (100% productivity)	$43.73
Total hourly income needed per employee (100% productive)	$21.86
Total hourly income needed if each are 45% productive	$48.58 SHOP BILLING RATE

By adding another employee but both working only 40 hours each week, you can achieve 45 percent productivity for the shop. Now you can reduce your hourly rate to $48.58 from the $49.19 you would need to charge if you ran your shop by yourself and worked 60 hours a week. Not much difference, but now you're working a reasonable 40-hour week.

Next, let's see what happens if you increase your staff by hiring two employees. Each employee will work 40 hours a week. More workers means that you can handle more jobs. Hopefully, you'll also earn more income for the shop. Table 6-4 provides the picture.

Table 6-4. Service rate calculation for a three-person shop.

Hourly Wages (6 + 7 + 15)	$28.00
Hours shop operated each year (40 hrs/wk x 52 wks = 2080 hrs)	
Overhead expense (52,000/2080)	25.00
Return on investment (10,000 * .1) / (2000 x 3)	0.17
Business Profit Desired [(28 + 25) * .1]	5.30
Total hourly income needed at 40 billable hours a week (100% productivity)	$58.47
Hourly income needed per shop employee (100% productivity)	$19.49
Total hourly income needed per employee if 50% productivity	$38.98
	SHOP BILLING RATE

Assume that you expect to earn over $130,000 next year. Your overhead has been running about 40 percent of gross income. You want to determine the actual hourly rate that you should charge to earn a desired profit and return on investment. Employee 1 is paid $6 an hour. Employee 2 is paid $7 an hour, and you (employee 3) get paid $15 an hour. Your annual overhead costs are $52,000 ($130,000 times 40 percent typical overhead = 52,000). Each employee will work 40 hours a week and take two weeks vacation. This yields 2,000 hours of work each year from each employee (40 hours/week x 50 weeks/year = 2,000 hours/year). Therefore, three workers will put in 2,000 hours each or 6,000 total hours annually.

Dividing the $52,000/year overhead costs by the 2080 actual shop operating hours (40 hrs/wk x 52 wks = 2080 hrs) yields $25 an hour as the amount charged to overhead each hour. Suppose that you want to earn a profit of 10 percent on overhead and wages. Adding labor costs of $28 (6 + 7 + 15 = $28/hr) and overhead of $25 results in $53/hour overhead and wage costs. The contribution to profit is 10 percent of $53 or $5.30 an hour.

Then, let's say that you want to realize a 10 percent return on your $10,000 start-up investment. The return on investment equals the investment times the desired return divided by the hours worked times the number of workers. This equals [(10,000 * 0.1) / (2,000 * 3)] or $0.17 an hour of billable fee that must contribute to ROI.

Adding the hourly labor costs ($28), overhead costs ($25), profit ($5.30), and ROI ($0.17) and then dividing by the number of employees, you get a total income required from each employee each hour of $19.49 ($58.47/3 = $19.49). This is the hourly rate that you must bill out if everyone is 100 percent productive as shown in Table 6-4. But, remember that a shop with only three workers will likely be 50 percent productive at best. If you don't put in extra (uncharged) hours to handle administrative functions, your billable hourly rate will shift to $38.98 per hour. This is what you need to budget and charge if you want to realize the 10 percent ROI and 10 percent profit on wages and overhead.

This brings your rates within the national average. The hourly fee for desktop publishing services in North America varies from $15 to $100 an hour. The median is about $40 an hour. Median means that most shops charge this rate. The $40 an hour median also means that many small shops with one or two workers are absorbing part of their overhead costs and are charging too little for their work. They are likely working more than 40 hours a week (even if they calculate on a 40-hour basis).

These tables show that you can operate a successful shop if you keep your costs low and your productivity high. Since your shop will be less productive with fewer employees, you must carefully analyze your costs and output if you want to bring your required hourly rate in line with what the current market (and your pocket book) will bear. Labor is your single biggest expense. This is why many shops hire freelance or part-time help and hold the full-time employee load at a minimum. Freelance and most part-time workers do not receive benefits.

A small shop simply will not reach the 50 percent productivity level without additional employees and added income, so most operators work more than a 40-hour week. They shoot for 45-50 percent shop productivity. And they also try to reduce their overhead to 35 percent or less.

Typically, wages are 60 percent of your costs. General and administrative expenses can average 32 percent of your expenses. Rent costs can be 5-9 percent of your total costs. You can keep rent low by operating out of smaller spaces, sharing a shop, or operating a home business.

The home office option has its own set of problems and challenges though. Initially, most DTPers operate out of their home, but as their business grows, space and electrical requirements usually forces them into office spaces outside the home.

Most owner-operators charge too little for products and services. These professionals must increase their hourly rates if they expect to earn a decent living and get a suitable return on their investment of time and money.

The advantage of pricing by the hour is that you get paid for all of the time involved. The downside is that it's sometimes difficult to know how long a job will take, so you can't give your customer a flat rate. However, if you have enough historical data, you can estimate a project based on similar jobs and be close enough to warrant the effort. Particularly in this case, experience pays. Budgeted hourly rates, as discussed in the last chapter, is a better method to use.

Charging by the Job Flat Rate Pricing

Clients, who are uncomfortable paying an hourly rate, will often accept a flat-fee bid. Some people just don't like giving work to professionals who charge by the hour. For these customers, it's better to express project cost as a total package price.

With flat rate job pricing, you can incorporate fees and charges that would stand out like a sore thumb on a price breakdown sheet. If you quote a price that's 25 percent lower than what a customer can find elsewhere, you can incorporate a price increase while still giving your customer the impression that they're getting your services for "peanuts."

On flat rate jobs, analyze the total number of pages involved, the complexity of each page, the volume of work this client brings to you, and the type of tasks that you will perform (data editing, grammar checking, spell-checking, illustrations, etc.). Then establish a price for the overall job. This approach uses the budgeted hourly rate technique described in the last chapter.

When a new customer with little or no desktop publishing or prepress experience comes in to discuss a job, you should incorporate several factors into the price that you quote. If you don't bid an hourly rate with a minimum fee, you may waste time "educating" and "hand-holding" that customer. New customers may have no concept of how much work is involved, or how a final document will look. They could start changing the design the moment you begin working on the project. This could impact your schedule and substantially increase your costs.

When you get a call asking how much a "simple" job will cost, avoid a snap answer. Telephone shoppers are typically price shoppers. (They could be your competitors price-shopping your business.) Assuming they're searching for the lowest price for a job. Recognize that with these people, quality comes second. But price is king. They look for this first.

You'll always have telephone shoppers who want to know what you'll charge to design and print a certain form, flyer, or document. When they call, get as much information on the job as you can. Ask a series of questions. Is the design complete? How many pages? How many columns? How many heads and subheads? How many tables, charts, and diagrams? Will columns need to follow a certain design form (e.g., line up at the bottom as well as at the top)? How much art? How many photographs? Is all the art and graphics camera ready?

The way the caller answers these questions will usually tell you how much of your resources will be required to complete that job. Take time to really study the project. Ask questions, and get all the clarity possible.

A snap response can appear unprofessional and make a customer think that you run a cut-rate "job shop" and not a professional graphics and document design organization.

However, if they insist on hearing a price over the phone, you can give them a conservative "ballpark" bid based on your worst-case conditions. Put bounds on the amount of effort you'll need to apply. Tell them the job could cost less if everything runs smoothly. And tell them that you can give them a final bid once you look over the material.

Not being willing (or able) to quote a "ball park" price for a job can signal a potential "rip off" or suggest that you're unsure of your own abilities and resources.

Steve Morris of Signal Graphics Printing Franchises described front counter tips in a recent *Instant Printer* article. When a customer asks for a "ballpark" figure, he gives them several. He uses a "good, better, best" principle. He gives them the "better" price first, based on his experience of an in-between cost to do the job. Then he gives them a lower price alternative based on using different, or lower quality materials. Finally he gives them a premium or "best" price based on using the best materials. This tactic removes the perceived need to shop around. And Steve has less need to negotiate a discounted price from those he quotes. Effectively the customer has completed all of the comparison shopping at Steve's front counter. No matter which option they choose, Steve gets the job.

Consider using the worst-case time scenario to form your cost basis. Then, if you can assign employees to their best tasks, you should complete the job in less time (closer to the best measured). This increases the profit potential for your shop. However, sometimes the best person for a job is already working on another project. In this case, a slower worker can be assigned the task and still be able to complete the job with acceptable profitability to the business.

Before you accept that next job, be certain that both parties agree on how the project will be delivered to you—in hard copy, on film, or on disk. If on disk, what is the application program and operating system format? Will conversion be required? Are proofreading and spell-checking needed?

Also, determine how the finished job will be delivered to the customer. Confirm print resolution, output form (paper or film), and how many copies of the galleys or camera-ready mechanicals are desired.

Be certain to clarify ownership of the disks, artwork, and film associated with a job. You may assume that you own these, but your customer may feel that they paid for these in their fee. Specify ownership rights in the agreement or job order that your customer signs. Be sure that they understand what they will receive upon payment for a job.

During the discussion process with a prospective customer, keep notes on how you calculate time and costs. Also note what you say to the customer and what the customer indicates they want. What they think they want and what they actually want are often two different products.

If there will be original artwork that you will create, bid by the hour. Avoid a fixed fee. In giving them a ballpark figure, allow time for an initial design plus several hours of alterations. You could negotiate minimum and maximum price boundaries. If they decide not to select your shop for the job, you may be lucky. Sometimes the winner of a bid ends up being the loser in income earned compared with the cost to perform and deliver.

Additional Charges

Because you've established how you will charge for each product or service, you're not done. Don't forget all the other things that you do before, during or after a job that take time, energy, and sometimes system resources.

The next sections deal with added charge items such as preflight, job difficulty, customer interface, and expedited work. It's your decision whether to offer these services free, as part of the total job price, or to include added charges to the job's basic price.

Preflight

The term *preflight* means to check out everything that the customer gives you—rough art, photographs, and electronic files. You should check the quality of hard copy, the quality and suitability of disk media and files, and that all job elements are there. If you're being asked to quote a price, you need a clear understanding on the condition of the initial job.

If the job seems more complex than you normally find, consider asking the customer to give you a small, but typical part of the job. This lets you work it and better understand how long it will take on the full job. Experimenting is especially helpful in color work.

The idea is to discover problems before accepting the job. Then you can give the customer the option of correcting problems or having you do the correcting.

Typically, customer-supplied computer files need correction. If conversion is required, you must build this into your proposal. If graphics need clean-up, or if files were generated on a PC and need to be converted to a Mac for layout, these are tasks that must be priced out and included in your estimate.

Dealing With Difficulty

One page is not necessarily equal to another page. One can be all text, while another may contain 70 percent text and 30 percent graphics. If you base your estimate on a page containing text and some heads, a keyboarding job whose pages are straight text, will cost out less than your standard page. You person can type faster if you don't have to deal with placing the correct head at the beginning of the right paragraph.

The NAPL deals with difficulty by assigning a percent difficulty—75%, 100% and 125%—to each function. For example, keyboarding entails: straight text - 75% difficulty; mixed text and heads - 100%; and mixed text and graphics - 125%. Single color layout includes: word processor output with no importing of text files - 75%; mixed text and a few imported graphics - 100%; mixed text and over 30 percent imported graphics - 125%.

By developing a table of difficulty considerations, you can apply a complexity factor to each function. This further refines your cost estimate. It takes longer to layout a page of 60 percent text, 40 percent graphics than it does to layout a text-only page. Thus the former costs out at 125 percent of the "standard" budgeted hourly rate.

Because of the toner used, even laser printer output pages can be assigned a difficulty rating. Text only with no graphics can be rated at 75 percent of the BHR value. Mixed text and graphics can be considered 100 percent or "typical." And mixed text with heavy graphics can be rated at 125 percent of BHR.

The use of the difficulty rating is especially useful in estimating a job containing multiple pages whose complexities vary. Establish a complexity standard defining the amount of text and graphic image on each page. Then assign a complexity rating to every page in a project and cost out each page accordingly. This pricing system works regardless of page count.

You could construct a difficulty rating sheet that can be used to quickly quote a price for a job. David Hornung, owner of The Graphic Center in Fond du Lac, Wisconsin described in an *Instant Printer* article how he uses a Composition Class Job Pricing sheet to make instant quotes a snap.

He made a counter Sample Composition Form by dividing an 8.5" x 11" sheet into five areas. Each area represents a page composition category (very light, light, medium, heavy, or extra heavy). By showing a sample of each composition category on his form, he can quickly determine how much a job will price out at and how long it should take to complete.

VERY LIGHT	LIGHT	MEDIUM	HEAVY	EXTRA HEAVY
ekc hfjdjsk eid eid ee id idi diek dhehdi dk did eivi	wlwidjdkfkej id e iel diel did dhid dhdh diei dd didi di deidndid eid ei	w iwi slsheueif idel diexi die die id dield ei die di ed dkdi eie didd dk dieos nsid diblo doe sum	hwl isleide ld;d dieldieh dield id die did didkd ei dleo dod do do dod od di sunbiscumdi	eid ielgi eithd dieldie edi die deoldoe doe d dd idi ekdi cd catjprod doe

SIZE	VERY LIGHT	LIGHT	MEDIUM	HEAVY	EXTRA HEAVY
4x6	$xx/pg	$xx/pg	$xx/pg	$xx/pg	$xx/pg
5x7	$xx/pg	$xx/pg	$xx/pg	$xx/pg	$xx/pg
5.5x8.5	$xx/pg	$xx/pg	$xx/pg	$xx/pg	$xx/pg
7x9	$xx/pg	$xx/pg	$xx/pg	$xx/pg	$xx/pg
8x10	$xx/pg	$xx/pg	$xx/pg	$xx/pg	$xx/pg
8.5x11	$xx/pg	$xx/pg	$xx/pg	$xx/pg	$xx/pg
8.5x14	$xx/pg	$xx/pg	$xx/pg	$xx/pg	$xx/pg
A4 size	$xx/pg	$xx/pg	$xx/pg	$xx/pg	$xx/pg
B4 size	$xx/pg	$xx/pg	$xx/pg	$xx/pg	$xx/pg
Tabloid	$xx/pg	$xx/pg	$xx/pg	$xx/pg	$xx/pg
(special)	$xx/pg	$xx/pg	$xx/pg	$xx/pg	$xx/pg
(special)	$xx/pg	$xx/pg	$xx/pg	$xx/pg	$xx/pg
(special)	$xx/pg	$xx/pg	$xx/pg	$xx/pg	$xx/pg
(special)	$xx/pg	$xx/pg	$xx/pg	$xx/pg	$xx/pg

Figure 6-1. Quick Quote pricing form.

On the reverse side of his form, Hornung designed six columns—the first column lists the paper size dimensions (in square inches of copy). Then he has a column for each of the five composition categories. Each category column lists a price for each paper size identified in the first column. By matching the paper size and print composition, he can quickly quote a price and close a sale.

This is a good idea because it reduces misunderstanding by your customer. Both of you know how difficult each page is. And both of you know what rate is being charged for each page in the project. Figure 6-1 on the previous page was designed based on the description Hornung provided in the article. You can adopt this form for your own business.

Use a Time in Tenths Chart

Many larger shops bill service by portions of an hour. Of these, some use the tenth of an hour increment. This means that they partition actual performance into hours and tenths-of-an-hour. Others build a twelfth-of-an-hour chart and bill out in five minute increments. They also round up to the nearest tenth of an hour when time-to-perform exceeds a tenth-of-an-hour increment unit.

Once you've established budgeted hourly rates for each service, you can add in profit and return-on-investment to get targeted prices. Then you can develop a chart that breaks down your shop hourly rates into incremental times. This quickly shows a customer what is owed on a job. As shown in Table 6-5, basing your chart on industry standards (incorporated in your baseline standard) helps add credibility to your pricing structure.

Table 6-5. Sample incremental time-pricing chart.

Incremental Pricing Chart
(based on Industry Production Standards)

Time Tenths	Minutes	$30	$36	$39	Hourly Rate $42	$45	$48	$52
0.1	6	3.00	3.60	3.90	4.20	4.50	4.80	5.20
0.2	12	6.00	7.20	7.80	8.40	9.00	9.60	10.40
0.3	18	9.00	10.80	11.70	12.60	13.50	14.40	15.60
0.4	24	12.00	14.40	15.60	16.80	18.00	19.20	20.80
0.5	30	15.00	18.00	19.50	21.00	22.50	24.00	26.00
0.6	36	18.00	21.60	23.40	25.20	27.00	28.80	31.20
0.7	42	21.00	25.20	27.30	29.40	31.50	33.60	36.40
0.8	48	24.00	28.80	31.20	33.60	36.00	38.40	41.60
0.9	54	27.00	32.40	35.10	37.80	40.50	43.20	46.80
1.0	60	30.00	36.00	39.00	42.00	45.00	48.00	52.00

If you have only a few shop hourly rates, then you can generate a simpler chart. The important thing is to have this in your counter price book so customers can quickly see what they'll pay.

Include the Cost of Meeting

As part of our zeal to think beyond traditional parameters in business—to maximize our bottom line profit, one often-overlooked activity is the meeting. In large and small organizations, the meeting is typically considered inefficient at best. The organizers often don't know how to plan and conduct such an interface. And some attendees often place meetings at low priority and thus arrive late, step out for "quick" telephone calls, or leave early. These issues, while frustrating and costly in themselves, affect only the overhead in a company.

It's the meetings with customers (or potential customers) that can have a direct bearing on the profit made on each job. I remember a series of meetings that I had with a prospective customer early in my business life. A printer asked me to meet with her to help a prospective customer understand the printing and publishing process. The "customer" was planning to publish a collection of articles that had been written by a well-known column writer for the local newspaper.

I was led (by both the printer and the prospective customer) that my company would be doing all of the book design and layout—that we would be providing camera ready art to the printer who would manufacture the book.

I participated in three meetings over a two-week period. Each meeting lasted one to three hours. Each meeting required over an hour of travel time. Throughout the experience, the prospective customer expressed his intent to work with both the printer and my company to complete the project. The printer and I solidly educated the man on the process and options.

On the last day, the prospect's closing remarks were that he would send us an invitation to bid on the job. We looked at each other in disbelief. We treated the prospective customer as a team member. We shared much with him. After six hours of consulting and three hours of travel time, I was faced with bidding for the job without opportunity to incorporate the time I had already invested in the project meeting with and educating this person. The printer faced a similar fate. We were snookered by a cut-throat, lowest-cost buyer who had led us down a path. Since the printer and I needed to cover our costs, our bids were above the bottom line price of the prospect's dredging operation. Ethics aside, neither of us got the job. But we did learn. We learned indeed.

When you agree to meet with a prospective customer, remember that you, too, may be facing an intelligence gatherer who has no intent of giving you the job unless you can meet or come under any and all competitor quotes. Cheap, unethical or uneducated sharks infest the business waters about you.

The point that I'm making is that every action related to winning a job has an associated cost. And meetings are often the hidden profit cruncher that make some jobs just not worth doing.

This is one reason some successful shops have two prices—one for the experienced, knowledgeable buyer, and a second, higher price for the complete novice. Time is truly money (into or out of your pocket). You must budget to cover all your costs. Then price to cover your budget and up to what the market will bear.

Agree to customer meetings with your eyes open. If you can, find the least expensive way to meet. Do a cost-benefit analysis. Do you know what the actual costs are for each meeting that you attend? Do you have an idea of the costs for each form of meeting that you can have—their site, your site, teleconference, videoconference, etc.? Are your meetings adding to the profitability of your business? Or are they merely another cost drain.

Here's a step-by-step approach to estimate how the costs of meetings relate to benefits for your company. This analysis can be kept in a spreadsheet file and used to plan for and track the cost of any meeting that you're considering.

As shown in Table 6-6, the information that you need includes: salaries of each person attending, fringe benefits, planning overhead costs, meeting overhead costs, desired profit and return on investment —for even a single meeting. In a minute, you'll see why even a single meeting is important to track.

Table 6-6. Costs associated with a one-hour meeting at a customer's site.

EMPLOYEE COSTS		HOURLY PAY
Computer Operator		$10.00
Designer		25.00
Project Manager		30.00
	TOTAL	$65.00
Salary Cost Per Hour		$65.00
Fringe Benefits (@38%)		24.70
HOURLY PAY & BENEFITS:		$89.70
PLANNING OVERHEAD		
Two hours prep for each person (200%)		
PLANNING OVERHEAD COST		$179.40
MEETING OVERHEAD		
Travel (30 miles @ 29¢/mile	$8.70	
Travel time (1 hour)	65.00	
Coffee (5 @ 90¢ ea)	4.50	
Laser printer paper (25 @ 25¢ ea)	6.25	
Overheads (6 @ 50¢ ea)	3.00	
MEETING OVERHEAD COST:		$87.45
PAY, BENEFITS AND OVERHEAD:		$356.55
PROFIT (planned at 10%)		$35.66
EXPECTED ROI (10%)		$35.66
TOTAL COSTS FOR ONE HOUR MEETING:		$427.87

First, estimate the costs of each person in your company who will attend the meeting. A $10-an-hour computer operator who sits in on a one-hour meeting costs the company $10 in labor. By listing all the attendees and their corresponding pay or salaries, you can have your spreadsheet calculate the total pay/salary cost per hour. If one makes $10 an hour, another $25 an hour and a third $30 an hour, your total salary cost per hour is $65.

Now add in the cost of fringe benefits—vacation pay, sick leave, dental and vision care, group health plans, retirement/pension plans and other added benefits that your company provides. Some costs such as payroll taxes, FICA, and SDI are not choices that you can make. They nevertheless must be included in your calculation. A good rule of thumb is to assume that your business has required deductions and fringe benefits that add about 38 percent to each person's hourly rate to form the total cost per employee. Thus, an employee earning $10 an hour actually costs your company $13.80 for each hour paid.

Program the spreadsheet to multiply the Salary Costs Per Hour by the percentage increase allocated to required deductions and benefits (in our case 38 percent). This results in a total pay and benefits cost of $89.70 for each hour of this meeting.

Next address the overhead costs associated with planning the meeting. How much time and materials does it take to get ready? This includes time spent discussing strategy, writing and designing the presentation, support by others, creating visuals, adjusting work schedules, and "invisible" expenses incurred by those who attend (e.g., interruptions away from another project).

Two hours of prep time for a one-hour meeting yields a planning overhead of 200 percent. If every person attending the meeting takes two hours to prepare, multiply the Hourly Pay & Benefits figure by two to get $179.40 as the preparation cost. If only one person must prepare, a major percentage is allocated to this person, and a minor percent (say 5 percent) can be allocated to each other attending staff member. For our example, we'll assume that all three people must prepare equally (hence $179.40). This moves us to the overhead issues related directly to meeting.

The meeting overhead costs can be defined as those expenses that everyone "sees" — transportation, equipment used, food and beverage, paper, transparencies, and other materials that are allocated to the meeting. One vehicle driven 30 miles, one hour of travel, five cups of coffee, 25 sheets of laser printer paper, and six overhead transparencies add to your meeting costs

In the example, a one-hour meeting with a prospective customer can cost over $400 (Table 5-2). This means that you must do all you can to make each meeting worthwhile. You can change the meeting length, use a different form of interface (e.g., teleconference), make planning less time-consuming, and have fewer people prepare for and attend. These affect your meeting costs.

It's sometimes tough to estimate the financial benefit of a meeting. What opportunity did you gain or lose by planning for and attending? Did the meeting actually produce a profit? Did the prospective customer come back to you months later and ask you to do a job that he felt you were best suited for because of what they learned at an earlier meeting? Was time saved because a face-to-face meeting clarified a misunderstanding by one or both parties? Did you obtain good market intelligence that helped you develop a successful strategy for penetrating a new area? Did the customer refer you to others who also benefited from your services?

To estimate the financial benefit, assign a value to each goal that you hope to achieve. If the meeting is to promote sales, did you indeed realize increased sales? By how much must you increase sales to make the meeting worthwhile? A job paying $325 after a meeting that cost $427.87 is hardly worth the effort—unless you also got follow-on jobs that let you amortize the meeting costs over more sales events.

If you meet to market your products and services, did you get their business? Since results from marketing can take weeks or months to materialize, you need a meeting model that will help you track the final outcome of each meeting. When you integrate intelligence snippets and referrals into your meeting tracker, your model can get complicated. And given the chaotic business lives that most of us face, your meeting model can be difficult to maintain. It's usually easier to take a macro view of the meeting process. Look at the big picture. Do you get the financial return from the time and effort spent? The analysis alone will show you how costly these events can be. If you can relate jobs won to a particular meeting or series of meetings, good.

Several years ago, Bernard DeKoven, director of the Institute for Better Meetings in Palo Alto developed a Meeting Meter program to display dynamically how much a meeting costs. The software is activated when the meeting begins and tallies up costs as the meeting progresses. It shows the destructive effects of arriving late and easily getting sidetracked during a meeting. Whether customer or colleague, metering your meetings can show the cost of interruptions, delays, and rambling.

And money is just one part of the cost. A discouraging meeting where frustration boils over into angry outbursts takes a toll on the attitudes and morale of those attending. Poor, useless meetings punish the participants. They bore people, they discourage people and make them so frustrated that it takes an hour or more to become productive and focused again.

Plan meetings better, make them effective, and you can significantly improve morale, mutual respect, and overall productivity. There's much that you can do to conduct effective meetings. Check your library and online services for other useful ideas.

If your customer is willing, start your meeting on time. Each meeting minute has an associated cost to both companies.

After the meeting, critique with your team. Discuss what you did right and where you can improve. Evaluate the success potential from the experience. Did you achieve your goals and objectives? Do both you and the customer feel good about the meeting?

On the day after the meeting, call the customer and thank them for their time. Discuss follow-up actions that you collectively should take. Go after their business while the opportunity is hot. Follow-up a week later may be too late to lock in the job.

Get on your computer and input information into your spreadsheet. Even a cost-benefit analysis—with all of it's detail—is well worth the effort. If you can rank your meetings in terms of financial payoff, you can link your meeting time and effort directly to the bottom line.

Set-up Fees

Time is money. Or at least you can earn money in each finite unit of it. But have you considered the time required to prepare to perform on a job?

If you've developed your own machine standards then you know how long it takes equipment to come up on line and be ready to perform. When you receive a disk from a customer, who asks for a high resolution printout, does your price incorporate the time it takes you to start the application, open the customer's file, set the output criteria and then command the system to produce printout?

Set-up times vary depending on the system and application program being used. You should incorporate set-up time in calculating the price for the first of each type of activity. For example, getting to the first page of printout can take four or five minutes. Subsequent pages of the same complexity can take a small fraction of this time.

Charging When Normal Time Limits are Exceeded

A related issue is the added time it takes for more complicated functions. For example, if an imagesetter takes between five and 10 minutes to produce film output, many shops charge a per minute rate for any output that takes more than 10 minutes to be produced. The type of RIP (raster image processor) installed will affect the output time.

For example, a desktop price list here on my desk says, "Output running longer than 10 minutes RIP Time will be charged at $60.00 per hour in 10 minute increments." Another desktop service bureau adds $1 per minute for pages requiring more than 10 minutes to output on a Linotronic L-300 imagesetter. They increase this per minute charge to $1.25 for using the L-530 and $1.50 per minute for the L-630. Our data suggests that the standard run time for imagesetting is five minutes for letter-size pages and 10 minutes for tabloid-size pages. Any printout taking longer than these benchmarks is charged at some set fee per minute.

I've seen this "added charge" concept applied to laser printer output. A local shop charges $1 per minute for run times exceeding five minutes on a 600 dpi laser printer. Therefore, if one customer wants text-only pages and another wants pages with heavy graphics, they pay different rates.

Charging a Minimum Rate

Although desktop publishing shops are slow to implement this concept, most service bureaus have a policy of charging a minimum price for any job. They realize that their objective is to earn revenue for every minute they work.

By setting a minimum price for their services, they also weed out many of the "one-zee, two-zee" type of low-volume jobs. If a person wants a single image scanned, they charge a minimum price regardless of their low quantity price. Thus they could advertise film imaging for $11.50 each in quantities of one to 10 with a $25 minimum per job. This encourages a buyer to purchase three films, increasing their revenue per sale to a profitable level.

Many shops set a minimum charge, but include free pick-up and delivery in the local area. A graphics business near me charges $10 minimum with no pick-up and delivery, but $20 minimum with free pick-up and delivery.

The idea is to guarantee at least minimum revenue for each sale while encouraging customers to purchase more that the minimum, effectively increasing the average dollars per sale.

Charging for Rush Jobs

There's an inherent inefficiency when work schedules are disrupted by customers who want service in less time than normal. If the typical workload comfortably accommodates scan completion in four hours, a customer who wants the disk containing scans now will impact work flow and schedule.

This person should be charged extra for the inconvenience to you—added convenience to them.

How are shops handling this issue? Table 6-7 lists

typical premiums by percent for five shops located geographically distant across North America.

Table 6-7. Rush charges for speedy service.

Standard Time	Less than 6 hours	Less than 4 hours	While-They-Wait
24 hours	25%	50%	100%
24 hours	-	50%	-
12 hours	50%	100%	-
24 hours	50%	-	100%
24 hours	50%	100%	150%

It boils down to how willing you are to work overtime to complete a job in the same day. Charging a premium for same-day service will provide incentive to work extras because it increases your income. Rush charges also cause prospective customers to re-think how fast they REALLY need the job done.

After instituting a premium charge for rush work, you'll find the added percentage on an invoice a nice perk for the extra pressure you endured.

The nicest thing about rush-rate premiums are their leveling impact on customer demands for "NOW response." "You want it now? Then, by George, you'd better be willing to pay the premium!"

Charging for Alterations and Corrections

A customer often only hears the first price quoted. Some grumble and argue when extra charges are added for changes—even when THEY are the reason that changes are made. You must be certain that your customers clearly understand that they will be charged for customer-directed (or customer-caused) changes. Then let them decide if what they are considering is really worth the added cost.

If your proof copy has errors, you should correct typographical or image errors without cost to the customer. But changes that vary from the original job specifications should be paid for by the customer. Perform to the original specs. Then, if the customer decides to alter the design, you charge for the additional work.

Alterations and corrections can be billed in various ways including by the word, by the line, by the correction, by the page or even by the job. If a customer insists on an hourly rate for handling alterations and corrections, quote an hourly fee that is lower than your standard shop rate. This makes the customer feel that they're getting a bargain (even though you still earn an acceptable profit).

Establish a shop policy for handling revisions and alterations. Many successful shops use a Design Acceptance form that they have their customers sign. This form establishes how changes or alterations will be handled. It becomes a basis of acceptance between buyer and seller. A sample design acceptance form is shown in Figure 6-2 on the next page.

Whenever you enter into an agreement with a customer, be certain that the agreement clearly specifies how many drafts will be covered by the contract. Also clearly specify when and how changes and alterations will be paid. If you agree to one complete rewrite, then state so in the agreement. Also state the charge that will apply when changes or alterations exceed the scope of the contract.

When it comes to making billable modifications to a design, there's an industry rule of thumb suggesting that you charge $2 to $5 for each change or correction that is directly caused by customer action (or inaction). This

ACCEPTANCE ACKNOWLEDGEMENT FORM

NOTICE: PLEASE READ CAREFULLY
If you O.K. errors shown on this proof without indicating what corrections are required, we cannot be held responsible.

If we make a mistake, and you indicate such on this proof, we will make the correction without charge to you.

But any changes or alterations that you make to your original specification will be charged to you at the rate of $_____ per _____.

A minimum of $_____ applies for any alterations or revisions.

Please acknowledge understanding of this policy by signing and dating this form.

I have carefully examined the attached proof and authorize you to proceed after making corrections and changes as noted on the proof.

Signed _____ Date _____

Figure 6-2. Changes and Alterations acceptance form.

includes changing typefaces and fonts, moving text, and shifting illustrations.

The key is to be paid for <u>everything</u> that you do. As described in *Desktop Production Standards*, there are some specific statements that you should print on your work order or work agreement form. It's important that both you and your customer know the ground rules and when additional charges will kick in. By getting the customer to read and sign these terms and conditions, and then to sign the acceptance of proof form, the lines of responsibility will be clear and defendable.

Summary

Pricing is a fascinating process. You can become successful and grow a thriving business by making certain that you are paid for each service that you provide. Don't let dollars fall between the cracks in a job. Get the most return for your efforts. Price with precision and charge for every service you provide.

7
Estimating, Bidding & Negotiating

"An estimate is NOT a bid."

The Basis for Good Estimating

Estimating combines art with science and business skills to produce a document that clearly describes project costs and provides sufficient funds for profit and return on investment.

In the world of estimating, there's no such thing as having too much information. The more information you have, the better your estimate.

In DTP shops and service bureaus, good estimating requires discipline and integrity. You must clearly understand your own staff and their capabilities before you can make a good forecast on time to perform and at what price you are willing to trade energy and expertise for customer need. It's critical to know how much time and material each operation actually requires. Estimating helps you use your true cost basis to determine the minimum price at which you can sell your services and still make some profit.

When a customer calls, asking for a verbal quote, many business managers can toss out a ballpark figure based on the customer's response to a series of questions and a detailed knowledge of the shop's capability. They use the cost per page or cost per piece concept. This doesn't make them accurate. It makes them responsive. It works on simple jobs. But for those real "money-makers," we need to accurately estimate the true costs to perform.

Three factors drive accurate estimating: job decomposition, team productivity, and estimating experience. The finer you partition a job into tasks—a process called *"functional decomposition"*—the easier it is to assign a difficulty weight and cost to each digestible piece. Breaking a large job down into simpler tasks is a form of "normalization." Every job is composed of a series of small tasks, and identifying each task makes project estimating much easier.

With each task functionally identified, you can then assign a difficulty weight to each of them. Some tasks will be complex, some difficult, some standard, and some easy. This step gets easier with experience and observation, but you must determine the rate at which a person should be able to complete each task. Then you can assign a time estimate and dollar value to the task.

Then factor in productivity. You should be tracking both shop productivity and the productivity of each employee. Shop productivity will be about 30-50%. The productivity of direct labor employees can be as high as 90 percent depending on the number of people on the staff and a myriad of motivational and attitudinal factors.

The final factor behind good estimating is experience. You get this by learning and by applying. As an estimator, you must clearly understand every task in each production center. You must also know the complexity of each software package that will be used—word processing, graphics, scan, OCR, layout and design, image manipulation, retouch, and even format conversion software. You should also understand how customer-generated files interface with your DTP and prepress software, how desktop publishing, mechanical art production, stats, and other prepress functions such as stripping all relate to the final product.

Before you can begin estimating a job, you must first possess a clear understanding of all the costs associated with performing on the project. You should have a good idea how long it takes to perform each task in your shop. Cost should be budgeted to an hourly figure. Use baseline standards as described in the last chapter, and be able to track your costs on a page-by-page and task-by-task basis. Then you can begin estimating in earnest.

Applied Estimating

With costs clearly defined and understood, you're ready to tackle estimating as a process. Your goal is to achieve a good hit rate on the quotes that you submit. Often a shop owner will have up to a dozen proposals in "the pipeline" waiting for prospective customer responses.

The only way to ensure satisfactory success in the proposal effort is to develop a quick and accurate way to estimate work. This means clearly specifying a job, checking the amount of work required before you can start, and having a way to deal with difficulty and complexity.

Specifying a Job

The process of estimating begins by clearly specifying a job. This means that you must gather all the information from the customer that you can. You want to specify each task that will be involved in completing the job. Then you'll develop a cost estimate using a worksheet form. There are various estimating programs on the market to help in this process.

Many factors must be considered when specifying a job—form of material provided, disk file formats, style sheets, skills required, special equipment, materials, required output, and how to handle additions and corrections,.

Every time you have an opportunity to quote on a job, it's important to clearly specify what is being requested. Job specifications provide details on each task to be performed—the number of text characters in the document, the estimated number of pages, the typefaces and fonts to be used, the graphics and photographs to be stripped in, the expected amount of graphic and image manipulation, the layout grid, and the type of output desired (laser paper, RC paper, film, etc.).

Some customers won't know what is possible in DTP design and production, so you may be educating and guiding your clients during the development of job specs. You'll have customers come in who have done little preliminary planning. Usually the graphic image or photo that they want to use is unrealistic or requires re-work or re-touching. It's critical that both you and your customer understand what job is being discussed and what final product to expect.

After gaining experience, you'll develop an ability to quickly ballpark the price for a job based on its characteristics.

Create a Form for Estimating

In your business, you'll find worksheets helpful—and in some cases very important. Most DTP shops and service bureaus construct a custom estimating worksheet. This form describes the job, the client and provides start and finish dates. Then it breaks the complete project into specific tasks. You'll probably find that you'll need an estimating form that is unique to your business. Figure 7-1a describes the activities associated with a job.

PROJECT RELATED COSTS

Indirect Costs
- meeting with a client
- communicating on the telephone
- communicating by fax or modem
- recording actions and times
- corresponding
- answering questions
- scheduling work

Direct Costs
- system power up
- program execution
- converting files to a useable form
- converting data for importing
- job preparation and setup
- downloading project data
- proofreading and spell checking
- editing
- text generation
- other keyboarding
- typography
- innovating a design concept
- developing a style sheet
- designing illustrations and artwork
- designing a logo
- designing clip art
- scanning art and photographs
- image manipulation and retouch
- developing a thumbnail layout
- creating a design
- implementing a design
- importing text and graphics
- importing clip art
- importing CD-ROM photographs
- more keyboarding
- adjusting the layout
- revising the draft design
- manual/electronic paste-up
- producing color proofs
- producing color separations
- typesetting/imagesetting
- generating camera ready output
- printing
- post printing

COSTS OF GOODS SOLD
- laser printer paper
- toner
- file conversion costs
- special typefaces and fonts
- stats
- illustrations
- film
- resin-coated paper
- telephone calls
- travel
- postage
- facsimile (fax)

Figure 7-1a. Costs related to a project.

Figure 7-1b shows a form for estimating project costs. List all the tasks associated with a job in a column on the left side of your form. In a column to the right of each task list the hours estimated and the price to charge for each hour or page. Usually, indirect and innovative times are billed at an hourly rate. Machine production times are often billed out on a per page basis.

On the far right, make a column to list the subtotal charge for each task. At the lower portion of the form, list each "out-of-pocket" expense. Add 10-20% to each of these expenses to cover administrative costs. Total all of the individual costs, and place this value in the lower right corner of your form. Remember that this is an estimate of what it will cost to do the job. If your hourly rates don't incorporate profit and ROI, you'll need to add a percentage for profit, and a percentage for return on investment to get a price on which you can base a quote.

Once your estimating form is complete, save your estimates of times and costs so you can compare these with actuals after project performance. This helps you refine your estimating skill. A spreadsheet program works well for performing this analysis.

PROJECT COST ESTIMATING FORM

PROJECT: _____ DATE: _____
CLIENT: _____

Indirect Costs   Hours x $/hour = Total/Task
  Proposal preparation
  Client kickoff meeting
  Follow-up meeting 1
  Follow-up meeting 2
  Draft submission meeting
  Final submission meeting
  Telephone calls with client
  Travel time
  Close-out project

Creative Costs Hours x $/hour = Total/Task
   Conceptual development
   Style template
   Manuscript preparation
   Writing copy
   Designing charts
   Designing graphs
   Designing tables
   Designing illustrations

Production Costs Qty x $/per ea = Total/Task
   Disk file conversion
   Manuscript download
   Spelling/Grammar checking
   Prepare/Format text
   Import text into layout program
   Typography
   Place graphics
   Layout document
   First draft
   Corrections/Alterations
   Paste-up
   Final proof

Out-of-Pocket Expenses Total
   File conversion support (____ files @ $___ ea)
   Laser proofs (____ @ $___ ea)
   Typeset output (____ @ $___ ea)
   Photographs (____ @ $___ ea)
   Illustrations (____ @ $___ ea)
   Stats (____ @ $___ ea)
   Color processing (____ @ $___ ea)
   Paste-up support
   Printing (____ cys @ $___ ea)
   Collating (____ shts @ $___ ea)
   Binding (____ pgs @ $___ ea)
   Travel (____ trips @ $___ ea)
   Delivery (____ trips @ $___ ea)
   Other

                Total Indirect Costs: _____
                Total Creative Costs: _____
                Total Production Costs: _____
                Total Out-of-Pocket Expenses: _____
                Shop Overhead Costs: _____

            TOTAL PROJECT COST:
                                            ======

Figure 7-1b. Sample Project Cost Estimating Form

Another approach is shown in Figure 7-2. Here the job is broken into functions and a percent difficulty is assigned to each function. Then cost and production rates are assigned for each activity and a total cost is calculated.

PROJECT TITLE

Specifications

Activities Required	# Pages at Each Difficulty Level		
	75%	100%	125%
Keyboarding	_____	_____	_____
Proofreading	_____	_____	_____
Scanning	_____	_____	_____
Retouch	_____	_____	_____
Design	_____	_____	_____
Layout	_____	_____	_____

Cost & Production Calculations

```
Keyboarding                                         COST/TIME EST
    75% Complexity:    _____ pages @ _____/page $_____  _____hrs
    100% Complexity:   _____ pages @ _____/page $_____  _____hrs
    125% Complexity:   _____ pages @ _____/page $_____  _____hrs
Proofreading
    75% Complexity:    _____ pages @ _____/page $_____  _____hrs
    100% Complexity:   _____ pages @ _____/page $_____  _____hrs
    125% Complexity:   _____ pages @ _____/page $_____  _____hrs
Scanning
    75% Complexity:    _____ scans @ _____/scans$_____  _____hrs
    100% Complexity:   _____ scans @ _____/scans$_____  _____hrs
    125% Complexity:   _____ scans @ _____/scans$_____  _____hrs
Retouch
    75% Complexity:    _____ images @ _____/each $_____  _____hrs
    100% Complexity:   _____ images @ _____/each $_____  _____hrs
    125% Complexity:   _____ images @ _____/each $_____  _____hrs
Design
    75% Complexity:    _____ pages @ _____/page $_____  _____hrs
    100% Complexity:   _____ pages @ _____/page $_____  _____hrs
    125% Complexity:   _____ pages @ _____/page $_____  _____hrs
Layout
    75% Complexity:    _____ pages @ _____/page $_____  _____hrs
    100% Complexity:   _____ pages @ _____/page $_____  _____hrs
    125% Complexity:   _____ pages @ _____/page $_____  _____hrs
Laser Print Output
    75% Complexity:    _____ pages @ _____/page $_____  _____hrs
    100% Complexity:   _____ pages @ _____/page $_____  _____hrs
    125% Complexity:   _____ pages @ _____/page $_____  _____hrs

                                TOTALS: $_____   _____ hrs
```

TOTAL COST: $_____

TOTAL TIME INVOLVED: _____ hours

NOTE: This estimate is for labor only. Materials are charged extra.

Figure 7-2. Cost estimating form.

So here's the concept. First develop production and machine standards. Then calculate budgeted hourly rates for each function performed in your shop. Establish a complexity rating for each function. Then develop an estimating form that uses your budgeted hourly rates and difficulty ratings to completely cost out a job.

Estimating Example - Brochure

Once you develop your own spreadsheet for estimating, you'll find yourself using it more and more. Figure 7-3 is an example of how the estimating form just described can be used to estimate a job to produce a six-panel brochure.

PROJECT TITLE: 6-Panel Brochure

Information Required
Characters to be keyboarded
Text characters or # final pages to proofread
Scans(grouped by size and difficulty)
Scans needing retouch
Pages to be designed
Pages for layout (group by complexity)
Pages to be laser printed

Specifications
2 pages - 8.5 x 11
2 colors each side (black & red)
3 panels each side
1800 characters to be keyboarded
4 graphic line art images to scan

CUSTOMER SUPPLIES
1. Concept drawing
2. Hand written text ideas
3. Line art drawings (4) on vellum

SHOP PROVIDES
1. Draft design for proofing
2. Camera ready art (4 separations @ 600 dpi)

QUESTIONS
1. Who corrects errors found in Preflight?
2. Who owns disk file containing design layout?

Estimating - 253

Activities	# Pages at Each Difficulty Level		
Required	75%	100%	125%
Keyboarding	2		
Proofreading	2		
Scanning		4	
Retouch		2	
Design			2
Layout		2	
Laser Printing	2	2	

Cost & Production Calculations

Keyboarding   COST   TIME EST
    75% Complexity: __2__ pages @ *$4.04/page* $8.08   0.2 hrs
    100% Complexity: ____ pages @ _____/page $_____ ____hrs
    125% Complexity: ____ pages @ _____/page $_____ ____hrs
Proofreading
    75% Complexity: __2__ pages @ *$13.50/page* $27.00   0.5 hrs
    100% Complexity: ____ pages @ _____/page $_____ ____hrs
    125% Complexity: ____ pages @ _____/page $_____ ____hrs
Scanning
    75% Complexity: ____ scans @ _____/scan $_____ ____hrs
    100% Complexity: __4__ scans @ *$10.00/scans* $40.00   0.8 hrs
    125% Complexity: ____ scans @ _____/scan $_____ ____hrs
Retouch
    75% Complexity: ____ images @ _____/each $_____ ____hrs
    100% Complexity: __2__ images @ *$15.00/each* $30.00   1.0 hrs
    125% Complexity: ____ images @ _____/each $_____ ____hrs
Design
    75% Complexity: ____ pages @ _____/page $_____ ____hrs
    100% Complexity: ____ pages @ _____/page $_____ ____hrs
    125% Complexity: __2__ pages @ *$54.13/page* $108.26   2.0 hrs
Layout
    75% Complexity: ____ pages @ _____/page $_____ ____hrs
    100% Complexity: __2__ pages @ *$29.43/page* $58.86   0.8 hrs
    125% Complexity: ____ pages @ _____/page $_____ ____hrs
Laser Print Output
    75% Complexity: __2__ pages @ *$0.019/page* $0.038   0.0055 hrs
    100% Complexity: __2__ pages @ *$0.026/page* $0.052   0.0055 hrs
    125% Complexity: ____ pages @ _____/page $_____ ____hrs

                               TOTALS: *$272.29*   5.31 hrs

TOTAL COST ESTIMATE: *$272.29*
TOTAL TIME INVOLVED: *5.31 hours*
AVERAGE COST PER HOUR: *$51.28*

NOTE: This estimate is for labor only. Materials are charged extra.

Figure 7-3. Cost estimation for six-panel brochure job.

The numbers on the form in Figure 7-3 aren't what's important. The key is the process. This is one way to generate an estimate on a job. To this estimate, you add profit and return on any investment to get the final target price that you quote. In this case, adding a 10 percent profit (assume your initial investment has been paid back) results in $299.52 that you quote.

A caveat. Your baseline production standards and cost basis determine what budgeted hourly rates and what specific production times are used in your calculation. Changing these can greatly affect the total cost estimate. It pays to do your homework well before you cost out a job. Many small business entrepreneurs do a poor job at this. Many bid "by the seat of their pants."

An Estimate is Not a Bid

A bid is an offer of price. It defines the dollar amount at which you are willing to exchange a product or service. Estimating and bidding are different.

In the optimum situation, an expert generates an estimate specifying all of the costs associated with a particular job. This estimating expert (called an *estimator* in larger companies) has no responsibility for setting the bid price or establishing profit. Instead, another person, probably a marketing type, independently establishes a rough bid price based on the competition, what the customer was charged last time, the work load, and the company's pricing strategy.

It is at this point, that the cost estimate and the rough bid price are compared. If the spread between the costs and the "could charge" is large, there is room to negotiate. If the spread is too narrow, the company may decide to pass on this job—or decide to live with the low margin for a strategic business-related reason.

Given the small staff in most desktop businesses, one person likely completes the cost estimate AND determines the price to bid.

However, the key here is that estimating and bidding are separate actions. An estimate is based on historical and empirical facts—actual performance averages and industry production standards. A bid price is based on judgement—interpretation of the external competition and the needs of the customer. Each process should be performed independently—not simultaneously— and then compared.

The key value of a cost estimate is that it should be used as a threshold for rejection on jobs that just don't provide enough profit to be worthwhile. The key value of a bid is that it defines the gross profit margin possible on a job. By clearly specifying costs and then bidding at what the market will bear, maximum profit will be realized.

Getting Bid Opportunities

Bid opportunities can be found everywhere. But you must be there when the opportunities arise, or you must make your prospective customers know that your support is available when their need arises.

To do this, keep prospects aware of who you are and what you can do. This can be accomplished by making cold calls in person, telemarketing, networking at trade shows and professional associations meetings, advertising in magazines, newspapers, flyers, inserts, and door hangers, going on-line, and by having your current customers, vendors, or colleagues tell others about your business.

The appendix to this guide provides valuable insights into what lead-generation method worked best for the businesses that participated in our recent survey.

For those interested in doing business with the government, get on a Qualified Bidders List. Contact the purchasing offices for each government organization that you want to serve. Once you get on their list, you may have to update your qualification each year to remain listed.

Be aware that government jobs may be plentiful, but the payment schedule is typically complex and slow. More than just a few businesses have folded after putting too many eggs (jobs) into the government basket and having extended payments restrict their cash flow too long to survive. You should spread your work over as many customer types as possible. A rule of thumb is that no more than 50 percent of your customers should be government-related organizations. Smaller businesses pay faster. They understand cash flow better.

Once you're on a qualified bidders list, you'll occasionally receive a *request for quote (RFQ)*, or *request for bid (RFB)* from one of your prospective government customers. These are similar documents. The buyer wants you to bid on a job or to bid on selling a specific product. Request for quotes are often used for product purchases. Request for bids are usually associated with service contracts.

The government organization could also issue a *request for information (RFI)* as a data gathering step prior to proceeding to the proposal and contract stages. When the buyer has a good idea what they want to purchase, government offices, large corporations and educational institutions may go out for bid using a *request for proposal (RFP)*. With the RFP, the client is asking that you generate and submit a proposal to perform specific work. The RFP results in an *invitation for bid (IFB)*, and this leads to the award of a contract to perform. For most small shops, the RFB is more common than the other buying documents.

A request for bid can come at any time—especially if you keep your company's name on a qualified bidders list. Typically the RFB will include a written statement of the job requirements and an indication of how long you have to respond. A good RFB provides a basis for understanding and on which you can make contractual commitments.

The request package should establish a competitive environment between proposed vendors. It's used by the client to develop a legally binding contract. Responding to an RFB places you in a competitive position where the price that you quote is usually less than the price you can give to individual prospects coming in off the street.

Responding to a Request for Bid

You can't make a commitment on response time and the form of output product or service without a detailed description of the complete job. Each aspect of the job must be itemized. All required specifications should be included in the bid request package that you receive. If they aren't, then ask.

Each task in the Statement of Work should be clear and concise. Each deliverable must be defined and described. If the customer didn't provide it in their RFB, include in your response your terms and conditions that tie payments to the acceptance of deliverables. Therefore, acceptance criteria must also be clearly cited.

In addition, the RFB should clearly explain what actions or conditions could void the agreement and any criteria for accepting one bid over another based on some factor other than price.

Some RFBs ask you to submit samples of past work. This is a good reason to make extra copies of those "really nice jobs" that have been very successful.

If the RFB asks for references, be sure to check with your clients before you put their name and telephone number on your bid response. You want strong supporters and very satisfied customers on your reference list.

The RFB should include a procedure for getting answers to questions, and it should identify the cutoff date and time, and where to return the bid.

Developing a bid response is time consuming, but once you master the process, you should be able to generate a bid quickly and professionally. Your word processor and spreadsheet programs are valuable tools in this process.

Your proposal should be clear and concise. Don't assume that your client understands any specification that was omitted in their RFB. Cover each aspect of the job and cover all the contingencies that you can imagine. Remember: Murphy is alive and well in the world of contract performance.

A final comment concerns the look and feel of your bid package. A professional look can impact its acceptance. Your bid package is often a prospective customer's first look at you and your work. Sloppy bid packages make for infrequent contract awards. Spend the time and money to give it the look of quality.

I put one bid in an expensive ($22) binder, where each sheet slid into a protective plastic holder. I got the job.

Symptoms of a Poor Bid Response

There are six things that can get you labelled non-responsive on a bid request.

1. You can fail to meet the terms specified in the RFB.
2. You may not be able to back up what you claim.
3. Your references may not be suitable.
4. You may be recommending a sub-optimum solution.
5. You may fail to consider the complete job,.
6. You may fail to consider a customer's actual needs.

When submitting your bid package, be certain that you have covered each of these factors. I go through each request and highlight the specific things that the customer wants. Then I make certain that each deliverable is clearly addressed in my response.

Bidding Against the Alligators

Estimating gives you a good feel for the potential net profit in a job. It's based on fact. Estimating is a science. Bidding is how you use your estimate. Bidding is based on diplomacy, tack, and skill. Bidding is an art.

There are many ways to bid a job. Just be certain that you don't bid too low. New desktop business owners tend to undercharge. They risk ending up with clients who feel that they don't have to pay much for your work. When these entrepreneurs become aware, they find that they must re-educate these clients or drop them and find new ones.

Desktop publishing and prepress mean different things to different customers. The wide range of talent and available skills makes comparing apples-to-apples difficult. You may estimate and bid based on logical analysis and clear understanding of what a job requires. A competitor may be just starting out—be completely naive, be business illiterate, or be after every customer that comes along. So they may bid aggressively and LOW. You're shocked by what they quote to do a job. You feel certain that they're not earning a living from their cutthroat pricing. You know that they'll be out of business within a year. Yet these types of competitors seem to flow endlessly out of the woodwork.

The primary reason that new businesses bid so low is that they haven't the foggiest idea what they should be charging. They look around at their competition and then set their rates far below everyone else.

As they wonder why they can't seem to make money in their business, you shake your head and move on to the next proposal. But should you? Perhaps you could help everyone in our profession by speaking with the low bidder. They may appreciate your words of wisdom. If they don't, call the customer to assure them of your support in case the shop that they selected fails to perform satisfactorily. It may be that the IRS will shut that competitor's doors long before delivery is made on the contract. This could be a golden opportunity for you. One customer was extremely upset because we couldn't deliver results overnight on a particularly complex job. They threatened to go elsewhere. We invited them to do so and even offered to give them names of competitors who performed similar services. After a week, the customer came back to us. The other shops that they contacted could not perform quality work and also could not deliver overnight as they had claimed.

Although desktop service is maturing, there are still enough alligators in the swamp to make estimating part magic. Hard disk drives still crash (usually at the most inopportune times) and incompatibility still rears its ugly head when we try to "improve" our system software.

If you've never performed cost analysis and have never met the "alligators," you can make some disastrous bids. The "new kids on the street" often learn by failing. There is a better way—careful cost analysis and street-smart pricing.

The Case for Market-Based Bidding

There are many factors on which you can base a quote for desktop services. Each adds advantage. Each adds some limitation. Knowing which factors to use takes time, experience and courage.

Many desktop shops price products and services as though they operate in a regulated economy. Each owner will add a mark-up to the costs and then price a job. These cost-driven owner-operators often multiply production standards by industry or custom cost rates to establish a baseline. Then they add mark-up to achieve the target price to quote. In fact, some industry standard tables already incorporate mark-up directly into each suggested price.

Quoting a job based on standard rates is relatively easy. But quoting a job based on market conditions may be more profitable. In a market-driven approach, you bid based on what the market will bear. You are constrained by what your competition is doing, but markup has little affect on your price.

The cost-driven entrepreneur establishes a quote using internal expenses. These costs are accepted as a given in this formula. Job prices are driven primarily by the expenses involved.

The market-driven entrepreneur uses the market place as the driving factor in price. Market driven estimators focus on knowing the competition and being sensitive to the perceived value of their work. By performing competitive pricing and customer value analysis, profitability can rise even while general prices decrease.

Successful desktop shop owners work hard to increase productivity and efficiency. They consistently strive to cut costs and reduce overhead. They seek ways to gain an edge over their competition by making their products or services unique. And they price jobs to optimize the use of all of their resources (people, equipment, software, facilities, and time).

The productivity of both the shop and of the employees becomes critical in this formula. Market price variations are countered by accommodating them internally in capital equipment and in business operation.

Most shops use both job cost estimating and market analysis to help determine price. Job cost estimating is one of your business tools. Some tools are better than others. Estimating a job based on cost predictions can provide a rough idea of potential profit, but it doesn't show how much you could be charging for the same job. Job cost estimating is best used to help weed out unprofitable jobs—to know when to decline (no-bid) work. It's a good analysis tool for making rejection judgements. Job cost estimating helps you determine your "rock-bottom" price.

The best approach is to use job cost estimating to establish your lowest price while using market forces to establish your top end bid. Use cost estimating tools to determine your break-even and to guide your bid decisions. But make your bid based on the maximum price that you can get in the current market condition.

In a recent *MSM* magazine article, Dan Evans, founder of a sales training and marketing development company, described a strong correlation between the actions to match the specific needs of a customer to your shop's capability and a successful sale. He says that the more specific you get about how your products or services will benefit a customer, the stronger this correlation becomes. Evans also points out that large contracts are lost or won during the probing of fact finding and the need-satisfaction process that occurs before your client has a chance to order. Therefore, ask questions, evaluate, match your products and services to the customer's needs, and then, if what you offer matches their needs, ask for the business.

If your market analysis suggests that you can succeed with much higher prices, go slow. Don't change your prices radically or you'll send shock waves through your customer base. Even if you improve your operation, continue to use the old base estimating standard to give you negotiating room during the bid process. You can back off on your quote without having to lower it to near break-even. Remember that your cost basis determines the minimum price at which you can accept a job and still make money. It does not define the maximum price at which you'd like to quote and be awarded a job. This is relegated to market-driven pricing.

Price is determined using external information. What you estimate and choose to quote is determined by analyzing conditions outside your company. By comparing price against estimated costs you can quickly determine the available margin.

If market-driven pricing consistently results in unattractive profit margin, you should analyze your operation to find ways to improve efficiency. Perhaps you're using obsolete equipment or out-dated software. Perhaps you need to reorganize your shop according to process flow so the work moves through your business in an optimal path. It could be that your overhead is too high and must be pared down. And it could be that you are simply expecting too much profit from a low margin world.

As productivity specialist, Roger Dickeson puts it: "You'd be ahead to dump the cost tables and load a price laundry list in your Macintosh and use the keyboard like they do at Burger King to pump out a quote. Be a quick pricer. But you'd better competitive-shop Hardee's and McDonald's to keep your computer price list updated for a quarter-pounder."

Submitting a Formal Quote

When a client asks for a formal bid, provide your response in writing. Usually this is done on office letterhead. Your bid should partition the job into broad categories and provide a bottom line price.

Figure 7-4 on the next page is an example of a quotation form that you can adopt for your own business.

```
                    YOUR BUSINESS NAME
                         Quotation
                      (Good for 30 days)
          To:    ABC Company              Date: _____
                 1177 Happiness Lane
                 Pleasant Valley, NY 11011
          For:
                      (describe project)
          1.                                    $
          2.                                    $

                       (describe tasks)
          3.                                    $
          4.                                    $
          5.                                    $


                                    Total:  $

          Accepted: _____    Date: _____

          This estimate is based on current labor and materials costs for the work
          described. Final prices are subject to revision if costs or specifications
          change. Alterations, and customer-directed changes will incur extra charges.
```

Figure 7-4. A sample formal quotation form.

Be sure to include a description of what the client will do and what the shop will do. Describe the terms and conditions under which the work will be performed. Standard terms and conditions are described in detail in our special report: *Desktop Production Standards*.

Include a caveat that your price quote is based on typical performance schedules. If your client wants faster response, you can put a RUSH on the job. Usually, this expedite action results in a 25-50% increase in the invoice billing.

Negotiating Techniques

The moment negotiations start, new business owners begin a process of becoming "seasoned under fire"—they occasionally "getting burned." But they learn. And the lessons can be relatively painless or excruciating trauma. Much depends on how well they prepare.

Each side in a negotiation wants to maximize its own position. However, negotiations should not be perceived as a form of mutual sacrifice. In this activity, buying and selling become opposite sides of the same coin. Negotiations produce the formula that helps both sides maximize their own interests. This process should result in everyone leaving the table a winner.

Your challenge is to find an arrangement that lets everyone win. The customer knows that you must make a profit in order to stay in business (although they don't like to admit this). And you know that each customer has a finite budget within which to operate.

Negotiation is a continuing process. No issues are irrevocable—even after agreements are reached and signatures are placed on paper. Both the buyer and the seller should understand and accept the business needs of the other party. And each should be flexible and willing to look at alternatives.

Cooperation creates harmony, and competition creates efficiency. The best negotiators don't try to manipulate. They try to understand and work out a mutual solution.

The problems occur when you discover that you are negotiating with a party that doesn't have the business ethics that you believe in and demonstrate. They push, cajole, persuade, and do their best to manipulate you to accept their rigid views and demands. Their actions stimulate the street smarts that you learned by being "burned" before (or by reading about and accepting what others have experienced).

How can you successfully negotiate a job so both you and your customer come out on top? First, do your homework. You not only need to know your job, but you also must know about the business that your customer is in. You must know what importance (and priority) your customer places on quality, form, substance, delivery, and price.

Then you need to understand what issues can be negotiated. These include:

- price
- terms
- delivery
- tasks
- materials
- time schedule
- level of service
- output form
- output quality
- warranty
- follow-on jobs

Identify your goals. What is it you want to accomplish? What is the minimum price at which you will accept the job? What is the highest price you think you can charge? Understanding and timing can be everything in this process.

If you can get a client to reveal the budget that they have for a job, you can use this as a yardstick for how far you can go with your bid. Try not to come in too low or too high relative to their budget.

From the moment you and your customer first communicate, you are negotiating. This means that you must be prepared to discuss service and support from the start. A chance encounter at an airport, in the line at the post office, or even during a business association meeting can become the beginning stage in the negotiation process.

From this point on, you move in a complex maze of tactics, strategies, and discussions. It helps to have previewed the issues that could be introduced during the process. You can do this by developing a response map to help you think out and structure answers to each question that might be posed.

The next time you meet, be certain that the right party is present. Negotiate with the decision maker, not the messenger.

Whether follow-on meetings occur at your shop or at the office of your customer, you should identify the issues that both sides accept and those issues that must be negotiated. Ask questions, and keep an open mind. Your questions should establish need, concern, and resistance. Your attitude should reflect a willingness to find a workable formula.

Listening is critical in this process. Learn where your prospect is and where they want to go with the project. And remember. You can't learn when you're talking. You must listen. Listen and observe first. Talk later.

Through dialogue and attentive listening, you can establish issues and create alternatives for your prospective customer. Neutral issues are usually handled quickly. For those issues that must be negotiated, have available alternative solutions—designs, terms, package deals, quality, quantity, and prices.

There are many formulas defining how a job can be performed and delivered. Be open to discussing different alternatives. Just be certain that both of you are speaking the same language. You should quickly overcome semantic and technical language difficulties. If you each have a different perception of a camera ready proof, clarity and agreement must be achieved before you can proceed. Produce a sample proof that is acceptable to both sides. This then becomes the criteria for suitability.

You should never begin negotiations unless you are willing to walk away. You need emotional detachment and a tough mental attitude to achieve your own negotiating objectives. The party who wants to deal the most, will deal from a disadvantage. So even if you desperately want that job, don't let the other party sense this. Be patient, but hold to a high standard of value for yourself and your shop's capability and performance.

The idea is not to close doors or limit what each will do based on the negotiation, but to clearly convey that you are providing quality service. You want open and friendly discourse. Therefore, try to clearly understand what they want and need. Then help them understand what you want and what you can provide.

Ask for more than you expect to get. This lets you give up less important issues while retaining the larger issues. If they want you to concede on some issues, give in slowly and reluctantly. But get something in return for each issue that you concede.

Be certain what issues you are willing to concede. Also know when you will be willing to make these concessions. You don't want to be the first to make a major concession because this puts you in an inferior position. Instead, give on small concessions slowly. A small concession that you give up reluctantly can seem like a greater win for the other side than it really is.

Try to keep the quote at a "whole job" level. If they want to break up each task into cost elements, they could be planning to "nickel and dime" you out of significant profit by negotiating each issue separately.

If they change the scope of the job, and increase the volume of work, be open to offering a volume discount. Many shop owners reduce their prices between five and 15 percent for quantity buys. If they don't ask for it, don't offer it, unless you are trading for something else during the negotiation.

Remain reasonable and stick to facts. This can encourage your prospect to accept the reality of the costs involved in providing the service or support that they seek. By getting them to understand your position, you can often get them to support your case and accept a price closer to what you want.

If they ask a question, be certain that you understand what they are actually asking. Have them repeat the question if you aren't sure what they really mean. Then only answer the question asked. A sharp negotiator will try to get you to talk more because it strokes your ego while it provides them information that they might use against you later in the negotiation process.

Instead, do the opposite. Listen more. Play dumb. Ask them to explain points and issues. Appeal to their knowledge of the subject matter. Build their ego so you can build a bridge to early agreement.

When they make their first offer, don't accept it—even if it is a great deal. When you feel like saying "yes," say "no." This serves as a sanity check for the actual bottom line of the other party.

Several important elements affect the final price that you reach—the payment terms and schedule, maintaining a lead over your competition, maintaining your work load near capacity, full employment for you and your staff, future business, and market timing.

The final price should not be unilateral. It should represent the consideration of both sides in the negotiation. It should be a win-win compromise where both parties come away satisfied. The agreement should not be a "splitting of differences" in which someone may remain dissatisfied.

Usually, a realistic price is realized long before the subject is directly addressed. At that point, asking your price becomes almost a ritual. You should never give your prospect the feeling that they have asked too little or demanded too much. Always treat them (and their package) with respect. No matter how great a win you achieved, always protect their ego. Help them save face. Treat the agreement as a true win-win for both parties.

When you do present your bid, show confidence and pride that you are agreeing to do the job at a price that is best for both parties.

If you just cannot come in below their target budget, see if they can do some of the work themselves. Perhaps they can do their own collating, or comb binding. Perhaps they can provide paper, bindings, disks, boards, or other required materials.

If this approach won't work, firmly, but gracefully announce an impasse and close the negotiations. Keep the options open to negotiate on other business opportunities in the days and weeks ahead. They just might call tomorrow and give you a better final offer on this same job. Don't burn your bridges. Your competitors may have been judged less qualified or responsive causing your bid to look better (at your price). You could win the job just by being open to future opportunities to bid.

Using Body Language

Much of the message that a negotiating customer conveys will come in the form of nonverbal communication—in the gestures and body language that they use, in the tone of their voice, in the way they move, and in the direction they look when you ask certain pointed questions.

With competition increasing, you need every possible tool to maximize your own profit potential. It's often not what you say that makes an influence on others; it's what you don't say. The signals that you send nonverbally suggest attitude, empathy, understanding and ethics.

Psychologists claim that 93 percent of emotion is communicated nonverbally. Most people literally "hang their emotions on their sleeves." If you can learn how to read their emotion—their body language, you can use this knowledge to lead them into accepting your proposal.

The master speaker, S.I. Hyikowa once commented that "In this era of television, image is more important than substance." Some say that Richard Nixon won the presidency because he was a master at using color to convey character. He wore a dark blue suit at a television debate in which the set background was light blue. The light blue background with Nixon in his dark blue suit produced an aura of honesty, integrity and sincerity. He won that election.

The moment a prospective customer approaches, they judge you by what they see and feel—facial expressions, gestures, posture, enthusiasm, etc. The process takes less than 10 seconds but the impression is permanent. Whether you make or break a sales opportunity can literally depend on the silent signals that you send.

It's critical for shop owners today to understand and use body language. Oriental business people are expert at using nonverbal signals. This ability makes them formidable negotiators. Most American's fail to recognize and use body language, although women are inherently better at sensing emotion and intent than men.

The human body can produce over 700,000 unique movements. These have been partitioned into about 60 discrete symbolic signals and around 60 gestures. A nodding head can signal yes. Pointing two fingers at your eyes can mean "watch me." Running your fingers through your hair can indicate frustration.

Some nonverbal communication can mean different things. Crossed arms can indicate defensiveness. It can also be a comfortable way to stand or sit. Touching the nose can suggest doubt in what the person is hearing. It could also be a response to an itch or soreness from a recent cold. Likewise, an unbuttoned jacket can signify openness and cooperation. But it could also be because an overweight person is trying to fit into an old suit.

Figure 7-5. Suggests closed to business.

The key is to take each nonverbal signal as a flag, not as a complete message. Look for a pattern of signals that mean the same thing. The body language should match the verbal expressions. It should match the context of what is happening in the situation. Body language should be read in clusters of signals with common meanings. It's critical in sales success. Once you understand body language, you can use this knowledge and actually sell using your voice *and* your body.

Use gestures and speak with a confident voice consistent with the conditions. Many negotiators adopt a "matter-of-fact" tone of voice. They use neutral terms that don't incorporate value judgements. Yet they're still open to explore many alternative solutions. The idea is to watch for those nonverbal messages from the moment you enter the negotiating room.

It starts with the handshake. A handshake can be soft, firm, brief, long, and sometimes painful. The way you shake hands gives clues to your personality. Aggressive people have firm handshakes. People with low self esteem often have a limp handshake. Politicians typically shake one hand while holding the same hand or elbow with their other hand (so you can't twist away, I suppose). Men often squeeze the hand of a woman causing the smart woman to move her index and little finger in toward her palm preventing a crushing handshake. Men like to feel powerful.

As a business person trying to sell, you should adopt a handshake that is firm, yet not crushing. You want to convey confidence and professionalism, not macho dominance.

Next, watch your posture. A slouch conveys lack of confidence. Standing straight with your weight balanced on each foot makes you look confident and relaxed. When you sit, sit up straight; don't slouch.

Rather than saying "Trust me," convey the message "I can be trusted" by how you use your body. Honest people have a mannerism that conveys honesty. Even animals sense this. One particular mannerism is that honest people show their palms more than dishonest people do. Holding a hand out to a dog with the palm down conveys dominance to the dog. It may snap at you if it doesn't know you. Reaching out to shake a negotiator's hand with your palm down conveys the same thing. Showing an open hand with palm up conveys honesty and sincerity. To an animal it conveys trust. Hands thrust into pockets convey hidden agenda or secretiveness. Show the palms. Help build trust.

The open hands with palms showing should be accompanied with an open posture and a sincere facial expression. Your arms should be unfolded, not crossed in defensiveness. And your eyes should be steadily focused on the customer. Darting eyes suggest deceit. Looking left as you speak conveys truth. Looking right when you speak conveys dishonesty. Always refrain from looking down when you speak.

Figure 7-6. An open palm is a good sign.

And get rid of the sunglasses. Dark glasses prevent a customer from seeing your eyes and "reading your soul." A person's eyes cannot hide a dishonest intent.

My best advice to women is to go with your feelings. Women have an innate ability to receive messages to both their right and left brains simultaneously. They can sense and they can feel emotion in others. A woman can "tell" if you're being insincere. Unfortunately, some women don't follow their instincts. This has gotten them in trouble. Your "sixth sense" is the part of your being that tunes in on nonverbal messages. Learn how to read these, and you'll substantially increase your sales success.

When you face a customer, use honest, open gestures. Outward and upward movements of the hands are positive actions. Putting the tips of the fingers on one hand against the tips of the fingers on the other is a form of "steepling" that conveys confidence.

Clasping your hands behind your head as you recline back in a chair can suggest arrogance and turn people off. Placing your hands on each side of your waist is called "standing at the ready." It conveys confidence and attracts others. This is why many catalog models are photographed in this pose as they show off new outfits.

Just by unbuttoning or opening a jacket in front of a customer will signify an open attitude—that you're willing to talk, to negotiate. Taking off your jacket is really powerful. And rolling your shirt sleeves part way up suggests that you're ready to get down to the final price.

As you talk with a prospective customer, watch their body language. If they cross their arms, use positive signals and words that will cause them to unfold their arms and become open to your sales approach. If their arms and legs are uncrossed and their hands are open, you're on track.

Figure 7-7. Watch for "mirroring" of your gestures.

When you notice them "mirroring" your movements and gestures, you've got them locked on your presentation. Mirroring indicates that there is maximum communication occurring between the two of you. If you move your arms apart, opening your palms, and they do the same, you are acting as one— synchronized. The messages and the words of the sale are being received and accepted by the other.

Try the technique called "tracking" to open them to your sales offer. Mirror their body language. Then gradually move them toward a more positive posture and psychological openness. As they shift their posture to mimic yours, their attitudes will shift, and you can close on the sale.

If they begin to cover their mouth, touch their nose or touch near an eye, they are withdrawing. Something that you said has turned them off. You must back up and resell using another approach. Gently re-focus on the prospective customer. Encourage them to share their concern. Open your palms to them and occasionally touch a palm to your chest as you speak. This is a strong signal of honesty. I was "told" by a deaf person that the way to tell if a signing person is actually deaf is to notice if they touch themselves. A hearing person will sign words, but seldom touch the body. A deaf person often touches their chest as they sign. The same with sincere statements. Touching a palm to the chest usually doesn't occur unless a person is expressing an honest opinion.

Avoid fidgeting or appearing nervous. Even if this is the first serious shopper in a week, you must act as though your business plate if relatively full. If they appear defensive or hostile, don't react in like manner. Use all positive signals. Lean slightly forward to put energy into the conversation. Open your hands and spread your arms with your palms up.

The old adage "Don't point" can be repeated here. Pointing at a person is an aggressive act. In my classes on communication skills, I present dozens of magazine photographs showing political leaders pointing at each other or chopping their hands down in a defiant gesture. Don't antagonize. Sell.

Think of your customer interaction as a traffic signal. Positive nonverbal messages signal "green" to go ahead and approach a close on the sale.

If the customer's body language transitions from positive to defensive or non-believing, the signal is "yellow" and caution must be observed. Slow down and advance carefully. Try to get them to exhibit openness.

A defiant, arms and legs "double-cross" with a scowl on their face is a definite "red" signal. You cannot approach closing negotiations unless you have a "green" light. If you can get your prospective customer to mirror your movements they'll be in synch with your presentation and receptive to closing on a sale.

If you are still unable to close, thank the person for the opportunity to bid. Approach sales like renting an apartment. It typically takes five showings before a rental is achieved. Likewise, it can take up to five inquiries before you close on a project. If that prospect is number four, the next person to call should be the one that buys. And the person who decided not to buy today, will consider you again if they are left with a positive impression of you and your shop. Impress them with your shop's professionalism and integrity.

Finally, don't get discouraged when a prospect decides not to buy. Your attitude can affect future sales. Take "turn downs" in stride. Use your body in the selling process and keep upbeat. If you believe in your product and the quality of your work, others will too. A positive, honest message conveyed by your nonverbal body language will win far more jobs than you think.

Using body language to move prospects from suspicion to being open and receptive can sway "fence-sitters" into buying. You can also use body language to calm hostile clients who are upset with mistakes or miscommunication even when it's actually their fault.

So, buy books on body language and nonverbal communications. Take a course at a local college. Learn how to read the signals. Then look in the mirror more. Watch how you appear when speaking on the phone or talking with someone else. Look for the signals that indicate openness. Watch the customers and follow their cues. Smile from within and without. They'll sense this and be comforted.

Be ready. As your customer's become more informed, they may just start using body language to read YOU like a book.

Getting Help on the Negotiation Process

You can significantly increase your success in the negotiation process by reading, studying, and practicing. One of the best teachers of negotiation has been Gerard Nierenberg. His book *The Art of Negotiation* and corresponding audio tape series are available through Nightingale-Conant Corporation, 7300 North Lehigh Ave., Chicago, IL 60648, (800) 323-5552.

Gerard's son, Roy recently developed a PC program with the same title as his father's book. Roy's software package works on MS-DOS computers. It helps you prepare for a negotiating session by presenting questions that force you to define and plan a strategy. The questions and answers can be ordered the way you want and printed out as a checklist that you can use during negotiations.

The program is available from Experience in Software, 2039 Shattuck Ave., Suite. 401, Berkeley, CA 94704, (415) 644-0694.

Put the Agreement in Writing

When you and your customer agree on performance and price, get your agreement in writing. The document you use can be an Agreement, a Contract, or even a Purchase Order. Just be certain that you both sign your names on a document confirming what you agreed during formal negotiations.

Be sure that each issue that you discussed and worked out is clearly described in the document. Be certain that it covers all aspects of the job.

List the specific tasks that will be performed on the job. With each task listed, identify who is responsible. Some tasks will be the responsibility of your customer (e.g., provide art and photos by a certain date and time). The majority of tasks will be performed by you and your staff. However, late delivery of the initial disks, art, or rough documents by your customer can affect the quality and schedule of your own performance.

Indicate when you will make delivery of a draft copy, the number of edit revisions allowed without added charges, how graphics will be received and handled, and when alteration charges will occur.

Allow flexibility for the customer to make changes (chargeable, of course) during the design process. Impromptu changes by a vacillating customer can create havoc when there isn't a clear understanding of change versus complete re-design alteration and the number and scope of changes allowed before extra charges apply. Design changes by waffling customers can be a lucrative way to increase job profits, but be certain that your customers are aware that their indecision and tendency to change are adding to the total job cost.

If any point is not listed on the agreement document, write it in. Each party should initial acceptance of the addition on both copies of the original agreement. The same goes for incorrect statements. Mark your changes on the original agreement forms. Then, both of you initial your acceptance. This eventually results in a document-pair that represents everything that the two parties agreed should occur.

The agreement should list each company's name, address and telephone number, and a point of contact for each party. For large companies, include their purchase order number (if provided). At this point, both parties should sign and keep a copy of the agreement.

With your signed copy in hand, begin work, and do your best to perform exactly as agreed or better. Remember the advice on early delivery. You want repeat business, and here's your chance to build a lasting relationship. Just don't inconvenience the customer by delivering too early.

Omissions in Many "Standard" Contracts

Potential problems can occur when critical factors are not included in a work agreement or contract for services. These omissions are like holes in "Swiss cheese." They become openings through which misunderstanding and poor perceived performance can flow out of a relationship. To avoid problems, be careful to:
1. Clearly specify the deliverables.
2. Tie payments to the acceptance of deliverables. (It's normal to get a 10-33% deposit on large jobs.)
3. Use wording that adequately covers defects and correction procedures.
4. Specify what customer actions will void your warranty.

5. Incorporate specifics on task descriptions, responsibilities, and schedule dates in the proposal and subsequent contract.
6. Provide fail-safe dates and provisions to cancel the contract if either party is unable to perform for an extended period of time.
7. Specify whether additional materials are being provided or will be charged extra.
8. Specify legal remedies if your customer "goes south" on you and refuses to pay. You'll appreciate having a clause in your "contract" that specifies that if you take legal action against them, whoever wins the case can recover all legal costs involved.

Forgetting any of these factors can set you on a risky course through rock-strewn waters. You may be able to navigate through, but it's much easier when the course is well established.

Follow Up On Your Estimates

Following up to determine how close an estimate came to reality is one of the most profitable things an estimator can do. Good follow-up produces a methodical comparison between initial cost figures and actual costs accrued during performance.

Careful follow-up will highlight deficiencies in your estimating strategy. It helps you spot loopholes and errors. It is also a way to confirm that all jobs have been estimated accurately. This process fine-tunes your estimating process and helps you avoid errors in future efforts.

By comparing actual costs with the expected costs, you are forcing yourself to apply critical reasoning and careful analysis to the process. You can't affect jobs that have been awarded, but you can certainly adjust your numbers and improve your win ratio on future opportunities.

Some professional estimators set performance goals for themselves. They try to get their cost estimates to come is within five percent of actual costs. A good ballpark range is three-to-five-percent accuracy.

As with most aspects of business, a computer spreadsheet is a valuable tool to use in performing post-production analysis.

When Estimating Your Next Job

Desktop publishers sometimes overlook important factors when preparing their estimate and quote package. Here are some things to remember when you prepare your next estimate.

Style Sheet. Establish a separate price for developing the style sheet. This part of the process can be time-consuming and involve a detailed understanding of layout and style sheet development.

Additions, Alterations and Corrections. Know in advance how you will handle the customer's alterations, printer's alterations, and customer-directed changes. Both you and your customer should know when additional charges will occur?

Job Characteristic. Pricing design work depends on the complexity of the job. A document with consistent layout can be priced at a different dollar amount than one with lots of design elements. Your budgeted hourly rate calculations help here.

Copyright. Usually when a business is hired to design a document, or some other form of product, the final product belongs to the client. They pay you for a service. You are essentially operating as "work for hire." If you are involved in a unique design with potential for multi-applications, make a conscious decision to discuss copyright ownership of the design and "other future use" rights regarding your work. You may be able to negotiate future residual rights (hence additional income) should the design be used in other products.

Art & Graphics. Try to determine the percentage of art that will be included. By knowing the number and complexity of figures, illustrations and photographs you can get an idea of the scope of the job. This lets you quote based on how much work you believe is involved. You can also estimate final page count based on a standard art size and the amount of artwork to be included.

Tracking Bids and Buyer Decisions

When you bid on a job and the bid goes to someone else, contact the buyer and ask for feedback on your quote. Even if you win the job, ask for feedback.

Explain that you consistently strive to improve, and you would like to find out where your bid stood among the competing bids. If a competitor beat you out, and their winning bid was half of your bid, probe to determine the experience level of the buyer. Sometimes a buyer has little understanding of what is really involved in a job. And sometimes a competitor is trying to "get their foot in the door" with the customer and plans to "recover" by charging a high fee for changes and alterations after the contract is awarded.

Try to track all the bids on a particular job. If you can, find out how the buyer decided the winning bid.

By following these steps for every job that you bid, you'll develop a historical database on both your customers and your competitors. This information can help you make even better bid decisions in the future.

If you decide to bid lower, keep your break-even point in mind. Recognize that, as the economy passes through down cycles, your customers will make extra effort to cut a tighter deal for themselves.

Summary

Estimating and bidding are part of a complex business process, and many people do nothing else. Estimators estimate, contract negotiators bid. Each has one primary responsibility. However, most desktop providers can't afford a dedicated person to handle each of these functions. The owner-manager is usually the person who takes on both of these jobs (with a myriad of other tasks).

Nevertheless, estimating and bidding can provide a substantial boost to your sales income. The better you are at these functions, the better your bottom line will look at the end of the business year.

After addressing strategy, bidding and negotiation, you're armed with some powerful tools for success. In the next chapter you'll find street smart ideas for maximizing your success potential. Chapter 8 covers operational ideas based on the best tricks in the trade.

8

Street Smart Operations

"Price is more than just a number."
Entrepreneur Magazine, February 1995

This chapter is about street tactics. It about ideas for implementing the strategy that you developed in earlier chapters. By using street smart techniques and various management tools, you can successfully set price and recognize when to pursue or decline a project. In this chapter you'll find tips, tricks, forms and worksheets that can help streamline your operation. And you'll learn how to design your own counter price sheet. Case studies will provide concrete examples of how to put strategy into action.

The successful shops are able to change rapidly and provide fast service. They appear capable and perform professionally. Chapter 8 shows you how to make every day an opportunity for extended success.

Do It By The Numbers

Financial illiteracy directly affects small business growth and income. In some cases, not knowing can cost dearly—a future for an aspiring owner-operator. Poor financial understanding is the Achilles heel of the entrepreneur. It's the bane of the desktop services professional. An old axiom suggests that a dumb competitor is the worst kind. There are many "dumb" competitors in the desktop services industry.

Success is not just knowing what to do. It's also in knowing how to do it. Let's improve your odds by tackling some economic and financial issues that directly relate to price.

Return on Investment

Understanding *return on investment (ROI)* can be tricky. There are several ways to calculate ROI—accountants seem to enjoy complicated formulas. The particular formula that they use depends on who they are generating numbers for—the stockholders or for upper management. Not being accountants, we need to make business calculations as simple as possible. Use a formula that someone in the trenches can understand.

Return on investment is the bang you get for the buck you spend. It defines the financial gain that you realize by investing money in your business?

This definition simplifies the ROI formula.

$$ROI = \frac{\text{net profit}}{\text{investment}}$$

If you put $10,000 into your business to get it started, you deserve a return on this investment just as if you had invested the money in mutual funds or treasury bonds. Today, you should be able to earn 5-10 percent on your money. This means that you should factor a ROI into your prices.

Take the investment and decide on an acceptable return. Then as we did in Chapter 5, integrate this return directly into your hourly rates. For a $10,000 investment, an expected return of 10%, and a 2080 hour working year, you should allocate 48¢ to each hour that is billed out. (See Table 5-3)

If you use the $10,000 to purchase equipment and software, the return then becomes a return on assets.

Return on Assets

In the world of financial analysis, people often use subjective decisions to make objective conclusions. They assume a given result and then base dollar investment numbers on the assumption. Although this seems silly, sometimes it's the best shot we can make at evaluating a business approach.

The concept of *return on assets* (ROA) is such a case. ROA is like return on investment. We want to realize a percentage of monetary good for an investment in something tangible like computer equipment or better software. In this case, we attempt to anticipate a revenue gain given we make a certain hardware or software investment. Our formula goes like this:

$$C = \frac{ER}{1 + r}$$

where C is cost, ER is expected revenue, and r is the expected rate of return (a percentage expressed as a decimal).

$$\text{Cost of Equip/Software} = \frac{\text{Expected Revenue}}{1 + \text{Expected Rate of Return}}$$

We're calculating the expected revenue value, so we rearrange the formula.

$$ER = C\,(1 + r)$$

If we spend $10,000 for a new computer workstation with all the latest and greatest features, and we want to get a return on this hardware investment of at least 20 percent, we drop these numbers into our formula and solve for what we must earn to achieve this return. (A spreadsheet program works great for this.)

$$ER = 10{,}000\,(1 + r)$$

$$ER = 10{,}000\,(1 + 0.2)$$

$$ER = \$12{,}000$$

Thus, we must earn $12,000 in each year of ownership to realize the 20 percent return that we feel is necessary to cost-justify the purchase.

Conversely, we can anticipate an income from making an asset purchase and then calculate the expected rate of return on this business decision. Again we rearrange the formula. Replace r, expected rate of return with ROA, return on assets.

$$C = \frac{ER}{1 + ROA}$$

$$C\,(1 + ROA) = ER$$

$$1 + ROA = \frac{ER}{C}$$

$$ROA = \frac{ER}{C} - 1$$

To illustrate this point, suppose that we are considering the purchase of a new color scanner. The purchase price is $6,000. We feel that we can sell $7,000 worth of scans in a year. What is our ROA?

$$ROA = \frac{7,000}{6,000} - 1$$

$$ROA = 0.166667$$

Expressed as a percent, our ROA is 16.7 percent. By making purchase decisions based on an expected ROA, we can optimize our asset investments. Remember that we are assuming how much additional annual revenue we'll earn using this new scanner.

An important factor to keep in mind is that technology and customer needs can change rapidly. To keep up, you should base your calculations on a 2-year replacement life. This means that you plan to buy new equipment in two years, so you must be able to resell the old equipment for enough (residual value) that you can make the replacement purchase while realizing a return on the initial investment. Some owners try to garner enough business so they can run two shifts. This gives them a better chance of increasing the return on their equipment investment.

In accounting books, you can find the same formula being used for both ROI and ROA. Desktop service businesses are unique. We apply our own application of these concepts. Thus the ROI and ROA formulas described above are for us.

Analyzing Financial Numbers

There is a certain symmetry to income statements. After you've looked at a hundred or so, you notice that the revenue a shop earns can be partitioned into various factors such as costs, taxes, and profit. In fact, these typical expenses can be partitioned out by percentage as shown in Table 8-1.

Table 8-1. Breaking down an income statement.

		PERCENT
Revenue		100%
Less Materials Costs	10%	
Less Manufacturing Costs	70%	
Gross Margin		20%
Less Sales Cost	10%	
Less G&A	6%	
Operating Profit		4%
Less Interest Expense	2%	
Pretax Profit	2%	
Less Tax (based on 40%)	0.8%	
NET PROFIT		1.2%

Given a total income for a year, it turns out that desktop service shops have a relatively low materials cost (toner, paper, film, etc.), but a relatively high manufacturing cost (labor intensive). Subtracting materials and manufacturing costs from our income yields the shop's gross margin. From this gross margin or gross profit, we must take out sales and general and administrative costs.

Sales costs for a shop typically comprise between eight and 12 percent of total sales revenue. In the desktop services industry, G&A costs take up five to eight percent of every sales dollar. General and administrative includes all the indirect costs, the administrative expenses to do business.

Depending on debt load, interest expense can be between one and five percent. Then if we subtract our sales costs and G&A from the gross margin, we can determine our operating profit.

From the operating profit, we deduct interest expense to get our pretax profit. Most shops face a tax rate (federal and state) of about 40 percent on the pretax profit. We apply the shop's tax rate to this pretax profit to realize a net profit on the bottom line. Does 1.2 percent look low? In most industry groups (including printing, prepress, and desktop publishing), the bottom line profit is typically between 0.2 and 3 percent. Achieving six percent net profit is terrific.

The government and several research groups monitor the breakdown of financial data for all of the major industry groups. The percentage for each category depends a lot on the type and size of the business. For example, in the world of the software developer, small software companies spend around 25 percent of their sales dollar on general and administrative costs. The larger software houses such as Microsoft spend as little as eight percent on G&A. Cooper Tire & Rubber Company comes in best with overhead running at only five percent of sales revenue.

This means that a small desktop services shop with one or two employees will likely spend much more on G&A than a larger shop employing over 10 employees. This explains why there's such a push to control operating expenses—in particular, general and administrative. Cutting down expenses is crucial to optimizing profitability. And operating expenses can be what separates the high- and low-profit performers.

Once we establish the financial profile for our own business, we can use this information to make some interesting comparisons. For example, we can use these percent ranges to analyze each job that our shop performs to separate the "wheat from the chaff." You'll probably discover that 80 percent of your profit comes from 20 percent of your customer base.

Comparing Your Shop With the Competition

We can also use these percentage breakdowns to compare bids on various jobs. This is a quick way to see who's losing their shirt by underbidding on a job. For example, assume that we bid $10,000 on a desktop design project but were beat out by a competitor who submitted a winning $7,000 bid.

If we assume that the competitor uses similar equipment (hardware and software) and has the same or similar costs that we do, then we can enter his winning bid into our spreadsheet and discover approximately how much that shop won (or lost) on the bid.

Look at Table 8-2. This breaks down the $10K and $7K bids just as we saw in Table 8-1. The competitor has a lower revenue level but the same outlay for materials and manufacturing (shop labor). This means that after the cost to produce are handled, this shop is already $1,000 in the hole, and it gets worse as we look down the column. By the time we factor in the cost of sales, G&A, and interest, they're losing over two-thousand dollars just by accepting the job.

Table 8-2. Breaking down DTP project award prices.

	Our Bid			Competitor		
BID PRICE	10,000	100%		7,000	100.0%	
Materials	1,000		10%	1,000		14.3%
Mfg Cost	7,000		70%	7,000		100.0%
Gross Margin	2,000	20%		(1,000)	(14.3%)	
Sales Cost	1,000		10%	700		10%
G&A	600		6%	420		6%
Oper Profit	400	4%		(2,120)	(30.3%)	
Interest	200		2%	140		2%
Pretax Profit	200	2%		(2,260)	(32.3%)	
Tax (40%)	80		.8%	0		0%
NET PROFIT	140	1.2%		(2,260)	(32.3%)	

Isn't it amazing? By taking a single data point (their winning bid) and dropping the bid value into your price breakdown spreadsheet, you can readily see that this competitor is losing $2,260 by taking on that job. Perhaps it's time to send cards to all of that competitor's customers telling them that your shop will be available to support them should problems occur on the job. You'll still be operating your business six months from now—when the IRS closes the door on this failing competitor.

The sad truth is that there are all too many shops operating today, who low-ball price and consistently operate on the razor's edge of survival simply because they don't understand these principles. No matter how you cut the pie, you still must pay for hardware, software, and professionals to make a project happen. For most shops, the numbers will pencil out remarkably similar.

Bidding below break-even can speed a shop's eventual demise. Unfortunately, many shops are doing this without even knowing it. Knowledge is power. Knowledge can also be profit.

Measuring Profitability

It's important that shop owners fine tune their intelligence gathering skills. Every employee in your shop must become sensitive to customer and competitor information. As the economy changes and as skill concentration increases, so does competition for existing business.

This means that owners must consistently evaluate their operations and financial results to determine where they stand relative to their competitors and then adjust their business strategies as necessary. As shown in Figure 8-1, the gross income of businesses providing desktop publishing services varies widely. Gross income is one way to compare businesses. But there's a better way. This one measures profitability per employee.

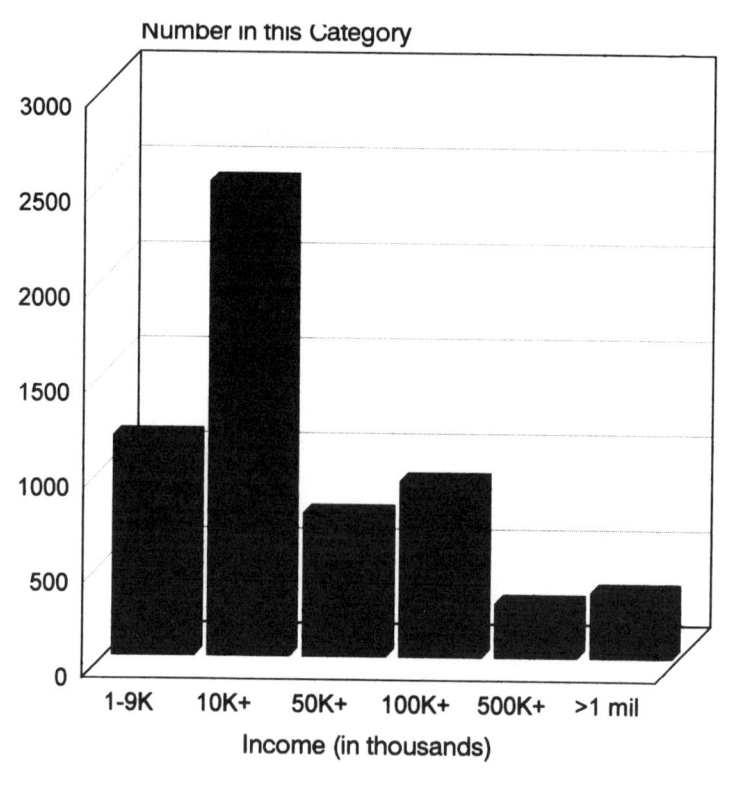

Figure 8-1. Relative number of desktop service businesses at various income levels.

An interesting way to evaluate a business is by using a barometer called the *economic model of business profitability*. This model measures profitability in terms of services sold rather than goods produced per employee. It's also a measure of productivity, so you may find it referred to as an *economic model of productivity*.

The model is normalized to what is called a "full time equivalent" (FTE) employee. By comparing the average income generated by a full time equivalent employee with the income revenue per FTE of competitors, you can determine if your shop has a profitability advantage or disadvantage. This can be equated to productivity per employee. The model takes total income out of the picture and lets you focus on how much an equivalent person in your shop earns. Looking at individual equivalent employee worth (profitability) can be a fascinating way to evaluate business success.

If your shop has six full time employees and earns $300,000 a year, it has a gross average income per employee of $50,000 (300,000 / 6 = 50,000). This gross measure can be applied against your competitor's earnings to develop an economic model for comparison. If a competitor is earning $750,000 annually with 10 full time employees, their sales per employee is $75,000. When compared with your $50,000 income per employee, your competitor has a 50 percent profitability advantage over your shop based on an apples-to-apples revenue-dollars-per-FTE basis.

When we investigated the economic model of sales per employee for other industries and companies, we found that the revenue per employee varies widely (Table 8-3).

Table 8-3. Income per Full Time Equivalent Employee

Company	$Income/Employee
Microsoft (software)	$289,000
Novell (LAN software)	288,000
Sony (electronics)	230,000
Stac Electronics (software)	224,000
Lotus Development (software)	206,000
Xpedite Systems (fax services)	179,000
Pro CD (CD ROM phone books)	153,000
Image Graphics, Inc. (prepress)	130,000
Local bank (financial)	120,000
Digital Equipment Corporation (elex)	108,000
George Lithograph (prepress)	100,000
Electronics for Imaging (software)	68,000
National Graphics (prepress)	62,000

Most $/FTE economic model data is calculated on larger companies. Microsoft, Lotus, and others are large companies. Yet, over 75 percent of all the companies in the U.S. have less than 10 employees. The $/FTE norm for the U.S. is typically reported as $100,000. A company with the same $/FTE may need to add staff when income per FTE exceeds the $100,000 threshold. Unless the company has a unique, high margin product or service, the existing staff may be overloaded and overworked.

We used our survey data and the limited trade publication information to evaluate the desktop services industry. Since our survey asked for income data and the number of full time, part time, and freelance employees, we could use survey and published industry data to calculate an average revenue per FTE for the profession.

Where do you stand when it comes to revenue per employee in your own business? The key to evaluation is to know where you are in relation to your competition. To find out, you must ferret out revenue and employee information on competing shops. Look for comparables. Watch for comments in news articles and business profiles printed in trade publications. Listen to industry speakers. Check the library and government labor department for industry norms. Since our company collects business information on desktop publishing and prepress, we analyzed our own data to see if we could define an average revenue per FTE for our industry.

Desktop publishing is a relatively new profession. We began in the middle of the last decade. Most of the shops started in the last five years. The number of these businesses is growing rapidly. They operate out of condos, houses, garages, light industrial office spaces, and store fronts. Their cost basis and earnings vary widely.

Since desktop services is a new industry, the average revenue per FTE employee should be below $100,000. There is a wide variance in the profiles of DTP shops. Some are well-established. Many are new and novice at everything. Analyzing this data can seem confusing. Yet, taken as a whole, the analysis yields fascinating insight into where desktop services stand today. The results described next are unique to the several thousand business profiles in our survey. A different sample size would produce different specific values but should produce relatively similar results since our tables are developed from actual numbers.

The range of income and number of employees in desktop services varies widely. New shop owners tend to undercharge for most services. Women owner-operators tend to pay themselves less than their male counterparts. They also tend to charge their customers less for desktop services. And counter prices tend to increase as a business matures.

They are primarily sole proprietorships with many of them operating out of the home. More women than men or couples are owner-operators. Their income varies from less than $3,000 a year freelance to over several million dollars a year in established full-time businesses.

Here's how we determined $/FTE for our data. We defined a full time equivalent employee as someone working 40 hours a week. Then a 20-hour part time worker is classified at 0.5 FTE and a 4-hour freelancer becomes 0.1 FTE (4 hrs / 40 hrs = 0.1). This provides a weighted scoring method for determining the total number of equivalent full time employees in a business. You can do this same analysis for your business and other shops near you.

By multiplying the number of full timers by 1, the number of part timers by 0.5 and the number of freelancers by 0.1, you can calculate the total number of

FTE employees for any business. A shop earning $500,000 a year with five full time, one part time, and three freelance employees will have a 5.8 FTE rating (5 x 1.0 + 1 x 0.5 + 3 x 0.1 = 5.8) and a revenue per FTE of $86,207 (500,000 / 5.8 = 86,207).

If a full time worker brings in $10,000 per month in sales and a part time worker earns $7,500 a month, dividing the income by the FTE basis means that the part time worker is actually 50 percent more profitable to your business (7,500 / 0.5 = 15,000) relative to a full time employee. This assumes that each expends a proportional amount of overhead budget and has the same earning opportunity. In addition, if a shop owner works 60 hours a week, this represents 1.5 FTE and this becomes that person's basis for calculation and comparison.

The FTE concept can be useful. We can evaluate revenue per FTE against various factors—overall shop earnings, design projects completed, scans performed and charged, typeset pages billed, etc.

In your economic model it is also useful to know the average revenue per FTE, the range of revenue dollars per FTE, and the average number of employees in a typical shop. In our survey, the average FTE in a DTP shop is 1.7, the average FTE for a prepress shops is 7.1.

Next we analyzed the revenue per FTE by income category. We partitioned the income data into categories as shown in Table 8-4. Then we determined the range of FTE employees in each category. Based on this, we had the computer remove outlier data (data outside a normal distribution curve) and calculate the average FTE for each income category.

Table 8-4. The FTE economic model for desktop publishing businesses.

FTE ECONOMIC MODEL
by Overall Shop Earnings

INCOME RANGE	FTE RANGE	AVG FTE	RELATIVE $/FTE RANGE	AVG $/FTE
$1 - $5 million	21-90	39.8	$55,556 - $83,333	$74,847
500K - 999K	5.3 - 12	7.7	56,818 - 133,929	87,732
100K - 499K	1.3 - 7.1	3.7	26,829 - 115,385	69,140
50K - 99K	1.0 - 3.6	1.7	16,556 - 100,000	45,348
25K - 49K	0.5 - 3.0	1.5	10,000 - 175,000	48,517
10K - 24K	0.1 - 2.2	0.9	5,682 - 50,000	26,841
1K - 9K	0.1 - 6.0	1.3	1,588 - 60,000	9,258

We determined the range of relative revenue per FTE in our survey data and had the computer calculate an average relative income per FTE. If a moonlighter works on a 0.1 FTE employee basis and earns $5,000 in a year, this represents $50,000 on a 1.0 FTE basis. Thus, in the $10,000 - $24,999 category, the average relative $/FTE came out to be $26,841 indicating that many of these owner-operators are working part time or just starting their business. The lowest income category is presented for information only. These shops are new or are maintained as freelance or second-job businesses.

As shown in the table, the top earning businesses averaged 39.76 FTE and averaged $74,847 per employee. In the $500K - $999K category, these shops averaged 7.73 employees earning $87,732 each. Between $100K and $499K, shops averaged 3.66 workers earning $69,140. As the total income revenue decreases, notice the resulting decrease in FTE employees. Except for the $25K to $49K category, the average relative FTE also decreases from the preceding value.

Discounting the lowest income category as representing new start-ups, this makes the $25K - $49K and $50K - $99K categories important. The average revenue per FTE of these two categories is $46,933. If we take this as a comparison basis, any shop that produces more than this value in revenue per FTE is more profitable (hence more productive) than the average shop. Likewise, a shop with less than $46,933 revenue per FTE is less profitable compared with this suggested standard. Thus this value can be used as a benchmark to evaluate your own business and that of competitors.

Since our data base was really humming at this point, we turned our analytical focus to the FTE and $/FTE based on the primary computer platform used in the business. This time, the data came out as shown in Table 8-5.

Table 8-5. FTE and $/FTE based on computer platform used.

	FTE ECONOMIC MODEL by Computer Platform				
COMPUTER PLATFORM	Average All Shops	$500K - $5 mil	$100K - $499K	$50K - $99K	$10K - $49K
MACINTOSH					
FTE	5.64	10.4	3.4	1.4	1.2
$/FTE	$57,382	$68,138	$63,082	$48,564	$26,895
PC					
FTE	1.47	12.0	2.9	1.7	1.1
$/FTE	$32,858	$83,333	$76,348	$52,257	$39,600
MAC & PC					
FTE	10.10	18.8	4.3	2.2	0.7
$/FTE	$91,410	$89,124	$56,316	$30,332	$8,058

As you can see in Table 8-5, the PC-based shops fared better than the Mac-only shops. At the high income end, using both PC and Mac machines is an advantage. Notice how the average FTE and average $/FTE track from one income category to the next.

Naturally, a different partitioning will yield different values, but the message from this data is clear. Most DTP shops (45%) have incomes between $10K and $100K. The PC-based shops seem to fare better than their Mac-based counterparts.

In its own way, the FTE economic model can provide the small DTP shop a way to compare profitability, productivity and competitive advantage with similar shops. It can show you that your business formula still needs tweaking.

In a general sense, the lower revenue per FTE in desktop services — lower than the accepted standard $100,000 per FTE for the U.S. in general — suggests a more disturbing problem. Perhaps the pricing strategy is out of line with mainline American business. Perhaps owners are only hurting themselves when they accept jobs paying lower prices than they could (or should) get.

In a cut-throat business world, business owners sometimes deal with razor-thin margins and struggle to remain profitable. Larger companies keep a tight lid on costs and use a common profit-boosting strategy — they hire fewer workers and focus on highly profitable projects. Owners can do more to make their projects more profitable. Pricing is key to the profit picture.

Making Your Own Profitability Model

Once you've had an opportunity to let the concept of revenue-per-full-time-equivalent sink in, you'll want to monitor your own shop to see how you stand relative to the rest of the industry.

Figure 8-2 is a sample production summary form that you can adapt to your own profitability/productivity monitoring program. It partitions each month into working days. Then it has a column for each employee in your shop or profit center. The form is used to record the dollars billed and the hours worked.

PROFITABILITY $/FTE
PRODUCTION SUMMARY

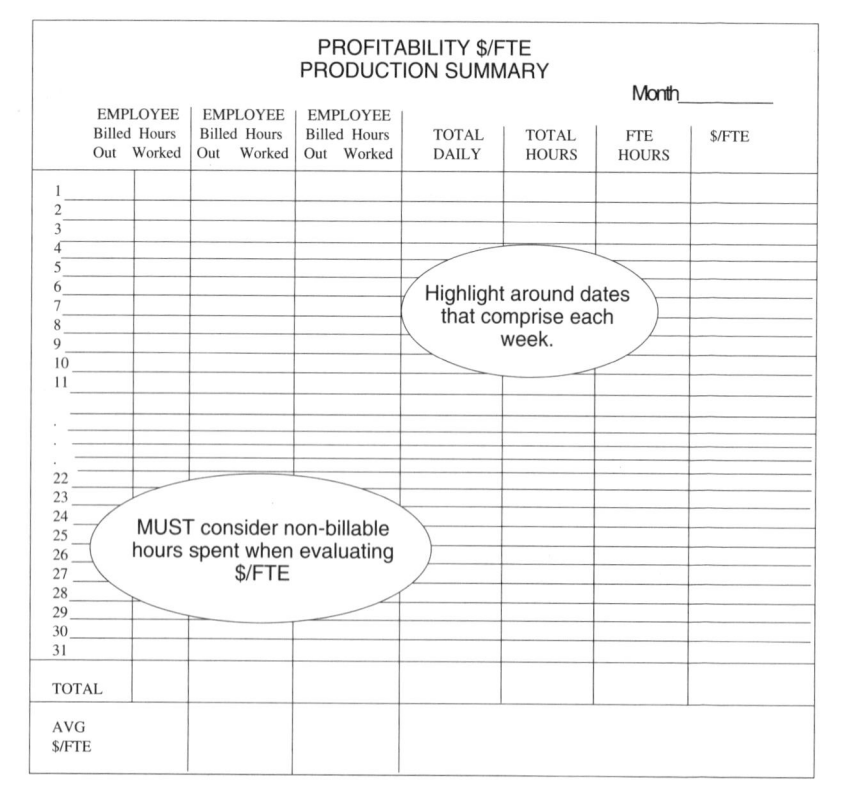

Month_____

EMPLOYEE Billed Hours Out Worked	EMPLOYEE Billed Hours Out Worked	EMPLOYEE Billed Hours Out Worked	TOTAL DAILY	TOTAL HOURS	FTE HOURS	$/FTE
1						
2						
3						
4						
5						
6						
7						
8						
9						
10						
11						
...						
22						
23						
24						
25						
26						
27						
28						
29						
30						
31						
TOTAL						
AVG $/FTE						

Highlight around dates that comprise each week.

MUST consider non-billable hours spent when evaluating $/FTE

Figure 8-2. Production summary form.

Each month a "highlighter" pen is used to outline the dates that constitute each working week. Then data is filled in for the days that work occurs.

On the right are columns that summarize the activity for each day. One column lists the total daily income, another lists the total hours worked, and another lists the total number of 8-hour FTE equivalent hours worked. The last column records the dollars of income-per-hours-FTE-worked ratio.

You could add a third column for each employee to normalize their output to a standard eight-hour full time equivalent.

At the bottom of form, the total dollars billed and hours worked for each employee are summarized. Then the hours are divided by the number of possible eight-hour work days in the month to get an equivalent-FTE-hour rating for each worker. This is divided into the total dollars earned to get a dollars-per-FTE value for each employee.

You could design this form to record weekly subtotals during the month with a final tally at the end of the month.

By associating the columns recording dollars billed and hours worked with the dollars-earned-per-hour-worked, you force your attention on the income that each employee earns for the shop.

At the end of the year, the total income-per-employee is added and the total hours-worked-per-year-per-employee are added to get annual values. The total hours worked are divided by a value representing the total hours possible to get an equivalent FTE rating for the year. For example, if Employee 1 worked 1,040 hours of 2,080 hours possible for an eight-hour worker, the ratio of 0.5 represents one half an FTE. If Employee 1 billed $30,000 for the shop during the year they represent $60,000/1.0 FTE for your business. This is good.

On the other hand, if they generate only $10,000 in billable income, they represent a $20,000/FTE worker to the shop.

If all workers perform non-billable work relatively equally, then all the employees can be compared with each other, and the shop in general can be compared with other shops to determine who is more productive, who is more profitable to the company.

What's the Maximum I Can Earn?

This is one of the most basic issues entrepreneurs face when evaluating the feasibility of starting a business. A good way to understand how to find this value is to consider an example.

The owner of a desktop service bureau operates in a strip center rented office. He has four full-time employees and shares the work load. He wonders what maximum income he can earn given that his fixed expenses are running $21,000 a year. His variable expenses are $11,000 a year and each employee has a different average productivity.

Table 8-6 shows how to calculate maximum possible income based on five employees at the following pay and productivity rates. Each employee is also billed out at a different rate.

Table 8-6. Maximum income possible.

DIRECT LABOR	BILLED OUT AT	HOURLY PAY	AVERAGE PRODUCTIVITY	PAYROLL	TOTAL POSSIBLE INCOME
Owner	$55	$20	32%	$41,600	$36,608
Designer 1	40	17	40%	35,360	33,280
Designer 2	35	12	38%	24,960	27,664
Operator 1	32	8	30%	16,640	19,968
Operator 2	25	7	30%	14,560	15,600
Shop Average:			31%	$133,120	$133,120

This may look fine until you realize that you must deduct both fixed and variable costs out of the total income. Thus, this business is losing over $33,000 a year. Bad business strategy.

The owner must cut costs or increase productivity. Or change the billing rate. What if, the owner billed out at a fixed shop rate of, say $54 an hour for the labor time of each employee? The result would look like Table 8-7.

Table 8-7. Maximum income possible (billing changed).

DIRECT LABOR	BILLED OUT AT	HOURLY PAY	AVERAGE PRODUCTIVITY	PAYROLL	TOTAL POSSIBLE INCOME
Owner	$54	$20	32%	$41,600	$35,942
Designer 1	54	17	40%	35,360	44,928
Designer 2	54	12	38%	24,960	42,682
Operator 1	54	8	30%	16,640	33,696
Operator 2	54	7	30%	14,560	33,696
Shop Average:			31%	$133,120	$190,944

Much better. Thus, it appears that the optimum formula is somewhere between the two—with maximum possible income between $133,120 and $190,944. The budgeted hourly rate concept will help set better billing rates. Then productivity gains will help improve the earnings column.

As a final view on what is possible, consider this shop with every employee working at 50 percent productivity and using individual hourly rates. Table 8-8 shows what CAN happen in a fully productive shop.

Table 8-8. Maximum income possible (50% productivity).

DIRECT LABOR	BILLED OUT AT	HOURLY PAY	AVERAGE PRODUCTIVITY	PAYROLL	TOTAL POSSIBLE INCOME
Owner	$55	$20	50%	$41,600	$57,200
Designer 1	40	17	50%	35,360	41,600
Designer 2	35	12	50%	24,960	36,400
Operator 1	32	8	50%	16,640	33,280
Operator 2	25	7	50%	14,560	26,000
Shop Average:			50%	$133,120	$194,480

This ($194,480) is the maximum possible earnings given the constraints. The gross profit (total income less wages) is $61,360 with a gross margin (gross profit divided by total income) of 32 percent. If fixed and variable costs remain constant ($33,000) the net profit (gross profit less fixed and variable costs) is $28,360 with a whopping 15 percent net margin percentage (net profit divided by total income). Typical net margin is about six percent.

Thus, you can see the dramatic impact that productivity has on the maximum income that a shop can earn.

Making a Counter Price Book

When customers ask to see your prices, some shop owners can reach for a sheet or set of sheets describing the services that they offer and the rates that they charge. If these price sheets are kept in a binder, the package is called a *"counter price book."*

There are many ways to structure the services described in your counter price book. Some shops use a simple one-page form. Others put the time into developing a detailed listing of services with volume discounts and various prices based on operation, complexity, and output desired.

There are several key things to include on your price sheets. First, the name of your business (telephone number included). Second, the date that a sheet was last revised. This helps you know how long it's been since you last updated your prices, and it lets the customer know that you probably DO occasionally update your rates.

Make your price sheets as functional as you can. Organize the information so related services are collected in the same area of the forms. For example, place design, conversion, input, and output services in their own areas on the forms.

Take the time to make your price sheets look as readable as you can. Use columns, rows, and bold typefaces on headings. And use boxes to separate and border various areas of your service. Some counter books include a time-increment hourly-rate breakdown chart on one of the sheets.

If you provide file conversion, chart out the type of conversion by file size and price. Since we're dealing with hardware, software and time, work up your billing rates and then charge by the amount of time the system is busy on that service — often time is represented by file size (10K, 100K, 500K, etc.). You can determine how long it takes to convert various block sizes of text, spreadsheet or graphics information. Then prorate your base billing rate and present your prices based on the size of file being converted. Make a note on the form how odd-number file sizes will be treated. And consider using a minimum fee for selected services that you perform.

Remember that it takes time to setup a job for a customer. It also takes time to close a job down after the work has been completed. You should consider charging setup fees for various types of jobs. The more successful shops use the setup charge and minimum fee concept sparingly—but firmly. Your shop should be paid for all the time and resources that are applied to a service.

If you're describing scanning or print output, show your prices for various resolutions and sizes. For example, laser printing can be described in a boxed row-and-column area with resolutions at the top of the columns and page sizes at the beginning of each row. This matrix gives a professional look to your form. If you also price print output based on the amount of toner on a sheet, provide small sample complexity drawings to help the customer recognize that everything has been considered and you will be charging a unique rate for those sheets that need more toner coverage.

If you provide imagesetter output, generate a chart like that for laser printer output based on dpi and output size — one for RC paper and another for film.

If you price your design based on budgeted hourly rates, you can list each service with its corresponding billable hourly rate. Various design services and rates can also be presented in chart form.

Every document that you produce for customer view is like a billboard for your business. Therefore, it's important to make each pricing sheet look as "professional" as possible. The idea is to let your price sheets advertise all of the services that your shop can provide. It does little good to have a unique capability and not let your customers know. Your price sheets should mentally seed ideas in the minds of your customers for other things that they may want your shop to do for them later. Knowing that your shop can do OCR scanning or PC-to-Mac and Mac-to-PC conversion can be valuable information for your customer. They not only will remember these facts the next time they perceive a need, they could also tell others about you and your services.

Sometimes little jobs can lead to large projects. If your customer knows for example that you can convert word processing and graphics file formats, they may bring some of their work to you. They could also include you in a major project that they are tackling because they know from your counter price book that your shop has the resources and ability to make their own job easier.

Job Scheduling Resource Allocation

Get a better handle on how you allocate resources and you can improve the profit on certain jobs. For example, if you must wait 10 minutes for a graphic-intensive file to print, why not perform other tasks or functions at the same time. Multitasking your efforts lets you leverage your resources and complete more work in the same finite time period.

I've watched employees sitting idly in front of computers while conducting time-intensive database searches. Rather than staring at a static "SEARCHING..." screen display, why not use the idle time to fold flyers or start a job on another computer. Consider doing two or three simultaneous jobs.

On occasion, I've been active scanning input on one computer, while printing labels from another, and at the same time, stuffing flyers in envelopes. If each of these functions are billable, I can significantly increase my productivity and dollars-earned in an eight-hour full-time equivalent (FTE) day.

The challenge is to accomplish more billable work in a finite time period. The solution (for the small 1-2 person business) is to multitask each employee. As shown in the work process flowchart in Figure 8-3 on the following page, some work can be done in conjunction with other jobs.

310 - Pricing Guide for Desktop Services

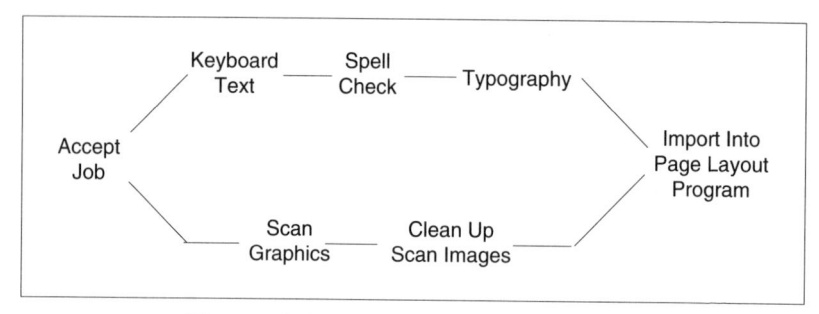

```
              Keyboard      Spell
                Text        Check  ── Typography
                   ╱  ─────     ─────            ╲
                  ╱                                ╲ Import Into
      Accept                                         Page Layout
       Job                                           Program
                  ╲                                ╱
                   ╲    Scan        Clean Up     ╱
                     ─ Graphics ── Scan Images ─
```

Figure 8-3. Work process flowchart.

By presenting your project visually, you can allocate best, worst, and expected times to perform each function. This enables you to identify the time path that is critical to the operation (Figure 8-4).

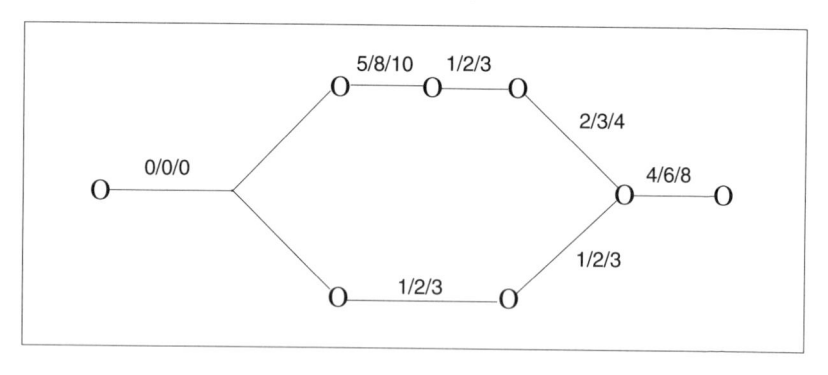

```
                        5/8/10    1/2/3
                       O────O────O
                      ╱            ╲  2/3/4
              0/0/0  ╱              ╲
            O──────O                 O     4/6/8
                    ╲               ╱ ─────── O
                     ╲             ╱  1/2/3
                      O────O──────
                         1/2/3
```

Figure 8-4. Critical Path analysis in job costing.

As shown in Figure 8-4, the top path takes longer that the bottom path. Therefore, any delays in the top path have immediate affect on the project completion. A small delay during the scanning and retouch functions may not affect the end time because the top path is the critical path on this project.

Figure 8-4 also shows that any spare time for those doing the bottom path functions can be used to advantage by putting those same resources to work on the top (critical path) functions.

Case Study:
Break-Even Analysis - Color Laser Copier

The following scenario will reinforce the concept of using break-even analysis in deciding what price to charge.

John had reviewed his strategic plan and had completed a tactical plan for operating his business for the upcoming year. His shop was located in a strip shopping mall, a few doors away from a post office store. There was a steady stream of customers using the services of the private post office. His strategy is to draw these customers to his shop for services that compliment those of the post office store. One service that seemed appropriate is to offer color copying and printing. He already offered black and white copying services.

After analyzing the available technology, John decided to install a color laser copier/printer. The machine that John selected can produce seven copies each minute and can interface to a desktop computer. It can accept originals in the form of computer graphics, still video images, black and white originals, original art, photos, and slides and negatives.

The copier/printer he selected has a suggested retail price of $42,000. John can obtain a three-year lease at 0.0175. This means that he pays 1.75¢ for each dollar of cost — a total of $735 a month. Foot traffic for his desktop publishing and black and white copy business is running 50 customers a day. The critical question is what to charge for each color copy produced.

He has a good handle on his shop overhead costs. And John has an average operational cost breakdown for the copier/printer provided by the vendor. His challenge is to find the point at which his costs are covered and profit can begin to accrue. This point is his break-even for the new service. John decides to perform a break-even analysis on his color copier/printer investment.

He has two ways to approach the analysis. He can compare his total expected sales volume with the associated costs or he can compare the total expected items (units) produced and sold with this same cost. In both methods, John must clearly understand his operating expenses.

Part of his expenses are fixed—they don't change as sales volume fluctuates. These fixed costs include rent, utilities, salaries, and insurance. Other costs vary with the job. These variable costs include hourly wages, the costs of paper, toner, developer, drum or photoreceptor, fusing oil, preventive maintenance, and additional utility expenses to produce the color output that he sells. To make a profit, John must pay both his fixed and variable expenses and then have some income left over. The residual income represents before-tax profit and return-on-investment (he loaned money to his company on start-up). John will analyze his color output business potential based on sales volume and on total copies sold.

First John must determine his total fixed costs. The machine will cost John $8,820 a year (735 X 12). He plans to use the copier/printer 1200 hours a year. About half the time, he will use the machine as a copier; the other half of the time, he'll use it as a printer connected to his computer. The hourly fixed cost contribution of the copier/printer is $7.35 ($8,820/1200 = $7.35). This cost becomes part of his shop overhead expense.

The computer that John will use with the copier/printer costs $5,000 and has a useful life of five years. This represents $1,000 depreciated cost each year. The computer is used continually during the work day — 2,080 hours a year. The hourly fixed cost contribution of the computer is 48¢ ($1,000 / 2,080 hrs = $0.48/hr). Of the 2,080 hours of computer use, 600 hours will be for color printing. The depreciated annual costs of the computer as used for color printing is $288 (600 hours times 48¢/hr). This costs also becomes part of his shop overhead expense.

Thus, to operate and use the color copier/printer, John pays $9,108 ($8,820 + $288 = $9,108) annually. Every hour of copier/printer operation costs John $7.83 ($7.35 + $0.48 = $7.83).

Now, John's overhead costs are running $17 an hour so the overhead contribution attributable to the color service is $20,400 ($17/hr x 1200 hrs). This makes the fixed part of his cost $20,688 a year. Now he analyzes his variable costs.

The average operational cost for the color copier/printer (including utilities) is 50¢ an hour—$600 per year. John's $6-an-hour employee will cost $7,200 a year for the time spent making color copies. This makes John's variable cost $7,600. His fixed and variable costs come to $28,288 a year.

At 1200 hours of operation, his color copier/printer is available 72,000 minutes a year. At seven copies per minute, John can get a maximum of 504,000 printouts in each year. This is if the equipment were in continuous use. It won't be, but this provides a best-case situation. In continuous use, John could break even on costs by charging 5.6¢ a copy ($28,288 / 504,000). However, John expects to use the machine only 10 percent of the available time — 50,400 copies.

This suggests that John needs to charge 56¢ for each copy to cover his costs (28,288 / 50,400 = 0.56). From a survey of local competitors, John found that color copy prices ranged from 60¢ to $3 each. The average selling price is $1.26. He tentatively selects $1.25 as his price. He also found that color laser printer prices range from $1.75 to $9 per page. It takes longer for his employee to set up the computer to print a color copy. He tentatively selects $5 per page as his color printing selling price.

His variable cost contribution is $7,600 divided by 50,400 or $0.15 per copy. John wonders how many copies he must sell to reach the copier/printer's break even point.

He subtracts his $1.25 selling price from the $0.15 unit variable cost and then divides the $1.10 result into his $20,688 fixed cost. This indicates that he will break even at 18,807 copies ($23,509 in sales).

This is shown graphically in Figure 8-5. If John sells color printer output at $5 a page, he can break even in one-fourth the volume (4,702 pages).

To check his math, John divides his average variable cost of $0.15 by the $1.25 average selling price and then subtracts this from 1 to get 0.88. Then he divides his fixed costs ($20,688) by 0.88 to get $23,509 as his break-even sales volume.

Therefore, at $1.25 a copy, John's copier/printer service will break even when his shop prints its 18,807th copy and earns a cumulative $23,509 in sales. For every computer-generated laser color printer output, John earns $5 instead of $1.25. If he sells scanned copies of photographs and transparencies, he can further increase his "per-output" price. Each higher-priced product reduces the sales volume required to reach break-even.

Nevertheless, John bases his calculations on the worst-case, lower income sale. Can he sell at least 18,897 copies a year? That's approximately 73 color copies each of the 260 days a year that his shop is open for business.

John changes the variables in his computer spreadsheet B-E model and determines new break-even points based on different selling prices and costs. He finds the computer model particularly helpful when performing "what if" per-copy price-change analysis.

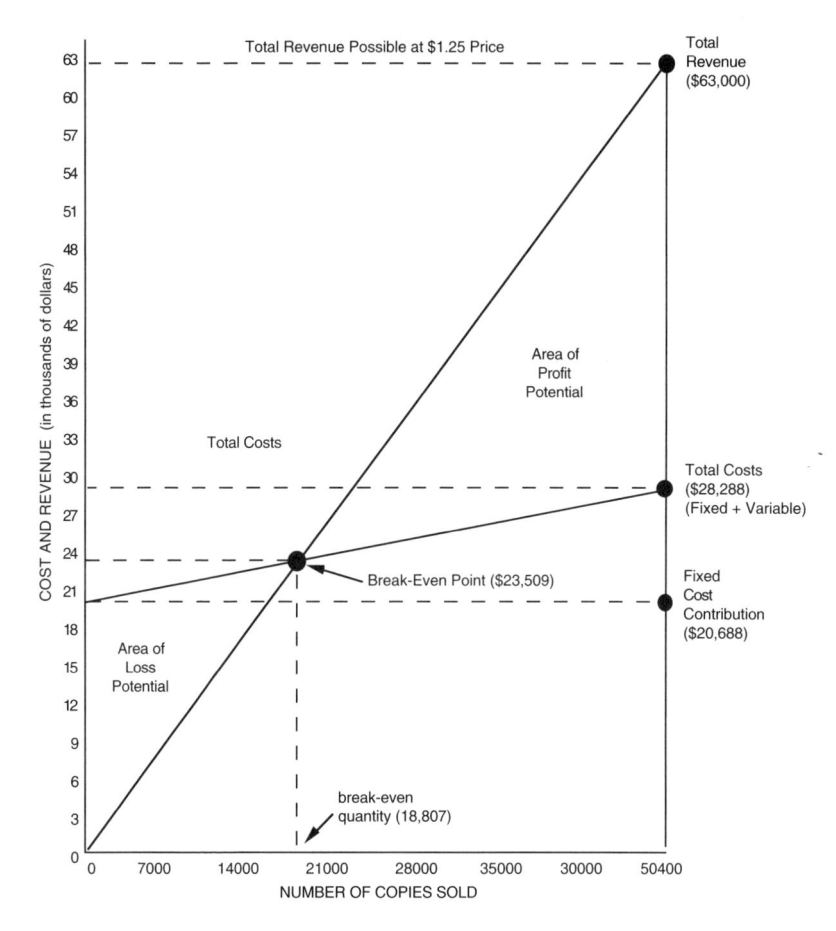

Figure 8-5. Break-even analysis for color copier/printer.

Break-even analysis helps him decide the viability of his copier/printer and at what price it becomes too costly to produce and sell copier/printer services. To increase the income generated, John raises the price in his computer model. He recognizes that this is not always possible. Competition may hold market prices too low to make this product or service worth selling. John's costs can also vary. And John realizes that break-even analysis doesn't consider discounting, customer demand (elasticity) and the pricing reactions by competitors. Nevertheless, it does help John quickly see the impact of various pricing strategies. And that in itself makes the analysis worth the effort.

Break-even is one of the analysis tools that John uses to manage his business. By knowing each break-even point, he can determine which products or services to offer. It also helps John decide if making an unprofitable sale to gain a long term customer is really worth the sacrifice. If John lowers his sales price, each sale contributes less toward paying his fixed and variable costs, and less remains for profit and investment return. In effect, a lower sales price pushes the break-even point further out along the horizontal axis in Figure 8-5.

Typically, the smallest 20 percent of John's orders will account for less than five percent of his sales income. It may not be worth making these sales at all. There's a point at which John's fixed costs exceed his income and he should decline the sale. John's break-even analysis shows him mathematically and graphically why some sales just don't make financial sense. A bushel of low quantity sales may generate revenue consistently below his fixed costs with a small variable cost added. This would suggest that John should decline these sales, or add a surcharge (charge a higher price) for low dollar sales.

Based on this, John selects a sliding scale of prices for copier/printer output. A lower price will be charged for larger volume jobs. He develops his pricing strategy to encourage an average sale of $25 or more. Thus, he wants customers to buy 20 or more color copies, or five or more color printouts with each order. Break-even analysis helped him determine this desired sales amount.

Case Study:
Job Estimating - Directory

Mary had just completed her weekly review of cash flow when she received a call from a prospect she met at a recent business networking meeting. The caller was the president of a local alumni club for a university. The club wanted to produce a directory of members. Having learned that Mary was a desktop publisher, the caller had decided to ask Mary to bid on the job. Mary was elated, but this would be her first directory. She needed to understand the job thoroughly before she could offer a price to do the work. She scheduled a meeting with the club president.

During the meeting, Mary wrote down the specifications for the job. The club had just under 300 members—all graduates of the university. The president of the club wanted a mailing list generated that could be maintained and updated. This mailing list would form the basis for the membership directory. During the meeting, the club president decided that the directory should have a coated cover, a title page followed by a list of club officers and the by-laws of the club, and then a listing of each member with graduation date and degree(s) earned. Both the home address and business address of each member would be included in the directory. The page size and binding weren't critical with this first directory, and the club president would rely on Mary to recommend what she felt is appropriate. The university logo would appear on the cover and first page of the document. The club president asked Mary to base her quote on producing 300 copies of the directory.

Upon learning that Mary had a bulk mail permit, the club president also asked Mary to include in her bid, the cost to mail the printed directory to club members. Mary was to provide all mailing envelopes and handle the complete process. The club president told Mary that $1,000 had been budgeted by the club. Mary returned to her shop, sharpened her calculating pencil and went to work on her estimate.

She broke the project down into functions. These included data entry, scanning of the university logo and by-laws provided by the club president, directory design, cover design, page layout, camera-ready print-out, directory printing, binding, shipping and mailing. First, she would have to enter partially typed, partially hand-written membership information into the computer. From this, Mary would generate a mailing list so she could print labels for mailing. From the same database records, she would print complete member information for the directory. Selected fields in her membership database would be printed to a separate file for importing into a word processing program where the data would be typeset for a two-column page. Mary would scan the club by-laws and save these in her word processing format. Then she would merge the by-laws with the membership data. Next she would scan the university logo and save it as a graphic file. She would design the cover and title page in her page layout program and then import the word processing directory file. But what size page should she design to?

Mary placed two columns of address labels over an 8.5" x 11" sheet of paper. Leaving room for top and bottom margins, she could fit 10 addresses in each column. She could also use font sizing and leading to make the information fit within the design footprint. If she designed to a 5.5" x 8.5" page, she could get eight addresses in each column. The club currently has 284 members. If it takes two addresses to list each member (home and work addresses), she would need 29 pages at

8.5" x 11" and 36 pages at 5.5" x 8.5" size. She can reduce the type size and leading to fit the data on each page.

If she designed at full size, she could mail each directory first class for 1.01¢ each. If Mary designed the directory for the smaller size and kept the document thinner than 0.25 inches, she can mail each directory as a bulk mail letter for between 18.8¢ and 22.6¢ each. Mailing 125 or more to the same ZIP code three-digit prefix would qualify the mailing for the lower rate. Since postage costs represent a significant part of the project, Mary decided to design to the smaller size.

She would use 10-point coated-one-side stock (10ptC1S) for the cover. It would be folded and saddle stitched to the directory sheets. The inside sheets would be 60# book stock. The entire job would be printed in black ink. She would generate camera ready sheets at 600 dpi and use a local quick printer to produce 300 copies of the directory. To cut printing costs, Mary would provide the cover and sheet paper stock to the printer avoiding the printer's markup and getting the lower trade rate.

For the mailing, Mary would purchase blank 6" x 9" envelopes and print a return address and mailing address label for each. She made a list of each function with a time estimate for completion. The labor tasks and time estimates are shown in Table 8-9:

Table 8-9. Total time estimate.

Client meetings	-	2 hours
Database design	-	1 hour
Database data entry	-	2 hours
OCR scanning	-	0.25 hours
Logo scanning	-	0.25 hours
File transfer	-	0.5 hours
Document design	-	2 hours
Cover and title page design	-	0.5 hours
Importing text	-	0.5 hours
Page layout	-	11 hours
Draft directory printout	-	1 hour
Changes & alterations	-	1 hour
Printing shop interface	-	1 hour
Label printing (return address)	-	1 hour
Label printing (mailing address)	-	1 hour
Applying labels to envelopes	-	2 hours
Stuffing mailing envelopes	-	2 hours
Bulk mail preps	-	2 hours
Post office mailing	-	1 hour
Customer follow-up	-	1 hour

TOTAL TIME ESTIMATED = 33 hours

Next Mary places a budgeted cost next to each function. She uses both standard rates for her area and actual prices for her own and the work of others. She plans to hire help at $5 per hour for the simpler jobs. She will hire a $12 freelancer to help desktop publish the project. Mary's budgeted labor rates are $20 an hour with a 40 percent productivity assumed and shop overhead incorporated. This results in a $50/hour billing rate for her shop. Mary applies the shop's $50 per hour billing rate to her own portion of the job. Her labor costs are as shown in Table 8-10.

Table 8-10. Budgeted labor costs.

FUNCTION	TIME (hours)	RATES ($/hr)	COSTS ($/hr)	TOTAL COSTS
Client meetings	2		$50	$100
Database design	1		12	12
Database data entry	2	$25	12	24
OCR scanning	0.25	35	12	4
Logo scanning	0.25	36	12	4
File transfer	0.5	40	12	6
Document design	2	35	12	24
Cover design	0.5	45	12	6
Importing text	0.5	45	12	6
Page layout	11	45	12	132
Draft printout	1	25	12	12
Chgs & alterations	1	40	50	50
Print shop interface	1	35	12	12
Label printing	2		12	12
Envelope stuffing	2	5	5	10
Applying labels	2	5	5	10
Bulk mail preps	2	5	5	10
Bulk mailing	1	5	50	50
Customer follow-up	1	50	50	50

TOTAL TIME: 33 hours = $546 estimated

Next, Mary analyzes the actual costs of materials that will be used during the project. Her materials costs were calculated as shown in Table 8-11.

Table 8-11. Actual costs of materials.

Laser printout - 100 shts @ 5¢ each (incorporates toner and paper costs)	$5
Envelopes - 300 @ 3¢ each	9
Cover stock - 1 pkg, 250 sheets 10ptC1S	22
Offset paper stock - 3,500 sheets 60# white offset	23
Labels - 568 @ 2¢ each	11

TOTAL MATERIALS COSTS = $61 actual

She will subcontract out for the printing, collating and saddle stitch binding at trade rates. Her printing cost estimate is shown in Table 8-12.

Table 8-12. Actual trade printing costs.

Printing, collating and saddle stitching (Does not include sales tax)	$235
TOTAL PRINTING COSTS = $235 actual	

Mary will mail the directories using her bulk mail permit. Her postage estimate is shown in Table 8-13.

Table 8-13. Actual bulk mailing postage costs.

Bulk mailing 284 pcs @ 22.6¢ ea	$64.18
TOTAL BULK MAILING COSTS = $64.18	

If she can collect the bulk mail into 125 or more pieces with the same three-digit ZIP code prefix, she can reduce her bulk mailing costs to $53.39, but Mary will estimate based on the higher cost.

Thus Mary's total cost estimate (rounded up) came to $898 ($546 + $61 + $235 + $65 = $907). Next she had to determine what she could charge and make a fair profit and return on her investment in hardware and software.

Mary marked each material cost up by 100%. And she priced each hour of work at her $50 billing rate. The project quote builds as shown in Table 8-14.

Table 8-14. Project quote (top and bottom end prices.

LABOR
All 33 hours of work performed at $50/hr shop rates
　　　　　　　　　　　　　　　　　　LABOR CHARGES = $1,650

MATERIALS & SERVICES
Database data entry - 20¢ per record, 284 records	$57
OCR scanning - 1 scan @ $6/scan	6
Logo scanning - 1 scan @ $6/scan	6
Label printing (return address) - 284 @ 5¢ ea	14.20
Label printing (mailing address) - 284 @ 5¢ ea	14.20
Camera ready 600 dpi - 20 sheets @ $1.50 ea	30
Laser paper - 100 sheets @ 10¢ each	10
Envelopes - 300 @ 6¢ each	18
Cover stock - 1 ream, 500 sheets 10ptC1S	44
Offset paper stock - 3,500 sheets 60# white offset	46

　　　　　　　　　　　　MATERIALS CHARGES = $245.40
　　　　　　　　　　　　(marked up as appropriate)

PRINTING
Print 300 directories, 2-sided, black ink, cover 1-side black ink, collate, fold and saddle stitch.
　　　　　　　　　　　　　　PRINTING CHARGES: $282
　　　　　　　　　　　　　　(marked up 20%)

MAILING
284 pieces @ 22.6¢ each
　　　　　　　　　　　　BULK MAILING CHARGES = $64.18

　　　TOTAL PROJECT PRICE = $2,241.58 (plus sales tax)
　　　　(Bottom End Price = $1,088.84 plus sales tax)

This is the top end of her quote range. This price does not include sales tax which is added to services and materials provided the customer. The bottom end quote assuming 10 percent profit and return on investment is $1,088.84 ($907 plus 10% profit and 10% ROI). By accepting a five percent profit and five percent return on investment, Mary can quote the job at $997.70.

By using part time help, Mary is able to bring her quote in below the $1,000 budgeted by the university club. She has some options that could also increase her profit. She could use remainder label stock that had already been purchased for an earlier project. And she could use the lowest-paid part time employee to do data entry, scanning, label printing, print shop delivery and pickup, and post office mailing. This will add another $85.50 to the bottom line. By lowing the costs to $812.50 and receiving $987.80 for the job, Mary can realize a 22 percent profit on this project.

Mary bids $987.80 for the job. She is awarded the contract. Her actual mailing costs are $53.39 (an additional $5.28 falls through to her bottom line). Label printing actually takes only one hour (another $12 in profit). And actual page layout takes two hours less ($24 more in profit). Thus, Mary gets the job for $987.80. Her actual costs are $768.75. Mary's achieves a 28 percent gross profit over her costs. Assuming a small cost for administrative handling of the part time workers, Mary still realizes a comfortable gross profit on the job. If the client wants the job completed on a rush schedule, Mary will add 100 percent more to her bid. Either way, Mary has a good understanding of her costs and her potential profit and return on investment.

The job went well. Mary provided a quality product to a new client. Bulk mailing within the county took only one to two days. Her client was happy. Mary enabled three people to earn money for their work. And she has the mailing list saved on her own hard disk, ensuring Mary of future jobs from this client.

Case Study: Trade Rate Ripoff

A colleague shared this one with me in hopes that you don't experience the same treatment. A photographer got an opportunity to design a catalog for a national race car organization. He asked my colleague if she would quote a price to design and layout the catalog.

She quoted an hourly rate of $30, which she felt was fair given that the standard rate in the area was closer to $40 an hour.

The publisher called her back and told her that he was awarded the job. He explained that he told the organization that he would charge them $30 and hour. Then he told my friend that he would pay her $18 an hour for her services and pocket the $12 an hour difference as his share. She was shocked and told him to "go fly a kite."

What could she have done?

Trade rate services are typically 20 to 25 percent of full retail. This weasel was planning to establish a 45 percent discount (in his favor). Based on a 20 percent trade discount, the photographer should been charged $32 an hour ($40/hr x 0.8 = $32/hr).

Before you ever agree to support on someone else's contract, state your full rate in writing and then show the discount that you will offer. Make your proposal in writing. On the bottom of your proposal have a line for an acceptance signature and another for your agreement signature.

Sign and date two copies. Send the two copies to the buyer asking that the buyer sign off on one copy and return to you.

Be very specific about what you will and will not do in support of the agreement. Also be very clear about how many "proof" copies you will provide and how alterations and revisions will be handled.

This process does two things. It drives away rip-off artists, and it establishes position for any small claims court action that may result.

Case Study:
What Billing Rate Should I Use?

Your company downloads graphic images from a modem, cleans them up and produces a 600 dpi laser printer printout of each image. These printouts are picked up daily by a local architectural company. You are paid by the printout. You have two employees and estimate that you and these two support people can clean up and print out 20 images a day. It takes an average of 30 minutes to download, clean up and print each image. You take a flat weekly paycheck of $600 gross and pay your support people $15 an hour each. The support staff works 40 hours a week. You also have a bookkeeper who works for you 10 hours a week.

See if you can answer the following questions related to this scenario. To make it easy, assume there are no holidays and no vacation days to take you away from this work. Also assume a shop productivity factor of 50 percent.

QUESTIONS:
1. What figure should you use to determine the annual number of hours used in your billing?
2. Should you include the $10 an hour that you pay your bookkeeper in your billing-rate calculation?
3. You rent your computer, modem and laser printer for $900 a month. Should this be included in the cost portion to determine your billing rate?
4. You pay $500 a month for your small storefront office. You also pay $130 a month for utilities and $65 a month for cleaning the office. What annualized amount should be included in your billing rate calculations?
5. Health insurance for each full-time employee costs you $300 a month. However, one of your staff is already covered under her husband's policy. How

much should you include at part of the billing-rate calculations?
6. Besides recovering all of your costs, you also want to make a profit this year of $18,000. Should this be included in the billing rate calculations?
7. Your company belongs to the National Association of Desktop Publishers. Annual dues are $95. Is this figure part of the billing-rate calculations?
8. All of your staff wear special lab jackets that you provide. These jackets have your company logo embroidered on them to provide a team appearance in your shop. Your company pays $1,050 annually for the cleaning these jackets. Should you include the cleaning costs in your billing rate calculations?
9. You send your employees to training classes to maintain their technical competence. This cost $1,500 a year. Should this be included in the calculations?
10. Assume that you pay $8,678 annually in payroll taxes and given all of the above, what is your billing rate per hour?

ANSWERS:
1. 7,800 hours — [(20 images x 30 minute/image) / 60 minutes/hour x 5 days/week x 3 people x 52 weeks/year = 7,800 hours/year]
2. Yes
3. Yes
4. $8,340 — [(500 x 12) + (130 x 12) + (65 x 12) = 8,340]
5. $7,200 — [$600 for you and $600 for one of your employees]
6. [600 + (15 x 8 x 5) + (15 x 8 x 5) = $1,800/week x 52 weeks = $93,600/year] [93,600 x 0.0765) + (93,600 x 0.0082) + (93,600 x 0.026)]
7. Yes

8. Yes
9. Yes
10. $39.58 — [93,600 employees + 5,200 bookkeeper + 10,800 auto + 8,340 office + 7,200 health insurance + 18,000 profit + 95 dues + 1,050 cleaning + 1,500 training + 8,678 payroll taxes] / 7800 hours = $19.79/hr. Then, based on 50 percent productivity, your billing rate should be $39.58/hour.

Getting Paid

Getting paid becomes stressful and unpleasant when customers don't put the check in the mail as agreed. Credit is fine when you're on the receiving end. It can be a cash flow nightmare when you're on the giving end.

To survive in business, you must get street smart in dealing with those who owe. An article in *Instant Printer* magazine described studies analyzing the payment history of accounts receivables aged 90 days or more. These studies show that accounts three months past due have only a 73 percent probability of being paid. After dragging a debtor along for 180 days, your chances of seeing payment drop to 57 percent. If 12 months go by without payment, you have a 26 percent chance of receiving payment. And if an account remains delinquent for 24 months, there's only 13 percent chance that you'll ever be paid.

While cash upon delivery is your best formula, you can increase sales by as much as 50 percent just by offering credit. Credit card sales yield greater volume but have their own risks—charges backed out months later and occasional credit card fraud with little or no recourse. A larger problem concerns getting some credit buyers to pay on time.

Naturally you want more sales, but how do you handle the credit issue without adversely affecting your cash flow? It doesn't take many "deadbeats" to drain your resources and threaten your own business survival. Sales may look nice on a ledger report, but only sales paid are sales actually made.

So how can you successfully add customers while maintaining positive cash flow? The first step is to ration credit like a miser tips a waiter—only when necessary, and to the least extent possible. Consider allowing credit purchases only for customers who represent volume business. Then check their credit history carefully before agreeing to terms. Credit customers tend to buy more products or services, but their ability and willingness to pay are critical in maintaining acceptable cash flow. If you can, consider credit only for those customers who consistently bring you sales with high profit margins.

Once you've decided to accept credit sales, collect copies of credit applications from every source that you can find. Adopt the "good things" on these forms, and generate a credit application form that is custom to your business.

Before agreeing to a credit relationship, analyze your customer. Your best sources for information on a potential credit customer are the companies that they already buy from on a credit basis. Check the applicant's bank references, and contact credit reporting agencies such as TRW to confirm the condition of their payment history. Place a higher weight on the most current information. Where possible, call the reference.

I use the "Reverse Three" technique with my credit customers. I ask an applicant to list three credit references. Then I call the references in reverse order—last one listed is called first. The last reference may have more reliable information for you than the first (most popular). This works well in the hiring process, too.

If a customer's credit history seems solid, discuss with them the terms for which you will conduct business. Establish ground rules before any work is performed. Don't jump on a 30 day payment schedule—called "net 30." Try to get agreement on a 15-day payment schedule. The sooner a customer pays, the better your cash flow picture.

Consider offering "price breaks" for paying early. IBM Credit Corporation has offered their customers 1 percent discount off invoice if they pay their bill within 15 days instead of 45 days as required by their credit agreement. On an invoice to a government organization, print a statement that they can deduct two percent from the invoiced amount if they pay before the net due date. Most government organizations require their contracting officers to take advantage of any discounts that are available. I've used this technique to receive payments for book purchases by the Government Printing Office in Washington, D.C. in just two weeks after receipt of invoice—unheard of in most "small business - big government" transactions.

Also, include a penalty clause in your credit agreement to cover payment made past the due date. Add a clause stating that, should legal action be necessary to collect on the account, the losing party must pay the attorney fees and court costs of both parties. The point is: You want to do everything possible to motivate customers to pay early—or at least on time.

When a job is complete, give the customer your invoice at the same time you deliver the project. Get the person receiving the work to check it for suitability. Upon acceptance, have them mark the invoice accompanying the work "OK TO PAY." Then immediately put the invoice into their payment cycle. It can take two weeks to move an invoice from the customer's department through the bureaucracy of a large company to final cutting of a check. I've encountered an amazing delay getting payment from some large, well-known companies. Their excuses run the gamut.

"Well, the department must approve the invoice for payment first, and that can take some time."

"We only cut checks on every other Friday."

"Why, the invoice has already been paid." This can mean the invoice has been accepted by the receiving officer and submitted to Accounts Payable for payment. Mailing of the actual check can be another week or two away.

Some large companies simply pay when they want to pay. These customers will agree to a payment schedule, but the Accounting Department in the customer's organization operates by its own rules—usually to their benefit and not yours as a creditor.

On large jobs, get the customer to finance the project by paying part of the fee up front. Then have them pay another portion upon successful completion of a specified milestone event with the remainder paid upon delivery of the completed work. I use the "1/3 - 1/3 - 1/3" rule with my large project clients. On a $6,000 job, I'll get agreement for a $2,000 payment upon signing the contract, $2,000 upon delivery of a completed draft (or another specified deliverable) and the remaining $2,000 within 10 working days of delivery of the final material on the project. When I work with printers and service bureaus, I usually pay them half up front and the remainder upon delivery of the work. We understand cash flow and its affect on a small business, and we must all cooperate to ensure mutual success. Most of your customers will understand cash flow and should be willing to work with you.

Before you establish credit relationships, develop a solid cost accounting and billing system to keep receivables under control. You need accurate and complete documentation and follow-up to keep this process moving. Before you accept credit work, be certain that both you and your client are clear on what you will do and how you will be paid. Put in writing what will occur if payment is not made or if payment is made with a check that is returned for insufficient funds. Then monitor your client's payment behavior, and take action as soon as danger signals occur.

After completing a job with net-pay terms, mark your calendar and then call your customer a week before the due date to thank them for the business and to confirm that everything was delivered properly. During the conversation, remind them when payment is due. You could even suggest that they take advantage of your policy providing discount for early payment.

Monitor each credit customer for signs that they may be in financial trouble. Danger signals include missing payment due dates with a history of timely payment, delaying comments such as "… check's in the mail," unreturned telephone calls, stonewalling by their Accounting Department, or catching them telling a "white lie." If payment is due in 14 days, make your first telephone call on day 15 to get the check number and confirm mailing of payment. Or arrange a specific payment schedule. If you receive a check that later "bounces," immediately call them to arrange their delivering a cashier's check that will be "good." If they want you to "run the check through again," agree to do so but explain to them that, as agreed by the contract between both organizations, an added charge will be levied for processing a check that was returned. Most banks charge between $15 and $25 for re-processing "rubber checks." Payment of this charge is due immediately.

When you feel that a debtor customer is in financial danger, call or visit the person who placed the order with you. Be pleasant, but professional. Explain that you have not been paid and that this is not typical with your customers (or with them in particular). Ask them if there is someone else that you should speak with to correct this delinquency situation. Be firm. You need to communicate a strong message that prompt payment is normal and expected. The more professional customers will contact you BEFORE a due date is passed to arrange another payment schedule. With delinquent clients, consider a "cash-plus" plan where they can continue doing business with you, but they must pay cash-on-delivery plus a portion of the delinquent balance for each job that you perform. Once they pay their account current, continue the "cash-up-front" policy for the next several jobs and then return them to a credit status if you feel comfortable about their payment intentions and capabilities.

Your best chance for collection occurs before the account ages delinquent beyond 30 days. This means that you should become the "squeaky wheel" to your laggard customer and perform most of your collection activity immediately within the first month after an account becomes past due. Start with a telephone call. Then send a friendly note attached to a copy of the invoice. If this doesn't work, call them and begin the verbal needling. Make it clear that you want payment. After a week, send them a formal appeal for payment. A week later, send them a telegram demand for payment. The next day, call them to determine when their check can be expected. If they stall, send them a demand letter by Certified Mail. Clearly state what was agreed and what is and is not happening. Hint that you may be open to a payment plan, but (without threatening) be clear that their immediate response is urgent. You want to pin them down to a commitment for payment.

If all else fails, begin the process of "playing hardball." Send them a certified "Pay Up Or Else" demand letter. Explain that you intend to initiate legal action for non-payment if you do not receive payment in full by the end of business 14 calendar days after the date of your letter. Call your local Better Business Bureau office and the American Arbitration Association to see if third party mediation is appropriate and possible.

If your "deadbeat" customer refuses to accept your Certified letters, send them a letter by regular mail indicating that you intend to prosecute for non-payment. Attempt to call them to convey this same message.

Wait two weeks then file a law suit in small claims court. If the amount is more than $5,000, hire an attorney and file a larger suit in the court the attorney recommends. If you don't want to pursue on your own, obtain the services of a collection firm. Select the collection agency based on their being bonded and/or licensed, time in business, and telephone responses by references that they provide to you.

In summary, ensure that the agreement that you and your customer sign clearly describes how and when payment will be made. And be certain that the term "payment" means "payment received by" and not "payment requested from an Accounts Payable Department by." This is particularly appropriate when doing business with government organizations, schools, and most large companies.

Never, NEVER take on a large job without getting "earnest" money up front. I like to work on a three-step basis—one-third of the agreed price is paid up front, one-third is paid upon submission of the first draft, and the last third is paid upon delivery of the final product. If a customer doesn't produce payment in full when you're ready to deliver, have them wait until they have the money before you turn over any work.

For those customers that pay on a net-<days> basis, be sure to invoice them immediately to start the clock. And be sure to provide the invoice to the correct department (e.g., Accounting Department). Some government organizations don't believe in starting their clock until their accounting department receives the actual invoice. If you go through the department for which you performed the work, they may take several weeks to "approve" payment, and then it may take several more days to get the invoice routed to the Accounts Payable desk in their Accounting Department.

On most net-pay jobs, I place a statement on the invoice that makes interest accrue and the whole amount due and payable on a day-by-day basis after the net-due date is passed.

When they fail to pay as agreed, go after the deadbeats. Every business struggles during what the government calls economic "readjustment periods"—"slowdowns" to most of us. But you can't let irresponsible customers take you to "the cleaners." Be willing to work with businesses that are dealing with financial problems. But remember. The profession as a whole benefits when you collectively keep customers honest, responsible, and accountable.

Financial liquidity is important. Just don't let it become flowing red ink on a spreadsheet of habitually late-paying customers.

Guerilla Operations for Business Survival

Business profitability runs in cycles depending on the agenda of the politicians in office, the mood of the country, and the conditions in the rest of the world. Cycles are natural. When the economic cycle is at the top, we're all happily busy depositing our sales success in the bank. But when the cycle turns down, things get scary. Business professionals become increasingly concerned when ominous black clouds form over our economy. When, each day we notice more "For Lease" signs posted in front of empty stores and tiny notes in local newspaper reporting increases in business bankruptcies our intuition tells us that the economy is heading into deeper trouble. We must act immediately to develop a survival strategy for our businesses.

In a down economy, survival can occur only by sticking to the basics and capitalizing on the strengths fundamental to your business. You should concentrate on those services that have the best potential for growth. You should also reduce expenses wherever possible. An analysis of your operation will identify areas where you can still lower costs, increase productivity, increase cash flow, and maintain or improve profit.

Your largest costs involve salary and benefits. Shop around for a better benefit package and shift to an employee cost-shared plan. Fewer medical claims directly translate into reduced health costs, so offer a cash bonus to those who keep healthy during the year. Pay a cash incentive to employees who improve their physical health — lose 10 pounds, reduce body fat by some percentage, or who stop smoking. Give them another bonus for maintaining their achievement for at least a year. Also pay a bonus to those who get an annual physical checkup. A healthier staff means healthier profit potential.

Adopt a "pay for performance" policy based on output quality, timeliness, and acceptance. Partition each employee's compensation into three parts—base pay, a performance bonus, and a customer evaluation bonus. Let an employee earn between five and 45 percent of their base pay by performing at optimum and making their customer happy with the service that the shop offers.

Consistently strive for maximum shop and individual productivity. To achieve this, establish weekly goals for yourself and your staff. Cross-trained each employee on the services that your business performs. Everyone should be given an opportunity to make suggestions, learn, and increase their skills and abilities. Loan manuals out overnight so employees can study at home. If they "forget" to bring them back the next day, send them home (on their time) to pick up and return the material. Inform each worker that survival of the business depends on responsibility, teamwork and "elbow grease."

Carefully monitor the output and performance of your team. Release less productive workers. Farm out energy-intensive jobs to freelancers to reduce salary-benefit expenses and cut utility costs. Set standards for job performance and then encourage workers to telecommute and work from home. By paying a set rate for a given job, you can transfer utility costs and work break delays to these home workers. Your employees gain by the convenience of working at home without the stress caused by freeway commutes. When you need more help, hire part-time hourly workers to avoid the additional salary and benefit package costs. Wherever possible, hire your own children to shift income to your kids while teaching them the value of thrift and hard work.

Became an expert at combining tasks. Batch, or combine jobs. Batch telephone calls, and batch errand trips. Make your errands on off times so you won't get caught in traffic jams. Became an expert at discount buying. After developing a list of expected prices, monitor office supply sales and watch for business-failure auctions. Be aware that some "sale" prices are only reductions from an inflated level. Also realize that some "auction" prices are often at or above retail. Became a smart shopper. Look for good deals on everything. Ask your suppliers for better payment terms and deeper discounts. Offer to pay cash for a "substantial" discount.

For the duration of an economic downturn, hold a tight rein on major purchases. Carefully analyze the cost versus benefit for each hardware and software product being considered. Require a substantial gain in earnings potential to justify any purchase. Consider renting during short-term hardware needs. And avoid buying "toys." A 14,400 bps modem is of little use if your clients are only using 2400 baud devices. Include the cost for consumables in your evaluation of hardware purchases.

If you want a software upgrade, try to wait until near the end of an upgrade offer before making the purchase. Call tech support and read magazine reviews to identify bugs in the software and to let corrective actions be made to the earlier version of the program.

Actively seek to reduce debt load. Convert high interest loans to lower interest options. Double-pay on the high-interest debt. And set a goal to reduce expenses by at least 10 percent within the first year. Eliminate things that are unnecessary. Before improving any activity, question if it should be done at all. Eliminate unprofitable products and services. If overhead expenses don't show a demonstrated return, try to minimize or eliminate them too. Only add products and services that relate to you basic business. And do this carefully. In each case, expect a return on your investment for every dollar that you spend.

To improve productivity, replace parts before they began to waste energy. Lighting accounted for much of your electrical costs. You may realize a 20 percent savings on your utility bill by installing task lighting and periodically cleaning the bulbs. By adjusting indoor light levels to the amount of daylight available, you can turn off overhead lighting. Also turn incandescent lights off when not in use.

Clean out your files to gain storage space and speed information processing. Organize your shop according to work flow to minimize bottlenecks and unnecessary steps.

Offer cash incentives to employees who make cost-saving suggestions in areas not directly related to their tasks. Pay them up to 25 percent of the first year's actual savings based on a four-year effective life of a suggestion.

When your vehicle needs replacement, buy a two-year-old model and save 25 to 30 percent on the total cost of vehicle ownership. Increase the deductibles on you vehicle's collision insurance coverage to lower ownership costs even more. And increase your gas mileage up to 30 percent by scheduling oil and filter changes and lubrication jobs based on the miles driven. Change the oil in your vehicle every 3,000 miles. Every 6,000 miles change both the air and oil filters and have a lube job performed on the vehicle.

To enhance cash flow, pay bills at the last minute. File them by date and pay them only when due. Take advantage of credit card grace periods and then pay your expenses in full. Increase your personal tax exemption to minimize the refund and provide more disposable income. Then help your employees do the same.

Change your billing and receiving procedure to make it easy for your customers to make payments. On large projects, bill more often so you collect more often. Keep the balances small so customers will be more prone to pay you first when they experience cash problems. Shorten payment due dates from net 30 to net 10 days. Offer a two percent discount for payments made before a due date.

Negotiate progress payments on jobs that extend for several months. Then invoice twice a month. Convince clients to pay up front for work in exchange for a discount.

Besides tightening your credit policy, quickly begin collection action on any overdue account receivable.

Work on a cash-basis with all new customers and be slow to approve credit terms. If you discover that a customer is about to "go under," operate on a cash-first basis with them. And be prepared for potential "price wars" by assessing how much you can cut your fees and still break even. By knowing how much profit you have in each job, you can negotiate with confidence.

Every week, call 10 old customers and attempt to revive business. Ask what you can do to get their business back, and then act on their comments.

Recycle printed fan-fold computer paper to use the reverse side. Design and used a stamp for the upper right-hand corner of the first page of each fax. It should identify the sender and receiver and eliminate the need for a separate cover page. Send more information by modem than by the U.S. Post Office to reduce mailing costs.

Analyze the use of paper, toner, envelopes and other office consumables. Establish a monthly average and then set a re-order point so you can buy during sales. Buy only what will be used within three months. By watching for announcements of product shortages or pending price increases, try to save 50 percent by volume purchasing from companies that are shutting down a line of things that you use.

Learn how to recharge your own laser printer toner cartridges and use these cartridges for standard office printing. Use commercial cartridges for client printing jobs.

To fill idle time, initiate staff training and increase preventive maintenance on your own equipment. Contact local businesses with similar hardware and software to offer your shop's support to them when they experience temporary work overload.

Increase your marketing and sales efforts. Keep in touch with your customers through postcards, phone calls, or personal visits. Query them on how you can serve them better. And act quickly on complaints. By visiting clients, you can reinforce your determination to maintain a high level of customer satisfaction.

To foster mutual support, refer leads to non-competing businesses who could return the favors. Join a support group and begin attending meetings of a local multi-discipline professional association. Encourage your staff to do the same.

To get recognition by local businesses, begin giving free presentations on how to reduce costs on desktop projects. Distribute fliers and donate services to local community activities. In every case, bring a large sign showing your business name and an ample quantity of promotional material.

Also encourage your staff to write short "What I Heard" notes that identify potential community business problems and opportunities. Follow-up and make these additional action items for your marketing efforts.

Fine tuned your listening skills and become sensitive to the needs and desires of potential business customers. Make you and your team experts in market intelligence collection. By recognizing problems in other businesses, you can research the subject and then quickly offer a solution. By building on these opportunities, you can increase your business activity and keep your staff working through the valley of a business cycle.

Homework, hard work, and good business sense can make you and your staff immune to the ravages of a down business cycle. By becoming a street smart guerilla, your business can not only survive, it can gain a significant share of the market.

Summary

This chapter covered street smart tactics of successful business owners. What you've read are the hidden secrets to maximum profitability. In the end, cost determines where you compete; perceived value by the market determines your price.

The Appendix provides demographics on desktop service businesses in North America based on a survey of over 26,000 businesses. Not only does it provide an insight into who they are and where they operate, but it descrbes how hard they work and what hardware they use. You'll also find the names, addresses and telephone numbers for popular trade publications and associations.

One Final Word

It's not over. In fact, it's never over. Pricing is a continuous process. The world that we live in and know is rapidly changing. Organizational structures are disintegrating. Companies are being ripped apart at the very core and being rebuilt as something entirely different. Sometimes whole companies disappear overnight—replaced by smaller, entrepreneurial teams. Layoffs are still happening—and the trauma will continue as the marketplace shifts, settles and then shifts again.

The world is finding new business, social and economic plateaus—new paradigms of what reality is all about. And it's frightening and wonderful at the same time.

As the information data highway transcends everything that we know about social interaction and work, the real power players are those who can handle information. There's great fortunes to be made by those who can convert mountains of data into useful visual messages. And there's no-one better at this than the designers, illustrators, desktop publishers and prepress operators of today. The future is literally yours for the taking. May the fonts be with you in this exciting adventure.

"Just name your price!"

APPENDIX

Other Useful Information

WHERE TO FIND IT

Typical Number of Employees - 343
Year Business Started - 344
Income Distribution - 345
Business Form - 346
Where Business is Operated From - 346
Gender of Owner - 347
Hours Worked Weekly - 347
Format of Incoming Work - 348
Type of Computer Used - 348
Popular Publications -349
Clubs & Associations - 355
Other Books Related to Pricing - 366

TYPICAL NUMBER OF EMPLOYEES

In conducting the survey for this edition, we asked for profile information on each participating business. One of the many things that we were interested in analyzing is the number of full time, part time, and freelance employees working in the typical shop. As expected, we noted that the number varied by the size of the business. We decided to partition the worker data by income category. The following is a breakdown of our results.

INCOME	FULL TIME	PART TIME	FREELANCE
$500-$19,999	0.65	0.48	0.37
$20K - $49,999	1.00	0.33	0.57
$50K - $99,999	1.25	0.60	0.61
$100K - $249,999	2.07	0.79	1.40
$250K - $499,999	3.89	1.07	1.19
$500K - $999,999	11.26	1.43	1.26
> $1 million	27.41	6.59	2.69
All	3.03	0.89	1.19

START YEAR

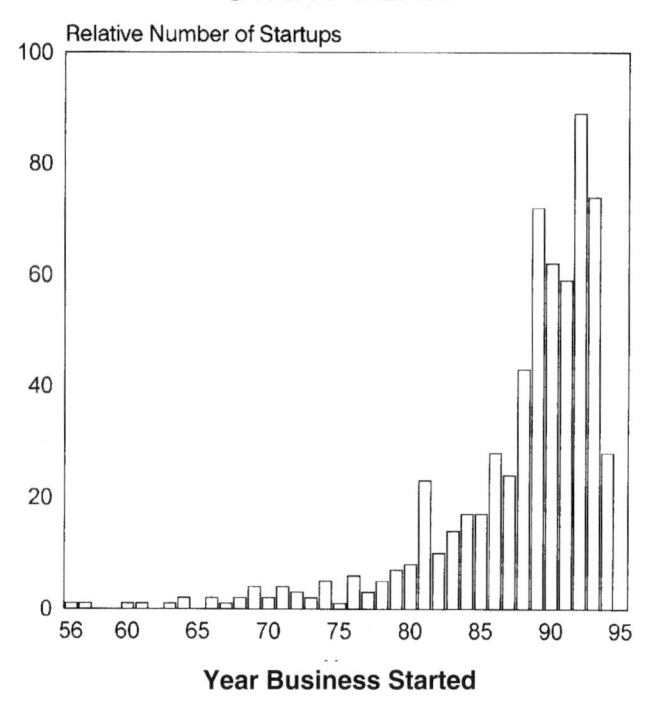

Relative Number of Startups

Year Business Started

INCOME DISTRIBUTION

The following chart describes how revenue is distributed across our survey population.

INCOME	% OF SURVEY PARTICIPANTS
$500-$19,999	41.4%
$20K - $49,999	23.9%
$50K - $99,999	11.7%
$100K - $249,999	9.2%
$250K - $499,999	5.3%
$500K - $999,999	4.9%
> $1 million	3.6%

BUSINESS FORM

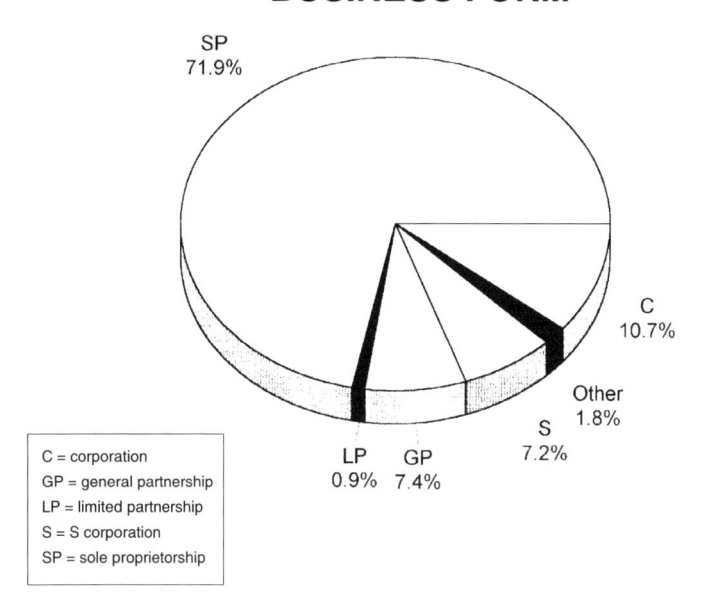

- SP 71.9%
- C 10.7%
- Other 1.8%
- S 7.2%
- GP 7.4%
- LP 0.9%

C = corporation
GP = general partnership
LP = limited partnership
S = S corporation
SP = sole proprietorship

WHERE BUSINESS IS LOCATED

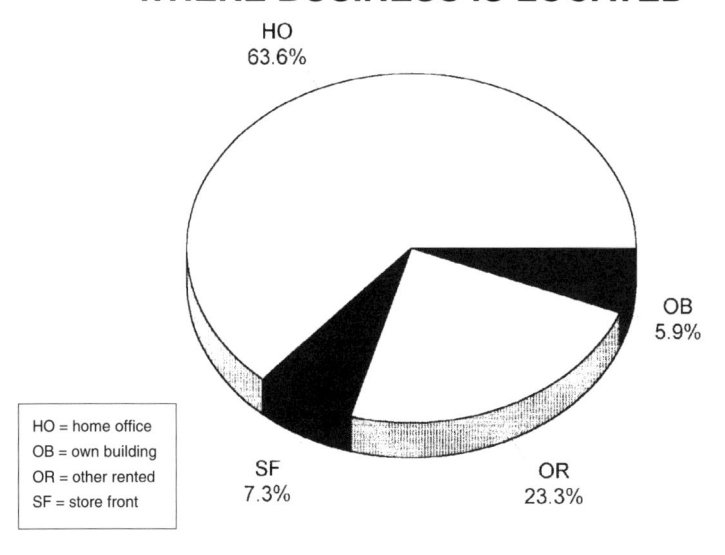

- HO 63.6%
- OB 5.9%
- OR 23.3%
- SF 7.3%

HO = home office
OB = own building
OR = other rented
SF = store front

GENDER OF OWNER

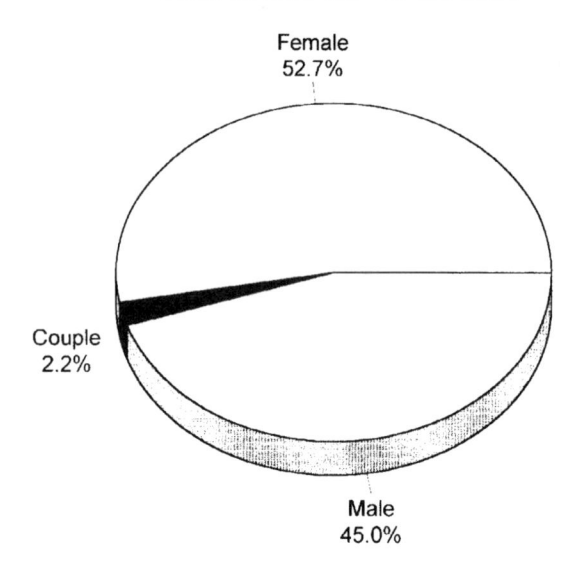

- Female 52.7%
- Couple 2.2%
- Male 45.0%

HOURS WORKED WEEKLY

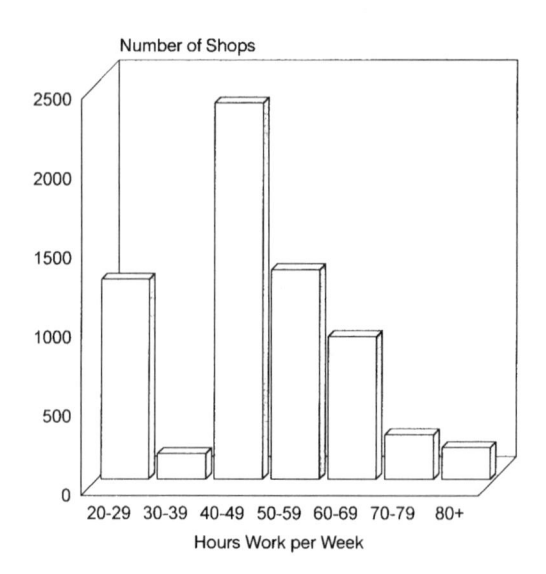

Number of Shops vs. Hours Work per Week (20-29, 30-39, 40-49, 50-59, 60-69, 70-79, 80+)

FORMAT OF INCOMING WORK

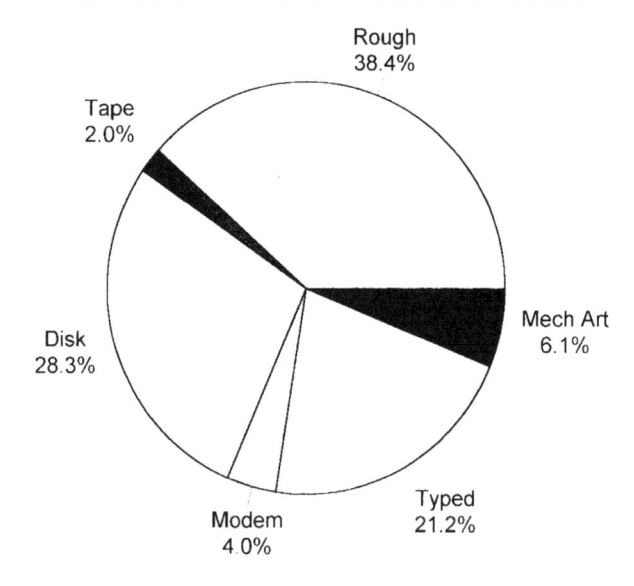

- Rough 38.4%
- Tape 2.0%
- Disk 28.3%
- Modem 4.0%
- Typed 21.2%
- Mech Art 6.1%

TYPE OF COMPUTER USED

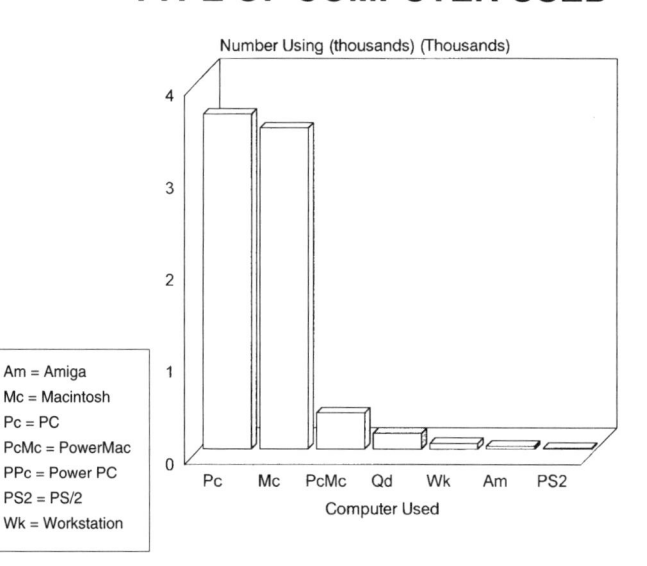

Number Using (thousands) (Thousands)

Computer Used: Pc, Mc, PcMc, Qd, Wk, Am, PS2

Am = Amiga
Mc = Macintosh
Pc = PC
PcMc = PowerMac
PPc = Power PC
PS2 = PS/2
Wk = Workstation

POPULAR PUBLICATIONS

Advertising Age
Subscription Dept.
965 E. Jefferson Ave.
Detroit, MI 48207-9901
fax (313) 446-0961

Aldus Magazine
Adobe Systems
411 First Avenue S.
Seattle, WA 98104-2871
(206) 628-2321

American Printer
29 North Wacker Drive
Chicago, IL 60606-3298
(312) 726-2802

Art & Design News
5783 Park Plaza Court
Indianapolis, IN 46220
(317) 849-6110 / fax (317) 576-5859

Artweek
12 S First Street, Ste. 520
San Jose, CA 95113
(800) 733-2916, (408) 279-2293

Beyond Computing
IBM Corporation,
590 Madison Ave., 32nd Floor
New York, NY 10022

Bottom Line Personal
Subscription Center
P.O. Box 58446
Boulder, CO 80322
(800) 274-5611

Business & Incentive Strategies
P.O. Box 1791
Riverton, NJ 08077-7391

Business Systems Dealer
14 W. South St.
Corry, PA 16407-1894

BusinessWeek
1221 Avenue of the Americas
New York, NY 10020
(212) 512-2000

BYTE
Subscription Dept.
P.O. Box 555
Hightstown, NJ 08520
(800) 257-9402

Communication Arts
P.O. Box 10300
Palo Alto, CA 94303
(415) 326-6040 / (800) 258-9111
fax (415) 326-1648

Communications Week
Circulation Dept.
P.O. Box 1094
Skokie, IL 60076
(708) 647-6834 / fax (708) 647-6838

Communication World
International Assn of Business
Communicators
One Hallidie Plaza, Suite 600
San Francisco, CA 94102
(415) 433-3400 / fax (415) 362-8762

Compute!
Subscription Service Dept.
P.O. Box 10955
Des Moines, IA 50950
(800) 727-6937

Computer Currents
P.O. Box 2339
Berkeley, CA 94702
(415) 547-6800

Computer Graphics World
P.O. Box 122
Tulsa, OK 74101-9966
(918) 831-9400

Computer Pictures
701 Westchester Ave.
White Plains, NY 10604
(914) 328-9157 / fax (914) 328-9093

Computer Reseller News
CMP Publications Inc.
600 Community Dr.
Manhasset, NY 11030
(516) 562-5000

Computer Retail Week
Circulation Department
P.O. Box 4312
Manhasset, NY 11030
(516) 733-6800 / fax (516) 733-6960

Computer Retailing
1750 Peachtree Road
Atlanta, GA 30357
(404) 874-4462

Computer Shopper
One Park Avenue, 11th Floor
New York, NY 10016
(800) 274-6384

Computer Street Journal
P.O. Box 200516
Austin, TX 78720
(512) 263-9166

Computer Telephony
12 West 21 St.
New York, NY 10010
(212) 691-8215 / fax (212) 691-1191

Corelation Magazine
Assn of Corel Artists & Designers
1309 Riverside Dr.
Burbank, CA 91506
(818) 563-ACAD / fax (818) 955-5867

COSMEP Newsletter
The International Assn of Independent
Pu **OUT OF BUSINESS**
P.(
San Francisco, CA 94142-0703
(415) 922-9490 / fax (415) 922-5566

Cost Controller, The
Siefer Consultants, Inc.
525 Cayuga St.
Storm Lake, IA 50588
(800) 747-7342

Creative Business
275 Newbury Street
Boston, MA 02116
(617) 424-1368

CWIP Clips
Chicago Women in Publishing
43 E. Ohio St., Suite 1022
Chicago, IL 60611
(312) 645-0083

Design Tools Monthly
2111 30th St., Suite H
Boulder, CO 80301
(303) 444-6876 / fax (303) 440-3641

Editorial Eye
Editorial Experts
85 S Gragg St., Ste. 400
Alexandria, VA 22312
(703) 642-3040

Editor's Workshop
Lawrence Regan Communications
407 S. Dearborn St.
Chicago, IL 60605
(312) 922-8245

Electronic Business
Circulation Department
44 Cook St.
Denver, CO 80206
(303) 388-4511

Electronic BusinessBuyer
P.O. Box 7537
Highlands Ranch, CO 80126-9337

Electronic Buyers' News
Circulation Dept.
P.O. Box 9054
Jericho, NY 11753-8954

350 - Pricing Guide for Desktop Services

Electronic Engineering Times
Circulation Dept.
Box 2010
Manhasset, NY 11030
(516) 562-5000

Electronic Publishing
P.O. Box 170
Salem, NH 03079
(603) 898-2822

Entrepreneur
2392 Morse Avenue
Irvine, CA 92714
(800) 864-6864 / fax (714) 755-4211

Federal Computer Week
Circulation Department
P.O. Box 3023
Northbrook, IL 60065-3023
(708) 564-1385

Forecast
Faulkner & Gray, Inc.
Eleven Penn Plaza
New York, NY 10001
(212) 967-7000

Fortune
P.O. Box 60001
Tampa, FL 33660-0001
(800) 621-8000

Graphic Arts Monthly
Cahners Publishing Company
44 Cook St.
Denver, CO 80206-5800
(303) 388-4511

Graphics Arts Products News
Maclean-Hunter Publishing Corp.
300 W. Adams
Chicago, IL 60606
(312) 726-2802

Graphic Design USA
1556 Third Avenue
New York, NY

HEPC Syllabus
Subscription Services
1307 S. Mary Ave., Suite 211
Sunnyvale, CA 94087

High Volume Printing
425 Huehl Road
Bldg. 11, Box 368
Northbrook, IL 60065
(312) 564-5940

Home Office Computing
P.O. Box 51344
Boulder, CO 80321-1344
(800) 288-7812

How
P.O. Box 5250
Harlan, IA 51593-4750
(800) 333-1115

Imaging Magazine
12 West 21 Street
New York, NY 10010
(800) 677-3435

In-Plant Printer
425 Huehl Road
Bldg. 11, Box 368
Northbrook, IL 60065
(312) 564-5940

In-Plant Reproductions
401 N. Broad Street
Philadelphia, PA 19108
(215) 238-5300 / fax (215) 238-5457

INC.
P.O. Box 54129
Boulder, CO 80322-4129
(800) 234-0999

Incentive
355 Park Avenue S
New York, NY 10010
(212) 592-6493 / fax (212) 592-6499

InformationWeek
P.O. Box 1093
Skokie, IL 60076-8093
(516) 562-5000

InfoWorld
P.O. Box 1172
Skokie, IL 60076
(708) 647-7925 / fax (708) 647-0226

Instant & Small Commercial Printer
P.O. Box 1387
Northbrook, IL 60065-1387
(708) 564-5940 / fax (708) 564-8361

Larry Hunt's Color Copy News
5325 Kelly Road
Tampa, FL 33615
(813) 886-9107

Macazine
Subscription Service Dept.
P.O. Box 6815
Syracuse, NY 13217
(800) 624-2346

MacChicago
515 E. Golf Rd., Suite 201
Arlington Heights, IL 60005
(708) 439-6575

MacGuide
Subscription Dept.
P.O. Box 13067
Denver, CO 80201
(303) 935-8100

Macintosh Business Review
Subscription Service Dept.
10 Holland Drive
Hasbrouck Heights, NJ 07604
(201) 393-6474/6475

Macintosh Buyer's Guide, The
Redgate Communications Corp.
Circulation Dept.
660 Beachland Blvd.
Vero Beach, FL 32963-1794
(407) 231-6904

Macintosh Hands On
52 Domino Drive
Concord, MA 01742-9906

MacUser
P.O. Box 52461
Boulder, CO 80323-2461
(800) 627-2247

MacWEEK
Customer Service Dept
c/o JCI
P.O. Box 1766
Riverton, NJ 08077-7366
(609) 786-8230

Macworld
P.O. Box 51666
Boulder, CO 80321-1666
(800) 288-6848 / fax (415) 442-0766

Magazine Design & Production
Globecom Publishing
4551 W 107th St., Suite 343
Overland Park, KS 66207
(913) 642-6611

Marketing Computers
Adweek L.P.
1515 Broadway
New York, NY 10036
(212) 536-5336

Micro Publishing News
21150 Hawthorne Blvd. #104
Torrance, CA 90503
(310) 371-5787

Microtimes
BAM Publications
5951 Canning
Oakland, CA 94609

Mobile Office
Circulation Department
911 Hope St., Bldg. 6
Stamford, CT 06907-0949
(203) 358-9900 / fax (203) 348-5792

Multimedia Monitor
P.O. Box 26
Falls Church, VA 22040
(800) 323-3472 / fax (703) 532-0529

Multimedia Today
IBM
4111 Northside Parkway
Internal Zip H4P-21
Atlanta, GA 30327
(800) 779-2062 / fax (404) 238-4298

NADTP Journal
462 Old Boston St.
Topsfield, MA 01983-1232
(508) 887-7900

NASS Newsletter
National Association of Secretarial Services
3637 Fourth St., N, Suite 330
St. Petersburg, FL 33704
(800) 237-1462 / fax (813) 894-1277

Network Computing
600 Community Dr.
Manhasset, NY 11030
(708) 647-6834 / fax (708) 647-6838

New Media Magazine
P.O. Box 1771
Riverton, NJ 08077-7371
(609) 786-4430

OnLine Design
Subscription Department
20 Borica St.
San Francisco, CA 94127-2802
(415) 334-3800 / fax (415) 334-4458

Package Printing and Converting
P.O. Box 12829
Philadelphia, PA 19108-0829
fax (215) 238-5412

PC Computing
P.O. Box 58229
Boulder, CO 80322-8229
(800) 365-2770

PC Graphics & Video
201 E. Sandpointe Ave., Suite 600
Santa Ana, CA 92707
(714) 513-8400 / fax (714) 513-8612

PC Magazine
P.O. Box 54093
Boulder, CO 80321-4093
(800) 289-0429

PC Publishing & Presentations
P.O. Box 5050
Des Plaines, IL 60019-9435
(312) 296-0770

PC Resources
IDG Communications/Peterborough
P.O. Box 50302
Boulder, CO 80321-0302
(603) 924-9471

PC Week
P.O. Box 1767
Riverton, NJ 08077-9767

PC World
Subscriber Services
P.O. Box 55029
Boulder, CO 80322-5029
(800) 825-7595

Personal Computing
P.O. Box 359110
Palm Coast, FL 32035-9921
(800) 423-1780, (800) 858-0095

Personal Publishing
P.O. Box 3240
Harlan, IA 51593-2420
(515) 247-7540

Personal Selling Power
P.O. Box 5467
Fredericksburg, VA 22403
(800) 752-7355

Plan and Print
International Reprographic Assn.
611 E. Butterfield Rd., Suite 104
Lombard, IL 60148
(312) 852-3055

PMA Newsletter
Publishers Marketing Assn.
2401 Pacific Coast Hwy., Suite 102
Hermosa Beach, CA 90254
(310) 372-2732 / fax (310) 374-3342

Portable Office
80 Elm St.
Peterborough, NH 03458
(800) 245-0804

Post Gutenberg
Lee Publications Inc.
P.O. Box 121
Palatine Bridge, NY 13428
(518) 673-3237

Presentations
23410 Civic Center Way, Ste. E-10
Malibu, CA 90265
(310) 456-2283 / fax (310) 456-8686

Presentation Products
23410 Civic Center Way, Ste. E-10
Malibu, CA 90265
(310) 456-2283 / fax (310) 456-8686

Presentations Magazine
50 S. Ninth St.
Minneapolis, MN 55402
(800) 328-4329

Print
320 Tower Oaks Blvd.
Rockville, MD 20852

Printing Impressions
401 N Broad St.
Philadelphia, PA 19108
(215) 238-5300

Printing Journal
1432 Duke St.
Alexandria, VA 22314-3436
(703) 683-8800 / fax (703) 683-8801

Printing Views
Midwest Publishing Co., Inc.
8328 N. Lincoln Avenue
Skokie, IL 60077
(312) 539-8540

Publish
Subscription Dept.
P.O. Box 55415
Boulder, CO 80321-5415
(800) 525-0643, (800) 685-3435

Publishers Weekly
P.O. Box 6547
Torrance, CA 90504-0457
(800) 278-2991

Publishing & Production Executive
North American Publishing Co.
401 N Broad St.
Philadelphia, PA 19108
(215) 238-5300 / fax (215) 238-5457

Reseller Management
P.O. Box 650
Morris Plains, NJ 07950-0650
(201) 292-5100

San Diego Writers' Monthly
3910 Chapman St.
San Diego, CA 92110
(619) 226-0896

Service & Support Management
Publications & Communications, Inc.
P.O. Box 399
Cedar Park, TX 78630-9820

Small Press
P.O. Box 3000
Denville, NJ 07834
(203) 226-6967

Small Publisher
c/o Nigel Maxey
P.O. Box 1620
Pineville, WV 24874-1620
(304) 732-8195

Southern Graphics
Zed Coast Center
1680 SW Bayshore Blvd.
Port St. Lucie, FL 34984-9985

Step-By-Step Graphics
Dynamic Graphics
6000 N. Forest Park Dr.
Peoria, IL 61614-3592
(800) 255-8800

St. Louis Computing
Wikman Publishing Inc.
1300 Hampton Ave., Suite 117
St. Louis, MO 63119
(314) 644-5854

Success
P.O. Box 10983
Des Moines, IA 50347-0983
(800) 234-7324

Target Marketing
P.O. Box 12827
Philadelphia, PA 19108-0827
fax (215) 238-5412

The Page
The Cobb Group
9420 Bunsen Pkwy, Suite 300
Louisville, KY 40220
(800) 223-8720

The Typographer
Typographers International Assn.
2262 Hall Place NW #101
Washington, DC 20007-1870
(202) 965-3400

The Writer
120 Boylston St.
Boston, MA 02116-4615

Upside
1159-B Triton Dr.
Foster City, CA 94404
(415) 377-0950 / fax (415) 377-1961

VARBusiness
Circulation Dept.
P.O. Box 2110
Manhasset, NY 11030-4309
(516) 733-6800 / fax (413) 637-4343

Word Perfect Magazine
Circulation Department
288 West Center Street
Orem, UT 84057

Writer's Digest
P.O. Box 2123
Harlan, IA 51593
(800) 333-0133

Writers' Journal
3585 N. Lexington Ave., Suite 328
Arden Hills, MN 55126-8056
(612) 486-7818

CLUB & ASSOCIATIONS

ABWA
P.O. Box 8728
Kansas City, MO 64114-0728
(816) 361-6621

Adobe Technology Exchange (ATX)
5201 Great America Pkwy, Ste. 441
Santa Clara, CA 95054
(800) 446-5622, (408) 562-6104

American Book Producers Association (ABPA)
New York, NY
(212) 683-0355

American Forest & Paper Association (AFPA)
1111 19th Street NW, Ste 800
Washington, DC 20036
(202) 463-2700

American Institute of Graphic Arts (AIGA)
3748 22nd Street
San Francisco, CA 94114
(415) 647-4700

American Institute of Technical Illustrators
2513 Forest Leaf Parkway, Ste 906
Ballwin, MO 63011
(314) 458-2248

American Newspaper Publishers Assn. (ANPA)
P.O. Box 17407
Dulles International Airport
Washington, D.C. 20041
(703) 620-9500

American Paper Institute (API)
260 Madison Ave.
10th Floor
New York. NY 10016
(212) 340-0600

American Society of Journalists & Authors
Northern CA Chapter
4603 Lincoln Drive
Concord CA 94521

Association for Computing Machinery (SIGGRAPH)
1515 Broadway
New York, NY 10036
(212) 869-7440

Association for Graphic Arts Training (AGAT)
c/o RIT T&E Center
P.O. Box 9887
Rochester, NY 14623
(716) 475-2737 / fax (716) 475-7050

Association for Information and Image Management (AIIM)
1100 Wayne Ave., Suite 1100
Silver Springs, MD 20910
(301) 587-8202

Association of American Publishers (AAP)
1718 Connecticut Avenue NW, Ste. 700
Washington, DC 20009-1148

Association of College and University Printers (ACUP)
Cal State University-Long Beach
1250 Bellflower Rd
Long Beach. CA 90840
(213) 985-4501

Association of College and University Printers (ACUP)
Pennsylvania State University
108 Business Services Bldg.
University Park, PA 16802
(814) 863-0580

Association of Corel Artists & Designers
1309 Riverside Dr.
Burbank, CA 91506
(818) 563-ACAD / fax (818) 955-5867

Association of Electronic Cottagers
P.O. Box 1738
Davis, CA 95617
(916) 756-6430

Association of Graphic Arts Consultants (AGAC)
P 0. Box 290249
Nashville, TN 37229
(615) 366-1094

Association of Imaging Service Bureaus (AISB)
5601 Roanne Way, Suite 608
Greensboro, NC 27409
(800) 844-2472, (919) 855-0400

Association of the Graphic Arts (AGA)
330 7th Avenue
New York, NY 10001-5010
(212) 279-2104

Baltimore Publishers Association (BPA)
Baltimore, MD
(410) 313-9338

Binders & Finishers Association
408 Eightth Ave., Suite 10-A
New York, NY 10001-1816
(212) 629-3232

Binding Industries of America (BIA/PIA)
Printing Industries of America
70 E. Lake St.
Chicago, IL 60611
(312) 704-5000

Book Manufacturers' Institute (BMI)
Wellesley, MA
(617) 239-0103

Bookbuilders of Boston (BOB)
Woburn, MA
(617) 933-6878

Bookbuilders of Washington (BOW)
Washington, DC
(202) 287-3738

Bookbuilders West (BBW)
Box 883666
San Francisco, CA 94188
(415) 546-4991

Business & Professional Women (BPW)
Greater Londonderry Chapter
25 Orchard View Place, Suite 12
Londonderry, NH 03053
(603) 432-8967

Business Forms Management Association (BFMA)
519 SW 3rd Ave, Suite 712
Portland, OR 97204-2519
(503) 227-3393

Business Group Network
P.O. Box 12280
Richmond, VA 23241-2280
(804) 783-9307

Business/Professional Advertising Association (BPAA)
901 N. Washington, Suite 206
Alexandria, VA 22314

Cahners Expo Group
999 Summer St.
Stamford, CT 06905
(203) 964-0000

California Press Women
PO Box 19667
San Diego, CA 92119
(619) 460-9488

California Writers Club (CWC)
2214 Derby Street
Berkeley, CA 94705

Canadian Printing Industries Association (CPIA)
75 Albert St., Suite 906
Ottawa, Ontario K1P 5E7 Canada
(613) 236-7208

CAP International
One Longwater Circle
Norwell, MA 02061
(617) 982-9500

Chicago Book Clinic, The (CBC)
Chicago, IL
(312) 946-1700

Chicago Women in Publishing (CWIP)
43 E. Ohio St., Ste. 1022
Chicago, IL 60611
(312) 645-0083

Computer Electronics Marketing Association (CEMA)
8650 Gennessee Ave., Ste. 100-502
San Diego, CA 92122
(619) 549-8881

Corel Creative Club
Corel Corporation
The Corel Bldg., 1600 Carling Avenue
Ottawa, Ontario, K1Z 8R7 CANADA
U.S. (716) 423-8200
CAN (613) 728-8200

COSMEP (Assoc. of Independent Book Publishers)
B **OUT OF BUSINESS**
San Francisco, CA 94101
(415) 922-9490

Dallas Society of Visual Communications (DSVC)
3530 High Mesa
Dallas, TX 75234
(214) 241-2017

Dataquest Inc. (DTQ)
1290 Ridder Park Dr.
San Jose, CA 95131
(408) 437-8000

DDAP Association
(Digital Distribution of Advertising for Publications)
1855 E. Vista Way, Suite 16
Vista, CA 92084
(619) 758-9460

Demonstrative Evidence Specialists Association (DESA)
(800) 522-DESA

Dunn Technology, Inc. (DTI)
1855 E. Vista Way
Vista, CA 92084
(619) 758-9460

Dynamic Graphics Educational Foundation (DGEF)
6000 North Forest Park Dr.
Peoria, IL 61614
(800) 255-8800

Editorial Freelance Association
P.O. Box 2050
New York, NY 10159
(212) 677-3357

Electronic Graphic Artists of Dallas (EGAD)
6440 N. Central Expressway
University Tower, Suite 506
Dallas, TX 75206
(214) 360-9072

Electronic Prepress Section (EPS/PIA)
100 Daingerfield Rd.
Alexandria, VA 22314
(703) 519-8168

Flexographic Technical Association (FTA)
900 Marconi Ave.
Ronkonkoma, NY 11779-7212
(516) 737-6020

Freelance Editorial Association
P.O. Box 835
Cambridge, MA 02238
(617) 729-8164

Graphic Arts Association (GAA)
1900 Cherry St.
Philadelphia, PA 19103
(215) 299-3300

Graphic Arts Literacy Alliance (GALA)
Graphic Arts Technical Foundation
4615 Forbes Ave.
Pittsburgh, PA 15213
(412) 621-6941

Graphic Arts Sales Foundation
113 East Evans St.
Matlack Building
West Chester, PA 19380
(215) 436-9778

Graphic Arts Show Co. (GASC)
1899 Preston White Dr.
Reston, VA 22091-4367
(703) 264-7200

Graphic Arts Technical Foundation (GATF)
4615 Forbes Avenue
Pittsburgh, PA 15223-3796
(412) 621-6941 / fax (412) 621-3049

Graphic Arts Marketing Information Service (GCA/PIA)
Printing Industries of America
(703) 841-1879

Graphic Arts Suppliers Association
1900 Arch St.
Philadelphia, PA 19103-1498
(215) 564-3484

Graphic Communications Association (GCA-PIA)
100 Daingerfield Rd, 4th Floor
Alexandria, VA 22314
(703) 519-8160

Graphic Preparatory Association (GPA)
501 N. Wesley Ave
P.O. Box 2
Mount Morris, IL 61054
(815) 734-4178

Graphics of the Americas
PIA of South Florida
P.O. Box 170010
Hialeah, FL 33017
(305) 558-4855

Gravure Association of America
1200-A Scottsville Rd.
Rochester, NY 14623
(716) 436-2150 / fax (716) 436-7689

Gutenburg Expositions
P.O. Box 11712
Santa Ana, CA 92711
(714) 921-3120

Houston Association of In-Plant Printing (HAIP)
1324 West Clay St.
Houston, TX 77019
(713) 522-2046

IBFI
(The International Association Serving the Forms, Information Management, Systems Automation and Printed Communications Requirements of Business)
2111 Wilson Blvd., Suite 350
Arlington, VA 22201-3042
(703) 841-9191

International Network for Women in Enterprise and Trade (INET FOR WOMEN)
6819 Elm Street #3
McLean, VA 22101
(703) 893-8541

International Publishing Management Association (IPMA)
IPMA Building
1205 W. College Ave.
Liberty, MO 64068-3733
(816) 781-1111

Institute of Electrical & Electronic Engineers (IEEE) Computer Society
10662 Los Vaqueros Circle
P.O. Box 3014
Los Alamitos, CA 90720-1264

International Association of Business Communicators (IABC)
1 Hallidie Plaza, Suite 600
San Francisco, CA 94102
(800) 776-4222, (415) 433-3400

International Association of Printing House Craftsmen (IAPHC)
7042 Brooklyn Blvd.
Minneapolis, MN 55429-1370
(612) 560-1620

International Business Forms Industries (IBFI)
2111 Wilson Blvd., Ste. 350
Arlington, VA 22201
(703) 841-9191

International Graphic Arts Education Association (IGAEA)
4615 Forbes Ave.
Pittsburgh, PA 15213
(412) 682-5170

International Prepress Assn (IPA)
7200 France Ave. S., Suite 327
Edina, MN 55435
(800) 255-8141, (612) 896-1908
fax (612) 896-0181

International Television Association (ITVA)
6311 North O'Conner Rd., LB51
Irving TX 75039
(214) 869-1112

International Thermographers Association (ITA/PIA)
100 Daingerfield Rd.
Alexandria, VA 22314
(703) 519-8100/8122/8136

Kenex
575 E. 4500 S., Ste. B240
Salt Lake City, UT 84107
(801) 263-3276

Key Productions
94 Murphy Road
Hartford, CT 06114
(203) 247-8363

Last Monday Club
3871 Piedmont Avenue
Oakland, CA 94611
(510) 450-4800

Leads Club
P.O. Box 279
Carlsbad, CA 92018-0279
(800) 783-3761, (619) 434-3761

Macintosh Consultants Network (MCN)
3600 Sisk Rd., Ste. 3D
Modesto, CA 95356-0539
(209) 545-0569
CONNECT and AppleLink address is "MCN."

Marin Small Publishers Association
P.O. Box 1346
Ross, CA 94957

Mid-America Book Publishers (MABP)
Lincoln, NE
(402) 466-9665

Midwest Secretarial Services Network
795 Office Parkway, Suite 118
St. Louis, MO 63141
(314) 993-8588

National Association for Female Executives (NAFE)
127 W. 24th Street
New York, NY 10011-1914
(800) 927-NAFE, (212) 645-0770

National Association for the Cottage Industry
P.O. Box 14460
Chicago, Il 60614
(312) 472-8116

National Association for the Self-Employed (NASE)
2121 Precinct Line Rd.
Hurst, TX 76054
(800) 827-9990

National Association of Desktop Publishers (NADTP)
462 Old Boston Road
Suite 8
Topsfield, MA 01983
(508) 877-7900, (800) 874-4113

National Association of Home Based Businesses
P.O. Box 30220
Baltimore, Md 21270
(301) 466-8070

National Association of Litho Clubs (NALC)
P.O. Box 1258
Clifton, NJ 07012
(201) 777-6727

National Association of Litho Clubs (NALC)
6550 Donjoy Dr.
Cincinnati, OH 45242
(513) 793-2532

National Association of Printers and Lithographers (NAPL)
780 Palisades Avneue
Teaneck, NJ 07666
(201) 342-0705 / fax (201) 692-0386

National Association of Printing Ink Manufacturers (NAPIM)
Heights Plaza, 777 Terrace Ave.
Hasbrouck Heights, NJ 07604
(201) 288-9454

National Association of Quick Printers (NAQP)
401 N Michigan Ave.
Chicago, IL 60611
(312) 644-6610 ext. 4716 / fax (312) 245-1084

National Association of Secretarial Services (NASS)
3637-4th Street North, Suite 330
St. Petersburg, FL 33704
(800) 237-1462, (813) 823-3646

National Association of Women Business Owners (NAWBO)
600 S. Federal St. Suite 400
Chicago, Il 60605
(312) 922-0465

National Business Forms Association (NBFA)
433 E. Monroe Avenue
Alexandria, VA 22301
(703) 836-6225

National Computer Graphics Association (NCGA)
2722 Merrilee Dr., Ste. 200
Fairfax, VA 22031
(703) 698-9600

National Family Business Council
60 Revere Drive, Suite 500
Northbrook, IL 60062
(312) 480-9574

National Foundation for Women Business Owners (NFWBO)
1001 Pennsylvania Avenue NW #435N
Washington, DC 20004
(202) 347-0978

National League of American Pen Women (NLAPW)
1300 17th Street NW
Washington, D.C. 29936

National Paper Trade Association (NPTA)
111 Great Neck Rd.
Great Neck, NY 11021
(516) 829-3070

National Small Business United
1155 15th St, NW, Ste 710
Washington, DC 20005
(202) 293-8830

National State Printing Association (NSPA)
Council of State Governments
Iron Works Pike
P.O. Box 11910
Lexington, KY 40578
(606) 231-1871

National Writer's Union
873 Broadway, Suite 203
New York, NY 10003-1209

Network of Entrepreneurial Women, Inc. (NEW)
P.O. Box 1100
Falls Church, VA 22041
(703) 435-4449

Network of Enterprising Women
P.O. Box 8204
Richmond, VA 23226

New England Women Business Owners (NEWBO)
P.O. Box 67082
Chestnut Hill, MA 02167
(617) 566-3013

Newspaper Association of America
11600 Sunrise Valley Dr.
Reston, VA 22091
(703) 648-1000

North American Bookdealers Exchange (NABE)
P.O. Box 606
Cottage Grove, OR 97424

North American Graphic Arts Suppliers Association (NAGASA)
1720 Florida Ave., NW
Washington, DC 20009-2660
(202) 328-8441

NPES, The Association for Suppliers of Printing and Publishing Technologies
1899 Preston White Dr
Reston VA 22091-4367
(703) 264-7200

Optical Publishing Association
P.O. Box 21268
Columbus, OH 43221
(614) 442-8805

Philadelphia Book Clinic (PBC)
Philadelphia, PA
(215) 664-2026

Print/New Jersey
75 Kearny Ave., PO Box 6
Kearny, NJ 07032
(201) 997-7468 / fax (201) 997-7063

Print Production Club of Kansas City (PPCKC)
Kansas City, MO
(816) 432-2600

Printing Association of Florida (PAF)
P.O. Box 170010
Hialeah, FL 33017
(305 764-8808

Printing Industries of America (PIA)
100 Daingerfield Road
Arlington, VA 22314
(703) 519-8100/8158 / fax (703) 548-3227

PIA of CT & Western Massachusetts
1 Regency Dr., P.O. Box 30
Bloomfield, CT 06002
(203) 242-8991 / fax (203) 286-0787

PIA of Georgia
5020 Highlands Pkwy.
Smyrna, GA 30082
(404) 433-3050   fax (404) 433-3062

PIA of Kansas City
702 Midland Bldg., 1221 Baltimore St.
Kansas City, MO 64105
(816) 421-7678 / fax (816) 421-7073

PIA of the Mountain States
900 E. Louisiana Avenue
Denver, CO 80210
(303) 744-6007 / fax (303) 698-1260

PIA of New York State
455 Commerce Drive
Amherst, NY 14228
(716) 691-3211 / fax (716) 691-4249

PIA of San Diego
3914 Murphy Canyon Rd., Ste A-107
San Diego, CA 92123
(619) 571-6555 / fax (619) 571-7935

PIA of the South
305 Plus Park Blvd.
Nashville, TN 37217
(615) 366-1091 / fax (615) 366-4192

PIA of Texas
910 W. Mockingbird Lane
Dallas TX 75247

Printing Industries of the Carolinas (PICA)
P.O. Box 19889
Charlotte, NC 28219
(704) 357-1150

Printing Industries of Maryland
2423 Maryland Avenue
Baltimore, MD 21218
(410) 366-0900 / fax (410) 366-1816

Printing Industries of Michigan
23815 Northwestern Hwy. #2700
Southfield, MI 48075-3366
(313) 354-9200 / fax (313) 354-1711

Printing Industries of the Midlands
11009 Aurora Avenue
Urbandale, IA 50322
(515) 270-1009 / fax (515) 270-8701

Printing Industries of Minnesota
450 N. Syndicate, Suite 200
St. Paul, MN 55104
(612) 646-4826 / fax (612) 646-8673

Printing Industries of New England
110 Tech Circle, PO Box 2009
Natick, MA 01760-0015
(508) 655-8700 / fax (508) 655-2586

Printing Industries of Oklahoma & Southwest Missouri
5200 S. Yale, Suite 101
Tulsa, OK 74135
(918) 496-1122 / fax (918) 496-2992

Printing Industries of Virginia
1108 E. Main Street, Ste. 300
Richmond, VA 23219
(804) 643-1800 / fax (804) 643-7482

Printing Industries of Wisconsin
P.O. Box 126
Elm Grove, WI 53122
(414) 785-9090 / fax (414) 785-7043

Printing Industry Association of the South
P.O. Box 290249
Nashville, TN 37229
(615) 366-1094

Printing Industry of the Carolinas (PICA)
P.O. Box 19889
Charlotte, NC 28219
(704) 357-1150

Printing Industry of Connecticut
P.O. Box 144
Milford, CT 06460
(203) 874-6793 / fax (203) 874-0291

Printing Industry of Illinois/Indiana Assn
70 E. Lake Street
Chicago, IL 60601
(312) 704-5000

Printing Industry of Metropolitan Washington, Inc., The
7 West Tower
1333 H Street NW
Washington, DC 20005
(202) 682-30001

Printing Industry of Ohio
88 Dorchester Sq., PO Box 819
Westerville, OH 43081
(614) 794-2300 / fax (614) 794-2049

Printing Industry of South Florida
P O Box 170010
Hialeah, FL 33017
(305) 764-8808

Professional Association of Secretarial Services (PASS)
Premier Office Services, Inc.
1116 Lyford Lane
Wheaton, IL 60187
(908) 668-3652

Professional Referral Services
20123 Nordhoff Street
Chatsworth, CA 91311
(818) 998-0182

Publishers' Marketing Association (PMA)
2401 Pacific Coast Hwy., Ste. 102
Hermosa Beach, CA 90254
(213) 372-2732

Publication Production Association of Southern California (PPASC)
Long Beach, CA
(310) 425-1721

Publication Production Club (PPC)
Chicago, IL
(708) 323-9490

Publication Production Group of Northern California (PPGNC)
Redwood City, CA
(415) 506-4763

Quad Cities Advertising Federation
P.O. Box 573
Moline, IL 61265
(309) 762-0732

Quad Cities Club of Printing House Craftsmen
2216 W. 54th Street
Davenport, IA 52806
(319) 386-6325

Reed Exhibition Company
999 Summer St.
P.O. Box 3833
Stamford, CT 06905
(203) 964-0000

Research & Engineering Council of the Graphic Arts Industry
Marshallton Bldg., P.O. Box 639
Chadds Ford, PA 19317
(215) 388-7394

Richmond Professional Network
P.O. Box 954
Richmond, VA 23207
(804) 355-7800

Rochester Institute of Technology
Technical & Educational Center
66 Lomb Memorial Dr.
Rochester, NY 14623-5604
(716) 475-5000

Sacramento Women's Network (SWN)
P.O. Box 13085
Sacramento, CA 95813-3085

Santa Cruz County Women's Network (SCCWN)
1822 Silvana Lane
Santa Cruz, CA 95062
(408) 479-0118

Screen Printing Association International (SPAI)
10015 Main St.
Fairfax, VA 22031
(703) 385-1335 / fax (703) 273-0456

Seybold Seminars
29160 Heathercliff Rd., Ste. 200
Malibu, CA 90265
(310) 457-5850

Society for Imaging Science & Technology
7003 Kilworth Lane
Springfield, VA 22151
(703) 642-9090

Society For Technical Writers
815 15th Street NW
Washington, DC 20005
(202) 737-0035

Society of Illustrators
128 E. 63rd Street
New York, NY 10021
(212) 838-2560

Society of Illustrators of Los Angeles
11480 Burbank Blvd.
North Hollywood, CA 91601-2301
(818) 784-0588

Society of Professional Journalists
P.O. Box 77
Greencastle, IN 46135-0077
(317) 653-3333

Society of Typographic Arts
233 E. Ontario, Suite 500
Chicago, IL 60611
(312) 787-2018

Southprint Printing Industry Association of the Southwest
P.O. Box 290249
Nashville, TN 37229
(615) 366-1094

State of New York Office of Minority & Business Development
P.O. Box 2072
Albany, NY 12220
(518) 474-6342

Technical Association of the Graphic Arts (TAGA)
68 Lomb Memorial Drive
Rochester, NY 14623-5604
(716) 475-7470

Technical Association of the Pulp & Paper Industry (TAPPI)
Technology Park
P.O. Box 105113
Atlanta, GA 30348
(404) 446-1400

The Creative Club
P.O. Box 983
Latham, NY 12110
(518) 449-4985

Type Directors Club
60 E. 42nd St, Ste 1130
New York NY 10165
(212) 983-6042

Typographers International Association (TIA)
2233 Wisconsin Avenue NW, Ste. 235
Washington, DC 20007
(202) 965-3400

Typographers International Association (TIA)
84 Park Avenue
Flemington, NJ 08822
(908) 782-4635

Ventura Users of Greater Boston
P.O. Box 517
Lexington, MA 02173
(617) 275-3592

Windows Prepublishing Association (WPS)
1804 Hayes St.
Nashville, TN 37203
(615) 320-9473

Wisconsin Publishers Production Club (WPPC)
North Lake, WI
(608) 838-9899

Women's Business Network (WBN)
P.O. Box 108
Berkeley, CA 94701
(510) 482-8583

Women for Women
849 23rd Street
Richmond, CA 94804
(415) 215-4202

Women in Business (WIB)
7358 N. Lincoln Ave., Ste. 150
Chicago, IL 60646
(708) 679-7800

Women in Communications
Georgia Chapter
P.O. Box 7763
Atlanta, GA 30357
(404) 482-0711

Women in Communications, Inc.
Portland Prof. Chapter
P.O. Box 3924
Portland, OR 97208

Women in Production (WIP)
New York, NY
(212) 481-7793

Xplor International
24238 Hawthorne Blvd.
Torrance, CA 90505-6505
(310) 373-3633

Other Books Related to Pricing

Business of Graphics Design: A Sensible Approach, Ed Gold, Watson-Guptill, New York, 1985 (ISBN 0-8230-0543-7).

Desktop Dividends: Managing Electronic Prepress for Profit, Philip K. Ruggles, Printing Management Services, San Luis Obispo, CA, 1993 (ISBN 0-9638203-0-3).

Desktop Dollars & Sense Publishing, Scott R. Anderson, Blue Heron Publishing, Hillsboro, OR 1992 (ISBN 0-936085-51-7).

Handbook of Pricing & Ethetical Guidelines, Graphic Arts Guild, ISBN 0-9321-02-07-7, 1991, $22.

How to Set Your Fees and Get Them, Kate Kelly, Visibility Enterprises, 11 Rockwood Drive, Larchmont, NY 10538. (914) 834-0602, 109 pp, $17.50.

How to Sell at Prices Higher Than Your Competition, Lawrence J. Steinmetz.

Negotiating Higher Design Fees, Frank Stasiowski, Whitney Library of Design, 1515 Broadway, New York, NY 220 pp, $22.50.

Pricing & Ethical Guidelines, 6th Edition, 208 pp handbook by New York-based Graphic Artists Guild. North Light Books, $19.95.

Price Wars, Thomas J. Winninger

The Pricing Game, Lyman Henderson, NAPL, $29.95.

Index

$/FTE - 306
2X pricing - 69
2.5X pricing - 70
3X pricing - 70
30-60-10 rule - 90

A

accepted custom - 30
adding products/services - 75
agreement - 279
associations - 355
average distribution cost per order - 109
average dollar per sale - 97
average variable cost per sale - 97

B

baseline production standards - 174
benchmarks - 159
BHR - 183
bid - 254
bid request, responding to - 257
bid, against competitors - 259
bid, opportunity - 255
bid, poor - 258
bid, tracking - 283
BIG survey standard times - 168
billing rate selection - 326
body language - 270
bottom pricing - 72
break-even - 96
break-even analysis - 97, 311
break-even order size - 109
budgeted hourly rates - 183
budgeted labor costs - 321
burden rate - 155
burdened hourly rate - 155
business form - 346
business start year - 344
business survival - 335
buy-outs - 159

C

calculated cost plus 70% - 59
charging - 207
charging by character - 209
charging by hour - 213

charging by job - 221
charging by line - 209
charging by page - 209
charging by shop hourly rate - 214
charging for additional - 224
charging for alterations - 239
charging for corrections - 239
charging for overtime - 237
charging minimum rate - 238
charging rush jobs - 238
Clayton Antitrust Act - 13
clubs - 355
comma pricing - 72
competing with competition - 61
competition - 10
competition, comparison - 292
competition, studying - 48
competition-oriented pricing - 29, 85
competitors, price - 56
complexitiy - 225
composite pricing - 31
computer used - 348
contracts - 280
contribution margin - 100
cost baseline - 149
cost of goods sold - 14, 108
cost of materials - 321
cost of services sold - 14
cost-based - 85
cost-oriented pricing - 21
cost-plus - 25
cost-volume - 25
counter prices - 24, 306
coupons - 112
critical path analysis - 310
customer base, analysis - 136
customer, commodity - 40
customer, solutions - 40
customers, wants - 53
cutthroat competitors - 138
cutting price - 110 cutting prices - 109

D

debt servicing - 51, 157
demand - 8
demand curve - 33
demand-backward pricing - 20

demand-oriented pricing - 17
demographic information - 343
determining demand - 47
differential pricing - 19
difficulty - 225
direct costs - 150
discounting - 115
discounting, legal - 119
distribution costs - 108

E
econom model of profitability - 294
economic model - 299
economy - 9
economy, studying - 49
elasticity - 34
elasticity factor - 34
employee loading - 343
esthetics - 11
estimate, follow-up - 281
estimating - 243
estimating a job - 317
estimating applied - 245
estimating costs - 50
estimating demand - 33
estimating form - 246
ethics - 77

F
Federal Trade Commission Act - 13
financial analysis - 289
financial numbers - 285
fixed costs - 150
flat rate pricing - 221
floor price - 58
floor price plus - 58
formal quote - 263
format of incoming work - 348
FTE - 294
full cost pricing - 23
full time equivalent - 294
function-time history - 172
functional decomposition - 244

G
G&A - 153
gender of owner - 347
general & administrative - 152
getting paid - 328
going-rate - 30, 85
gross margin - 2, 103
gross profit - 2, 104, 108

gross profit margin - 108
guerilla operations - 335

H
high price myth - 57
hours worked weekly - 347

I
IFB - 256
income distribution - 345
income vs profit - 88
income, maximum possible - 304
incremental cost - 23
indirect costs - 150
industry production standards - 164
inelastic demand - 34
invitation for bid - 256

J
job estimating - 317
job scheduling - 309
job-outs - 159

K
keystone markup - 2

L
labor rate - 155
law and government - 12
leadership pricing - 66
list price - 115
location - 11
loss leader jobs - 120
loss-leader pricing - 31

M
machine standard - 160
margin analysis - 106
margin curve - 106
margin of safety - 192
marginal cost - 106
marginal revenue - 106
mark-up pricing - 21
mark-up, accepted reference - 24
mark-up, calculated - 24
mark-up, standard - 24
market, monopolistic - 6
market, monopolistic-competitive - 7
market, oligopolistic - 6
market, purely competitive - 6
market-based bidding - 260
markup - 1

meeting, cost of - 229
minimum charge - 186
MOS - 192

N
NAPL standards - 171
NASS standards - 172
negotiating - 274
negotiation process - 286
net revenue marginal analysis - 61
net revenue, inventory sell off - 61
new product pricing - 66
new service pricing - 66
no-bid - 271
nonverbal communication - 280

O
odd/even pricing - 20
one-half pricing - 69
operating location - 346
operating profit - 290
overhead - 103, 150
overhead factor - 155

P
payment, getting - 328
penetration pricing - 18
percent capacity plus margin - 60
percent gross profit - 108
preflight - 225
prestige pricing - 19
pretax profit - 290
price cutting, when works - 120
price increase, objections - 130
price leader - 66
price lining - 19
price points - 127
price skimming - 18
price, factors affecting - 5
pricing objectives - 46
pricing problems - 82
production summary form - 302
productivity - 89
productivity, factors affecting - 94
productivity, individual - 93
productivity, shop - 91
profit center - 187
profit, top - 144
profit-oriented pricing - 27
profitability model - 302
profitability, measuring - 293
project quote - 323

project time tracking - 173
proof acceptance form - 241
publications - 349

Q
quick pricing form - 227

R
raising prices - 122
raising prices, how much - 126
raising prices, subtle ways to - 126
rebates - 114
request for bid - 256
request for information - 256
request for proposal - 256
request for quote - 256
resource allocation - 309
return on assets - 287
return on investment - 51, 286
return on investment, selecting - 50
reverse three technique - 329
RFB - 256
RFI - 256
RFP - 256
RFQ - 256
ROA - 287
Robinson-Patman Act - 12
ROI - 51, 286

S
sales-volume method - 97
selling, general & administrative - 153
service contracts - 73
service, donating - 74
service, pricing of - 52
set up time - 186
set-up fees - 236
setting price - 46
SG&A - 153
Sherman Antitrust Act - 13
single price, any customer - 61
specifying a job - 245
standard benchmarks - 159
sticker price shock - 131
strategic thinking - 39
strategies, pricing - 58
subjective pricing - 31

T
tactics - 81
target profit - 27
target return on sales - 28

targeted return on investment - 29
tiered pricing - 62
time in tenths chart - 229
total time estimate - 320
total units sold method - 100
trade discount - 115
trade rate ripoff - 324
transaction pricing - 65

U
unique selling proposition - 144
unitary elasticity - 34
USP - 144

V
value, added - 56
value-based pricing - 68
variable cost percentage - 97
variable costs - 150
volume discounts - 118

W
work process flowchart - 310
worker performance production standard - 164

Y
year business started - 344

Other Useful Tools

Pricing Tables: Desktop Services
$49.95   ISBN 0-929535-16-2

Based on extensive survey of desktop providers
Business distribution by state
Income distribution by business type, location & gender
Business revenue by type of job
Regional pricing tables list billing rates by task and job
Covers every aspect of creative design, DTP and prepress
Also includes pricing for multimedia and Web services
Includes up-front and post printing activities
Tables list average price and range of prices for each category
Heavy poly 1" three-ring binder available for $5 more
Binder can used for custom counter price book

Desktop Production Standards
$49.95   ISBN 0-929535-17-0

Laser printer, scanner, and imagesetter processing times
Develop machine timing standards for your equipment
System operator and designer production times
Covers writing, editing, and creative design
Also covers desktop publishing, web page design and more
Develop your own employee performance standards
Shows how to develop your own budgeted hourly rates
Use your timing standards and BHRs for flat rate pricing

TO ORDER
Call toll free

(800) 811-4337

or
visit our Web site at
www.brennerbooks.com